THE BOYS OF BALLYKELLY

THE BOYS OF BALLYKELLY

Gordon Blair

Additional material provided by Norman Lindsay

Book Guild Publishing
Sussex, England

First published in Great Britain in 2010 by
The Book Guild Ltd
Pavilion View
19 New Road
Brighton, BN1 1UF

Typesetting in Garamond by
Keyboard Services, Luton, Bedfordshire

Printed and bound in Great Britain by
CPI Antony Rowe

A catalogue record for this book is available from
The British Library

ISBN 978 1 84624 405 6

Dedicated to my wife Pam who unstintingly put up with most of the reprobates in this book — sometimes she could have seen them put down! Happy days.

Contents

Shackletons Don't Bother Me   xi

Prologue   xiii

PART I: Ballykelly and North Atlantic

1   The Arrival   3

2   The Social Vipers   20

3   Aircraft Handling and Rectification Flight   26

4   The Introduction   33

5   The Bigot   38

6   Bodo Bound   43

7   The Gourmet   51

8   Snow Storm   54

9   The First Party   65

10 Gnashers in Gibraltar   75

11 The Stripper   86

12 Love's Labours Lost   93

13 Engine Change in Bodo   99

14 The Crock of Gibraltar   106

15 The Storemen   131

CONTENTS

PART II: Sharjah

16	Sharjah Bound	139
17	The Swimming Pool	147
18	The Graduate	151
19	Going Home	162

PART III: Majunga

20	Unilateral Declarations	173
21	Something Lost, Something Gained	176
22	Majunga Bound	186
23	Khartoum	192
24	The Battle of Omdurman	200
25	The Zoo	203
26	The Consular Party	206
27	The Birthday Party	213
28	Departure	218
29	Nairobi	220
30	Majunga	226
31	Majunga Nights	230
32	The Wing Commander and the Sergeant	234
33	The Halo of the Reverend Curry	242
34	The Darts Match	245
35	The Outcome	252

CONTENTS

PART IV: Before the Demise

36	The Troubles	257
37	We Are the Champions	262
38	Irish Hospitality	268
39	Engineering Officers	277
40	The Driving Test	283
41	The End	296
Epilogue		300

Shackletons Don't Bother Me

Sung to the tune of 'The Long and the Short and the Tall'

Shackletons don't bother me
Shackletons don't bother me
Clapped out abortions with holes in their wings
Four piston engines and with two rudder fins
Their bomb bay is too bloody small
Three eighths of four fifths of sod all
You'll get no enjoyment on coastal employment
So cheer up my lads sod them all.

They say that the Shack is a very fine kite
This we no longer doubt
If you should find there's a Mig on your tail this is the way to get out
Just keep cool, calm and sedate mate
Don't let your British blood boil
But don't hesitate, slam it straight through the gate*
And splatter the bastard in oil!

---

*The 'gate' refers to a physical point on the movement of the engine throttles that had to be overcome to get the engines up to their maximum supercharged boost pressure and ultimate power utilising water methanol injection. Griffon engines were renowned for oil leaks!

Prologue

The Royal Air Force, that bastion of British military might that in the 1940s fought in the white heat of battle in the Second World War, found itself in the 1960s in what was commonly known as the 'Cold War'. What was this Cold War? Most people understood it to be subterfuge and military action to keep the might of the USSR away from our doorsteps, but how did the RAF play its part? There were many factions that undertook different roles, but none was as intrepid as Coastal Command, which was constantly in the front line in the war against the new Dreadnoughts of their day – nuclear submarines.

The common denominator and inspiration behind this book is the love–hate relationship experienced by almost everyone who maintained, and flew in, the Coastal Command submarine-hunting AVRO Shackleton, also known by many other names from sentimental terms of endearment to the downright blasphemous.

This is not a technical book about the AVRO Shackleton aircraft, but rather an account of the lives, times and exploits of some of the RAF people who serviced these great beasts. I say great because the Shackletons were so great, and their very being brought together a mélange of mainly good-natured men, some of them hard working and others of a more delicate and malingering disposition, who somehow gelled more than they might have done had they been working on other types of aircraft. Why this was is an enigma. Perhaps it was because all the military aircraft that had come before the Shackleton were extremely spartan and functional, and all the aircraft that were to come after it were mainly jets and were therefore soulless and even more functional. Perhaps it was the fact that there had to be a great deal of interaction between man and the machine to keep the machine airworthy, invoking a hands-on understanding of the component parts in much the same way as a surgeon knows the human body. Or perhaps the Shackleton was evocative in the same way that steam railway engines are – because they could be observed in operation and they both carted a restaurant and some beds around with them. Whatever it was, the Shackleton design evolved out of the Second World War Lancaster and Lincoln bombers, and this fact somehow heightened certain emotions in those who were close to them.

The first Shackletons came into service in April 1951 and they lasted in one form or another right through to 1991, thus showing their robustness and versatility if not their potency. They were the ugly ducklings in the era of the new emerging jet-powered aircraft, and despite their long period of service they never managed metamorphosis into a thing of beauty even though there were several versions throughout the years.

The Shackleton was not an easy aircraft to keep serviceable as it was derived out of thirties technology. In fact the most modern things in the Shackleton, apart from some of the electronic wizardry, were the 'bone-dome' helmets worn by the aircrew. These helmets were worn, not in fear of the aircraft being attacked by an enemy fighter, but to keep the crews' heads from being jellified by the constant noise and vibrations of the aircraft as they traversed the skies looking for quarry.

This aircraft was cobbled together to make a robust flying machine that could stay aloft for many hours in the slim hope of encountering a submarine somewhere in the vastness of the oceans. Towards the end of the war, most German U-boat 'kills' were by aircraft and this gave rise to the objective of having an aircraft like the Shackleton to replace the Sunderland flying boats and converted Liberator bombers that had been so successful in disposing of these submarine 'wolf-packs'. However, the Sunderlands and Liberators were only successful because the diesel–electric-powered U-boats had to stay on the surface of the sea for the majority of the time, their time submerged being limited by the need to 'snorkel' for air on a regular basis. When on the surface the U-boats were sitting ducks for the aircraft to bomb or shoot and it was this vulnerability that destroyed them. Later in the war some submarines were destroyed by depth charges or air-launched homing torpedos, but in essence the submarine invariably had to be spotted on the surface by radar or eyeball before it could be targeted for attack by air.

By the time the Shackleton had been established as the British submarine hunter in the early 1950s the world was moving on by constructing nuclear-powered submarines that did not have to surface at all, from the moment they left their base until they returned. This was very sad for the Shackletons as they were now very unlikely ever to encounter their nuclear-age prey, except in combined naval exercises where submarines were positioned in areas where they had the potential to be found.

These shortcomings did not deter the Ministry of Defence from keeping up the pretence that the mighty submarine hunters were a potent force. After the war they even sold most of Britain's wartime diesel-powered submarine fleet to unsuspecting third-world nations in the hope that the Shackletons would be able to find them if and when those nations turned against the West.

This then gave a reason to have a potent submarine hunter. The groundcrew of these beasts regarded themselves as a potent force, but more often than not this potency was realised in the bars and other nefarious establishments near the airfields all over the world where the Shackleton had managed to touch down – and there were many! There are probably still airfields today where the Shackleton's characteristic trademark of large oil stains on the concrete dispersal areas are evident and witness to the passing of this ancient relic, in much the same way as fossilised dinosaur dung is evidence of their passing. The oil stains were caused by leakage from the powerhouse for these aircraft, the Rolls-Royce Griffon engines of which each Shackleton had four, not all necessarily working at the same time. These engines were derived from an earlier Rolls-Royce Buzzard configuration helped by the development of the famous Merlin engine that had powered the Spitfire, Hurricane and Lancaster bombers during the war. Similar to the Merlin, it was a water-cooled, V-twelve, two-speed, supercharged piston engine, but bigger and more powerful, and the last of this acclaimed line. The noise that emanated from these power plants gave rise to the everlasting name for the Shackleton – 'The Growler'.

Because the power output from these engines was so great, the blades of conventional propellers would have had to be extremely long to absorb its power. This would have necessitated an extremely long undercarriage, thereby making the front of the aircraft sit very high off the ground, as it was originally designed with a tail wheel, giving it the 'sit up and beg' attitude. This problem was avoided by fitting the engines with two shorter propellers on two shafts, one integral to the other, turning in opposite rotation. These shorter 'contra-rotating' propellers then allowed everything to be kept in proportion but added to the novelty features of the Shackleton and gave rise to another nickname – 'The Contra-Rotating Nissen Hut'.

While the Griffon engines were robust and powerful, they were also temperamental and needed a lot of tender loving care and attention from their adoring keepers – engine fitters nicknamed 'sooties', as they were invariably covered in a mixture of exhaust grime and oil after working on the engines or ancillaries and therefore looked as though they swept chimneys for a living.

Shackleton squadrons were stationed all over the world in defence of the realm and major sea routes. Singapore, Hong Kong, Aden, Gibraltar and Malta were the main overseas bases. At home, St Mawgan in the south, Kinloss in the north and Ballykelly in the west were the three bases that unerringly preserved the home coastline from the threat of submarine attacks and delivered mail to weather ships stationed in mid-Atlantic. The Shackletonsalso carried out a successful and valuable role in maritime search and rescue operations and many stricken sailors have welcomed the distant growl of the Griffons in the sure knowledge that the Shackleton had tracked them down.

The 'factional' anecdotes in this book recall the life and times of some of the people who lived and worked on the Shackletons based at RAF Ballykelly on the shores of Lough Foyle some fifteen miles east of Londonderry in Northern Ireland. Ballykelly was not the easiest place in which to live at that time, as it was remote from the rest of the British Isles and there was always the stretch of Irish Sea to cross if the mainland had to be reached. People either loved or hated living in this part of the country, as it could be construed as being an overseas posting without any of the monetary or climatic benefits that real overseas postings would give. The unmarried men, or 'singlies', on the base probably felt even more isolated than the married men, and because of this they tended to stick together and make their own entertainment on the base. The sense of isolation was somewhat exacerbated by the Irish political struggles that were just re-starting around 1968, and even although there was no real threat to Ballykelly itself this did add a certain pressure to the tenuous hold that some of these boys had on Guinness-adjusted reality.

This isolation and the fact that the forces personnel tended to keep themselves to themselves made for a close-knit community that relied on its own company for entertainment. And entertain themselves they did, both at home and away. Any Ballykelly Shackleton detachment that involved groundcrew was a flying party just waiting to happen on landing. The parties revolved around drinking of course, leading to lots of singing and party capers. The singing was especially good as most of the Irish folk songs made popular by the likes of the Clancy Brothers and The

Dubliners were known and sung with gusto, and these authentic songs were complemented by many of the ribald rugby variety. There were not just the cheery songs but also the old tearjerkers that had men maudlin in their beer with thoughts of home – even if they *were* at home! This is a Scottish and Irish trait mostly unknown to other races.

The RAF never posted WRAF ladies to Ballykelly for the comfort of the poor sex-starved men who were stationed there, so there was always an abundance of testosterone around the place. There was always the willingness to use this testosterone with any lucky lady, married or not, of a sympathetic nature, but in reality the use of the 'five-fingered widow' prevailed in keeping a degree of sanity among the exponents of the art.

It is well known that 'travel broadens the mind' but in the case of the boys from Ballykelly it was also an opportunity to exploit the different moral standards of far-away places to disperse some testosterone for very little money. Military historians will search in vain among these pages for events of earth-shattering importance but between these lines, and many sheets, is evidence that many a knee trembled as young men in uniform performed acts of outstanding physical bravery only inches, sometimes less, from some of the deadliest sexually transmitted diseases known to medical science. In fact, at the time of some of these actions, a lot of the diseases were not known to medical science. Some others, thankfully, were still a long way over the horizon. In addition, today there are probably numerous middle-aged people of mixed race in various parts of the world still looking for their fathers.

Friends and comrades from those far-off days, with whom many a pint of Guinness was supped and many a song sung, who think they recognise themselves in these pages either by physical description, by exploit or both, and might be considering legal action in these days of 'compensation culture', should remember a couple of points before throwing their money at lawyers. Your name has been changed to protect your guilt, and the author is flat broke and has emigrated to a place far, far away. However, this book is dedicated to you for your unstinting support of the best medicine of all – humour and laughter!

Cheers!

The photograph shows the last steam train to cross the runway at RAF Ballykelly in Northern Ireland circa 1969. The railway intersected the runway near the northern end and the passages of the trains were given priority over any aircraft ready for take-off or landing. This was just one of the little quirks of this RAF base which claimed the distinction of having the only runway in the world where a sheep was run over by a train!

For more information on Shackletons, visit www.shackletonassociation.org.uk

Shackletons in Action

To see the Shackleton in action you might like to visit
www.youtube.com/watch

Search for 'Shackleton Tribute'. This is a very good video and is an insight into much of the content of this book.

PART I

Ballykelly and North Atlantic

1

The Arrival

Looking back over the years to this particular day, I see myself becoming embroiled in a surreal situation that was entirely unexpected, yet was to be the start of a chain of events over a period of three years that I have subsequently always regarded as the best of my life.

We are all victims of circumstance. Some circumstances are thrust upon us and we can do nothing about them, others are of our own making, where we are willing participants heading towards our individual aspirations, and yet others when we are seemingly pulled along by some irresistible force, towards what would seem to be our ultimate unknown destiny. In these circumstances, like a rabbit caught in a beam of light, it seems impossible to divert the course of that destiny, even though we have the power to do so. The circumstances that I found myself in on that bleak January morning in 1968, I now believe, were certainly engendered by destiny.

I dislike boats. They are noisy and vibrate continuously with a contorted motion that goes in every direction like some great egg whisk moving through the water. They are smelly with a combination of fuel oil, engine exhaust fumes, cooking and restaurant smells all mixed in with the body odour of a million people who have sailed before. I had crossed the Irish Sea overnight from Heysham to Larne in one such hateful beast of a ferry and spent a very uncomfortable night in what was laughingly called a 'reclining seat'. As is usual there was the inevitable piece of metal framework or hard plastic on the chair that got stuck into my body somewhere, making comfort and sleep impossible. Bloody chair designers should be made to sit in their seats for more than a cursory couple of minutes to make them realise the torture that they can inflict on a long-term user. I had always been able to sleep on a clothes line but with the discomfort of this particular recliner seat and the motion of the boat there was no way that the arms of Morpheus would embrace me. I walked the decks and in the early morning light my first reaction to seeing the emerging Emerald Isle was that it did indeed look very green, as did the faces of a few of my fellow passengers as they hung over the deck railings shouting for deliverance as the last of their bile was whipped away on the wind.

The green of Ireland is caused by lots of rain falling on this fair land and it was certainly raining as the ferry bumped its way into the Larne dock. After the gangway was secured there was a rush by the foot passengers to disembark and many loaded themselves onto the waiting train on the dockside that would transport them through the Northern Ireland countryside and deposit them at their various destinations. The train was to be pulled by a tired-looking, ancient and asthmatic steam engine. The cull of the British Railways stations and steam engines in the early sixties by the good Dr Beeching had obviously not reached this far out in the Atlantic. The smell and sounds of the engine brought back a certain nostalgia for real steam 'express' trains, before the euthanasia administered by the dear doctor, and the memories of having to either stand in the corridor or hide in the toilet to get a seat on long-distance journeys from, say, Cardiff in Wales to Perth in Scotland that took seventeen hours. We can get from Cardiff to Perth Australia in that time now!

The train eventually wheezed its way out of the station and the journey through the soft wet terrain passed very slowly with frequent stops along the way – not so much 'Inter City' as 'Inter Village'. Eventually after some three and a half hours the train shuddered to a stop once more at Limavady Junction, the station that served Royal Air Force Ballykelly. I had arrived at last, after what seemed an epic journey nearing twenty hours duration, and it was with little enthusiasm that I stepped onto the platform on that bleak morning, which was still semi-dark because of the low cloud cover scurrying over the station. At least it had nearly stopped raining. I put down my kit bag to pull up the collar on my coat against the biting wind.

I was a fully paid-up member of Her Majesty's Royal Air Force and had just returned from two and a half years' tour of duty in the Far East. For the first fifteen months of that tour I had been based at the Royal Australian Air Force base at Butterworth in north-west Malaysia servicing Javelin jet fighters. My wife Pam, our two daughters Deborah and Alison and I had lived as a family on the tropical island paradise of Penang.

Living in paradise was merely a front, as in reality we were there on a semi-war footing due to the fact that Malaysia, supported by British and Australian forces, was in 'confrontation' with President Sukarno's Indonesian forces. As a family we would have liked to have stayed in Penang for the whole of the overseas tour, which would normally have lasted for two and a half years, but the squadron flight I had worked with had been disbanded after Sukarno was deposed by military coup in 1965 and the new leaders of Indonesia officially recognised the new government of Malaysia in 1966 – they had obviously heard that I had arrived in this theatre of war and had given up their ideas of land grab.

The squadron flight had moved back to the main base at RAF Tengah in Singapore. I didn't go with the squadron to Tengah but was posted instead to RAF Changi, also in Singapore. So for the past thirty months we had languished in the tropical heat and reasonably well-paid and decadent lifestyle of the British services overseas.

What was I doing here in Ireland, I had to ask myself? When about to leave Singapore I had been given a choice of posting in the UK and I was about to ask for anywhere but Ballykelly; however for some reason I didn't do it. I now had some three and a half years left to serve and found myself in the very place that I didn't particularly want to be.

Yet again, because of the short time that I had left to serve, I could have requested a final posting to anywhere in the UK that would have benefited me prior to being ejected into civilian life. I didn't take up this option either, and somebody at central postings office obviously had a wry sense of humour to have sent me here to the furthest outpost of the United Kingdom that would do me no good at all in preparing myself for the future. In this matter, instead of making a fuss, I had reasoned with myself that it would be worth giving Ballykelly a trial period and if I didn't like it I could always ask for a last posting transfer sometime later. So you see, I could have chosen to change my present circumstances, but something was calling to me and that, I believe, was destiny.

At this juncture I was twenty-three and had already served eight years in the RAF, having joined in January 1960 at fifteen years and eight months as a Boy Entrant, Engine Mechanic. The route to Ballykelly had taken me from the technical training school – interspersed with drill, bed-packs, jankers and bullshit – at St Athan in south Wales – hence the long train journeys from Cardiff to Perth, to Kinloss and Leuchars, both in Scotland – to Butterworth and Singapore. I now held the exalted position of Junior Technician, Engine Fitter.

During my three-year tour at Kinloss I had worked on the Shackleton aircraft similar to those that were being operated out of Ballykelly. At Changi in Singapore I had worked in the engine bay servicing the Griffon engines and propellers that were the power plants for these dinosaurs of the air. So, all in all, I had some four and a bit years of experience on this type of aircraft and was therefore deemed by the same misguided soul at the drafting office to be the right fodder to inconvenience with further exposure to them.

Why was I on the train at all? I had a perfectly serviceable car lying at my wife's parents' home in Doncaster, where we had been staying since our return from Singapore on New Year's Day. The reason was foot and mouth disease – not that I had suffered a bout of it myself, of course! The disease had broken out on the mainland sometime during the winter of 1967 and the Irish authorities were quite rightly restricting the access of vehicles into Ireland. The car was a Ford Zodiac Mark 3, a brute of a thing with a very thirsty six-cylinder engine. Too thirsty for a mere junior technician, married, with two hungry children, but the car had been given to us as a present by my wife's father on our return from abroad. He had just been employed as a biscuit salesman selling 'Wagon Wheels' and 'Jammy Dodgers', which entailed the use of a company car. I don't think he could sell the Zodiac, so he gave it to me to get it out of his garage, as his brand new company car had taken priority.

How I wished then that I was in the car or had been denied entry to these fair shores because of the foot and mouth scare. I wished this because, as I prepared to pick up my kit bag from the platform, I had unexpectedly espied Chic McGurk who I had known slightly from my previous life at Kinloss. I knew his reputation even better.

Chic was a brute of a Glaswegian standing six foot three inches, with a great ruddy complexion and a look in his eyes that indicated the razor-wired border between the two states of sanity and insanity. His bent nose, the dent in his forehead and the various scars and nicks around his face made him look like the victim of a shark attack. His complexion was highlighted by drink of course, and he had broken veins all over his face and especially his nose. He had a thirst greater than my Zodiac. For a young man he had been completely ravished by his best mate – alcohol.

Chic was quite amiable and reticent when he was sober but he was one of those terrible, violent drunks. Unfortunately, nobody ever remembers him being completely sober. His looks did not in any way reflect his trade in the RAF as he was a 'fairy' – the name given to any of the

6

wishy-washy electronic trades that never did a full day's work in their lives. Chic was an air radar technician.

When stationed at Kinloss he had gone out on a bender one night and had wrecked a bar and several of his fellow drinkers in the local town of Elgin. For his efforts, Chic had sustained some damage to his cranium, which had affected what little pickled brain was left, and he had disappeared from work for several days. In the military, being absent without leave is an extremely heinous crime and Chic was court-martialled and given three months in Colchester military prison.

Colchester at that time was renowned as one of the harshest prison regimes in the world. It was like that because the sadistic bastards in charge of the prison were there to give the inmates a short sharp shock, bootcamp style, to bring them back on the straight and narrow, and it was supposedly 'good for morale and discipline'. Whether it was good for the morale of the inmates or for the sadistic guards was open to question. It was said of anyone who had ever experienced Colchester that they came out a changed man, mentally and spiritually broken. Chic was also changed but his experiences had made him worse. It was claimed that the three months of sobriety enforced by the prison sentence had knocked him over the edge and that when he came out he was perpetually trying to make up for all the drink he had not been able to consume while inside.

On this day, Chic was living up to his reputation. He had obviously been partaking of a few cool libations on the ferry across the Irish Sea and in the train buffet car coming up from Belfast. I could only guess at this but I think my guess was probably correct, as he was being physically bundled off the train by the guard and the buffet steward with whom he had obviously had some altercation. His bag was unceremoniously thrown out of the carriage door at him. He failed to catch it and it landed on the platform with the ominous clink of breaking glass. This was undoubtedly his reserve stock of alcohol now being soaked up by his underpants. On the platform he was 'stottin' drunk and falling about among the other passengers who were trying to keep clear of him, rapidly departing the scene, shaking their heads in disdain. If he saw me I knew there would be trouble ahead, and I was not to be disappointed.

At Limavady Junction there were no places to hide and there were no immediate signs of how I could get off the platform without meeting him, as he was between me and the exit. So with my head bowed very low I tried to pass Chic to make good my escape. Unfortunately for me, for some reason he recognised me, even although I hadn't seen him for at least four years. Whether he had seen me and recognised me earlier on the train or ferry I shall never know.

He staggered up to me and put his hand on my chest for the dual purpose of stopping himself staggering and stopping me from getting away from him.

'How the fuck's it goin', big man? Ah hivna seen youse in fuckin' ages! Youse should a come an' had a wee bevvie wi me on the train. It wis fuckin' great in at. Where is youse goin' by the way? Youse is no posted tae this hell hole, is youse – it's worse than bein' in fuckin' jail here, so it is.'

I stammered a few words of inane greeting through an extremely embarrassed set grin on my face. My embarrassment was made even worse as the train had not departed the station yet and one of the boarding passengers was a high-ranking air officer who was surveying the scene with some interest.

'How's youse getting' doon tae Ballykelly by the way?' Chic inquired. I replied that as this was my first trip here I thought I might be able to get a taxi or a bus. I was also thinking to myself, 'Why me – why do these drunken bastards always latch on to me?'

'Fuck that!' said Chic. 'I've got a mate that'll tak us yins tae ra gate an' at, c'mon wi me, we'll gie him a ring.'

I think I did try to make some excuse to try to extricate myself once more, but to no avail. Chic had a hold of me around the neck, my head nestled very uncomfortably in the crook of his arm, and he was leaning heavily on me as he pulled me down into the station car park. This was very ungainly and I had to drag my full and very heavy kit bag along after me, as there was no way I could carry it with Chic draped all over me.

At this point the train started to pull out of the station.

'How's it goin' an at hen, any chance o' geein us a ride doon tae Ballykelly gate an at? Or on second thoughts maybe just a ride wid be enough – hoos aboot it?' This tirade was directed towards the very attractive WRAF driver of a grey Standard RAF staff car who was removing the high-ranking officer's flag from the small mast on the car's front wing. She had obviously driven him to the station.

'Go and stuff yourself!' she replied in her best south-east accent. 'This ain't a taxi or a bleedin' bonkin' wagon, anyway, wot d'ya fink I am?'

'I'm very sorry,' I said. 'My mate's a bit under the weather as he was a bit seasick from the ferry crossing and had to have a couple of drinks to settle his stomach. Could you tell me where I could phone for a taxi? This is my first trip to this part of the world.'

'Oh, you seem to be all right. I suppose I could take you down to the village and drop you off before we get to the gates into the base, as long as you behave yourselves though. Get your stuff in the back.'

'That's the fuckin' game!' said Chic, bouncing off the side of the car with his holdall and leaving a bloody great scratch on the rear wing from the zip. He eventually got the door open and lurched into the back seat, sprawled himself all over it and immediately appeared to go to sleep. There was a very strong smell of alcohol coming from both his bag and his breath.

With him sprawled over the back seat it meant that I had to travel up front with the dolly bird, not that I was complaining. We set off and I made some small talk to the girl, which was immediately interrupted by some belching and farting from the back seat. I remember saying that I thought she should hurry up as anything could happen with the state he was in.

'I didn't think there were any WRAF at Ballykelly,' I said.

'No, there ain't any. I'm driving Roger – I mean the Air Marshal – on a trip round Ireland. We've been here for a week now and are going back home tomorrow,' she replied coyly.

I thought to myself that she was probably doing more for the Air Marshall than just driving.

As I mused on this fact there was an almighty retch from Chic and ten pints of Guinness, several vodkas and a meat pie were ejected onto the floor of the car. The girl gave out an almighty scream, became hysterical and nearly crashed the car into the ditch before I pulled on the steering wheel and the handbrake, stalling the car near a gateway in the process.

'Wot the hell am I goin' to do now,' wailed the girl. 'I'm really goin' to be in trouble for sure. I wish I had never given that ugly pig a ride in my car. Whew, what a bleedin' stink!' She waved her hand in front of her face and wound down the window at the same time.

I tried to calm her down but in reality there was little I could do. I simply could not think of anything. I got out of the car, opened the back door, pulled the mat and the remains of Chic's stomach contents, still steaming in the morning cold, out onto the road and tipped them into the ditch. I wiped off the more solid parts with some grass but it still left a hell of a mess on the carpet and seat in the back of the car, all of which I could do little about.

'You'll have to get that ignorant pig out of the car,' she said. 'I'm not goin' another inch with him in there and that's for sure. I need to go into the garage in Limavady to get this mess cleaned up before I go back to my hotel in Ballykelly.'

I tried to reason with her that nothing else would happen as he had done his worst, but nothing would persuade her to carry on.

Christ, what a job we had getting Chic out of the car. He was utterly comatose and weighed a ton – even without his stomach contents. We eventually got him to the side of the road and laid him up against the fence in the recovery position. I got his and my stuff out of the car and was still trying to apologise to the girl when she drove off in high dudgeon. I had asked her to try to phone for a taxi to come and pick us up but I had little hope of her doing so, as her two-fingered salute indicated, and who could blame her? I bet she and Roger never used the back seat of that car again.

So here I was stranded by the roadside, only about half a mile from the railway station. I could easily have walked back to phone for a taxi, but with the state Chic was in I didn't want to leave him in case he began to choke on his vomit or something. I kicked at the grass at the side of the road and probably had a sly swipe at Chic into the bargain. I cursed my bloody luck.

As providence would have it, within about three minutes, which seemed like an eternity, a farmer driving an ancient David Brown two-seater tractor and a low-slung trailer loaded with some milk churns came trundling down the road at some speed. I did not wave the man to stop – but stop he did, like the Good Samaritan. He got down from the tractor and came across to me.

'Jeez boys, yon feller looks in some state, it looks like drink's bin taken,' he shouted over the non-existent exhaust silencer of the tractor. 'Diz yez need a hand?'

'I'd be grateful for a lift down to the gates at Ballykelly.'

'No problem at all, boyo! Let's get your friend up onto the trailer.'

I was about to respond that this was no friend of mine but the noise of the tractor put me off saying anything. My main worry at this time was how it would look arriving at the Ballykelly guardroom in a tractor and trailer along with a comatose drunk. I was glad of the help though.

Once again providence came to my rescue. As we tried to lift Chic up off the ground he gave a grunt, appeared to become conscious once again and struggled to his feet. However, stability and gravity are not the friends of drunks. The laws of physics prevailed and Chic lurched along the road with his head parallel to the ground and went headlong into an iron gate, sustaining a two-inch cut to his upper forehead. He gave out an almighty 'Fuck!' and became comatose once again. There was a fair amount of blood flowing from the wound, but it was nothing too serious.

I was saved! Now I had the excuse to bring him to the guardroom, the trailer substituting as an ambulance.

After having rearranged some of the milk churns we finally got Chic back into the recovery position on the trailer, only this time there was blood covering most of his face and soaking his shirt and overcoat. Why do head wounds bleed so much? I tried to staunch the flow with my 'dirty' hanky but there was nothing more to be done at this stage.

I got onto the seat on the tractor beside the driver and with a violent lurch of the clutch we were off. As we sped along the road at what seemed like breakneck speed, I was getting covered in non-combusted diesel smuts that were emitted in a constant stream from the inefficient and ancient engine, and lumps of dirt that were being thrown up from the front wheels of the tractor. I glanced back at the trailer to see if Chic was still with us. The trailer had been used quite recently for muck spreading and poor old Chic was in direct contact with the muck on the floor, which was mixing with some spilt milk. As the trailer moved along the road at a fair rate of knots he was bounced and vibrated more into the mire. However, I was relieved to be on my way and even more relieved that I had the excuse to get Chic into the base without too much trouble.

We reached the main Limavady to Londonderry road and turned right, and after half a mile or so we were in the village of Ballykelly. The tractor took a right turn into the road leading down to the main gate of the base, tucked some two hundred yards away. I shouted to the farmer that he should stop and let me off the tractor before the gate. He said something in return but I could not understand him above the din of the exhaust. Still he gave me the thumbs up sign so I knew he had got my message. My intention was that I could go up to the guardroom and present my ID card, and tell those inside of the predicament of our recumbent and comatose passenger. We pulled in to the side of the road and stopped. I dismounted from the tractor, trying not to get any more dirt or manure on my clothes. I got my kit bag down and walked confidently through the open and unguarded gate up to the guardroom. The farmer stayed on his tractor, leaning on the steering wheel as he patiently surveyed the scene.

The guardroom was manned by RAF Police, commonly known as 'Snoops' for obvious reasons. These people were not the smartest in the land, but they believed that they had a divine right to be as nasty as they possibly could to anyone that came within their range. Their ultimate goal was probably to become a guard at Colchester.

I went up to the window where a corporal Snoop was pretending to write something on a piece of paper attached to a clipboard. He eventually decided to recognise that I was there and looked up from his clipboard. I was immediately shocked and at the same time had to stop myself laughing when I saw his face full-on for the first time. He had two of the most enormous ears sticking straight out from the sides of his head, accompanied by a very monkey-like face. I could have sworn that I had turned up at the zoo instead of an RAF station. The proportion of ears to face made him resemble an oversized wingnut.

Stifling back laughter I produced my ID card. 'Corporal, I am Junior Tech Blair, just been posted here and I need some help with an injured guy who is lying in the farmer's trailer over there.'

'Just a minute, mate,' he replied, quite civilly I thought to myself. He disappeared into the guardroom and came back with another clipboard.

'Right, who the hell are you then?' he barked. 'What's your name, rank and number?'

I supplied this information and also repeated that there was an injured man in the trailer who needed urgent attention.

'You say you're posted here – you're not on my friggin' list mate and if you're not on the friggin' list you can't come in – can you?'

'I can assure you that if I had not been posted here I wouldn't be here, would I?' I said producing my transfer documentation which I was glad I had with me.

'It's all very well you havin' this documentation but we have not been notified that you have been posted here and you are not on the friggin' list. We've got a heightened security level here because of some IRA trouble, who's to say that you're not one of them with false papers?' he screamed. I shrugged – but I knew that I had just walked onto the base through an unguarded gate so where in hell's name were the measures for the heightened security?

'Look, never mind me for the moment, there is an injured man in the trailer over there and he needs urgent medical attention. He is stationed here at Ballykelly. I met him on the railway station platform and we've travelled here together.'

'Where is this fucker that you keep on about?'

I pointed once again and he had to poke his head out of the window to see what I was pointing at. Just then the head of Chic McGurk, or what purported to be the head of Chic McGurk, poked itself above the sides of the trailer. It was an awesome sight. One side was covered in dried blood and the other was plastered in milk mixed with manure slurry. This had made one side of his hair stand up, so he looked like some grotesque gargoyle that had been shat upon by a thousand pigeons.

'What the friggin' hell is that?' snorted the Snoop. 'Injured you say – has he been run over by the tractor?'

'No, no, as I said, I met him at the station – I know him slightly and we travelled from the station to here together. He has had a slight collision with a gate on the way and has quite a deep cut on his forehead. The farmer was good enough to give us a lift in his trailer otherwise we might not have got here for a while.'

'It's a pity you even arrived here at all with the state of that fucker – and you not bein' on the friggin' list. How come he had this – what did you call it – collision with the gate, did you beat him up or somethin'? You say he's stationed here – who the friggin hell is it anyway?'

All this time, McGurk had been sitting up in the back of the trailer looking around him with uncomprehending eyes – mainly because they were bunged up with blood and manure and tears were pouring down his cheeks making his mask even more grotesque.

'No, I did not beat him up,' I retorted, 'and his name is Chic McGurk.'

'Oh no! Not friggin' McGurk again!' wailed the Snoop. 'Couldn't you have killed the bastard while you had the chance? We had better get him off that trailer before he comes round fully. Otherwise there will be trouble like the last time.'

I never had the chance to ask what the last time was, as the Snoop called out to his colleagues inside the guardhouse to come and give him a hand with 'that bastard McGurk'. I was forgotten in the ensuing rush to restrain him.

Four Snoops in total came rushing out of the guardhouse and ran across the road to the trailer, their hobnailed boots crunching on the road like tank tracks. However, when they reached the vicinity of the trailer they slowed down markedly and a certain amount of tension was in the air as they talked among themselves, obviously deciding how to tackle McGurk to get him off the wagon.

McGurk was still sitting up in a very dazed condition, whether from the effects of the drink or the head-butt on the gate it mattered not. Two Snoops got onto the trailer from the tractor end, which positioned them behind our hapless warrior. Their job was obviously to get hold of his arms and slide him towards the rear where the other two were waiting to lift him to the ground. This was a good plan and would have worked if McGurk had not partially regained some sense. Through his drunken haze he undoubtedly thought he was being attacked. He grabbed at one of the lads on the trailer and brought his legs from under him. This guy fell into the space between McGurk and the front board of the trailer and this position gave him a good purchase to push with his feet on McGurk's back.

He must have pushed with all his might, as McGurk and the second Snoop from the trailer came shooting off the rear along with one of the milk churns that the Snoop had taken hold of in order to steady himself. McGurk, along with several pounds of manure slurry, went sliding into the two other Snoops standing on the road waiting to catch him. At the sight of the slurry coming towards them, there was no way that they wanted to get any of it on their immaculately pressed trousers or their highly polished boots, so they jumped out of the way – they failed on both counts and missed McGurk into the bargain. McGurk hit the ground with a crunch and his condition was worsened by the Snoop from the cart falling on top of him, followed by the milk churn. He was out cold again but what a rare sight he had left behind. Four Snoops plastered in blood and shit all over their nice shiny uniforms and boots, and they still didn't have McGurk in a safe place.

'Get a ground sheet quickly!' cried one of them. 'There's no way we want to be carrying this shitty bastard into the guardroom.'

One of them came running back across the road and plunged into the building, returning with a ground sheet, which was duly spread out next to McGurk. Collectively the Snoops used their feet to kick and roll him over onto the sheet. Once he was on they each grabbed a corner of the sheet and started to half lift, half drag him around to the back of the guardhouse where there was a high, wired compound.

'He needs medical attention for that cut on his forehead,' I shouted after them.

'Don't worry, we'll get the Doc out after we have cleaned him up with the hosepipe.' Christ, the Snoops had some humanity in them after all.

As they disappeared round the corner, it was the last I saw of Chic McGurk for a while. I was going to make some protest about the use of the hosepipe but thought better of it and anyway it was possibly the best thing for him.

I went across to the farmer who was replacing the milk churn on the trailer, and thanked him for his kindness. 'Jeez boy, no thanks required – it's the best laugh I've had in ages,' he replied, and all things considered, I had to agree with him. He climbed back onto the tractor and revved the engine, turned round on the road and disappeared in a puff of soot.

However, I was not finished at the guardhouse. I went back to the window where I heard some awful cursing and swearing coming from the rear – McGurk had obviously come to, due to the effects of the hosepipe I presumed. I waited for several minutes. Wingnut came back to the window still brushing detritus from his trousers and obviously concerned about the state of his boots.

'Oh it's you again – what is it this time?'

'Same thing as last time, I need to book into the base as I have nowhere else to go and it's a bloody long way back home.'

'No need for the friggin' swearin' – let me look at your transfer papers again.'

I handed them over. 'I am posted to 203 Squadron so can't you phone or let me phone the squadron adjutant?' I asked.

'That's a problem as there are no friggin' squadrons any more as they have gone over to centralised servicing.'

Oh Christ, I thought, and my heart sunk to my boots – not the dreaded Handling and Rectification (H&R) Flight philosophy that I had worked at Kinloss all those years before – it was unpopular with aircrew and groundcrew alike, as the groundcrew were not part of a particular squadron but serviced all squadron aircraft collectively from a central point.

'Well, in my experience, there will be a H&R flight commander or a warrant officer who should be able to tell you that I am expected to report onto the base today. Can you please give them a ring?'

He disappeared once more into the bowels of the guardhouse and it was several minutes before he came back.

'They've never friggin' heard of you either. They say they are not expecting anybody as they are over-manned with all this squadron change-over and that. If they don't know who you are then what chance do I have?'

'What chance indeed,' I thought. 'Look, I have identified myself and have shown you my transfer papers – what more do you want me to do? I am here and I can't go back, can I? So are you going to let me onto the base to at least get a bed for the night so we can sort this out later?' By this time I was near shaking with tiredness, frustration and anger at all that had happened.

'I'll need to get a hold of the friggin' station warrant officer before I can make any decision.'

'Now that's a good idea,' I said and I could see his chest physically swelling with this compliment.

He disappeared into the guardhouse once more. 'He'll be along from Station Headquarters in about ten minutes,' he called from inside.

'Thanks,' I replied.

Ten then fifteen, twenty, thirty minutes passed, and it seemed like an eternity. I reflected back to when I had left Doncaster the previous day for the drive to catch the Heysham ferry and that seemed like longer than eternity. I had had very little to eat since docking at Belfast and I could have murdered a cup of tea.

After about thirty-five minutes had passed, the station warrant officer came pedalling very unsteadily on his bike down the road from the direction of the village. I was to learn later that 'Station Headquarters' turned out to be Mickey's bar next to the betting shop on the main road.

Station warrant officers were always stern characters, carrying the full weight of the operational airbase around on their shoulders – or so they thought. In essence they were mainly jumped-up discipline jockeys who knew little more than how to count blankets in the blanket store and how to prop up the bar in the sergeants' mess. They were even worse with drink in them! More importantly for any groundcrew personnel, they were to be avoided like the plague, as they would issue a charge at the drop of a hat for some minor indiscretion or misdemeanour. Like a cat with a mouse, once cornered there was little hope of escape from their clutches for a long time.

He gave me a very uncompromising look and did not respond to my 'Good morning, sir,' as he walked straight into the guardroom.

'Whew! What is that fuckin' stink in here? Strewth look at the state you lot are in, you'd think you had all been down the fuckin' midden! I'm not goin' to stand for this – not on my station. You all had better have an excuse for this!' He had obviously had a fair skinful of drink for his mid-morning break and looked decidedly pissed.

'It was the fault of that guy standing outside, sir. He brought that fucker McGurk in here on a manure cart driven by a farmer. His head was split open.'

'How did the farmer get his head split open, did McGurk do it?' asked the SWO.

'I don't think the farmer's head was split open but McGurk's was,' said Wingnut. 'Did anyone see if the farmer's head was split open?' he asked the other Snoops.

'Well, if McGurk did split open the farmer's head then you better get the evidence so we can sling the book at the bastard. He's not getting away with making a mess of this fuckin' guardhouse and you lot will be on a charge if you don't get this place and yourselves cleaned up. Where is McGurk now?'

'He's out the back soaking wet as we had to put the hosepipe on him to get the worst of the shit off him. We've called the Doc and he should be on his way to attend to him.'

'Well, can't you ask McGurk if he split open the farmer's head? Still I don't suppose he would admit it in any case – we'll need hard evidence. Is this why you called me here to find out who split the farmer's head?'

'No, not really, sir. We didn't know that the farmer's head was split open before you came in but we will certainly find out who did it. The reason we got you across here is that there is a guy outside who reckons he has been posted here and has come all the way from Singapore or somewhere but nobody knows anything about him. He brought McGurk in on the cart with the farmer with the split head.'

'Well, did you ask him if he saw who had split open the farmer's head – I bet you didn't, you clueless bastards – bring him in so I can ask him.'

I was duly escorted into the guardhouse and felt very uncomfortable and vulnerable among so many brain cells – they must have had a dozen between them. The atmosphere was highly charged – with the stink of manure but little else. In reality there was no need for me to be inside, as anyone in Limavady five miles away could have heard their conversation.

'The corporal here tells me that you brought in McGurk on a manure cart and that McGurk had split open the head of the farmer who was driving the tractor. Did you see this happen?' There was a definite slur in his voice and he had difficulty focusing because his eyelids kept closing.

I relayed the whole sorry tale to the SWO, although I left out the bit about the staff car. However, I did have to say that McGurk was drunk otherwise I had no excuse for him head-butting the gate. I also passed an opinion that I did not know whether the farmer had arrived on the scene with a split head or not – there was no evidence either way but certainly McGurk did not do it.

This seemed to perplex the SWO as he was now convinced that there was an Irish farmer running about the countryside with a split head.

Funny thing is, he never asked if I knew the name of the farmer or where he might live. However, he seemed quite pleased that he could get McGurk on a charge of Drunk and Disorderly and Conduct Prejudicial to Good Order. To be honest I thought Chic would probably get off quite lightly and it would not have bothered him in the least.

After several fruitless phone calls the SWO eventually allowed me onto his station and he directed me to the bedding store. I am sure I detected a lump in his throat and a small tear in his eye at the very mention of the place. I was sure glad to get away from there before the SWO sobered up!

In the bedding store I was allocated to room 246. I left the bedding behind to collect later because I was carrying my heavy kit bag as I went in search of my new home. I found 246 at the end of a line of very old and weary-looking single-storey buildings. To call them buildings was a compliment, as they looked more like hovels that were in dire need of some care and attention – like demolition. The entrance to these hovels was in the centre of the building, with the toilets and shower room directly ahead. I poked my head round the door and looked round to see what was on offer. Two urinals, two cracked and crazed sinks, two toilet bowls behind rather dilapidated doors, two showers bedecked with very mouldy shower curtains made up the salubrious suite. All this to service the ablution requirements of eighteen men!

Back in the small corridor, on either side was a door that led into the rooms that shared these magnificent facilities. I took pot luck and turned to the right as I left the toilets. This one action sealed my destiny. I entered a dingy room that had eight beds with very old service-type wardrobes and side lockers arranged around them. One of the beds was without bedclothes, so I dumped my stuff on it and collected my bedding from the bedding store. I made my bed and opened the locker to hang up my clothes – there was no back to the bloody thing. I looked at the other lockers and they were all the same, but they had padlocks on the latches at the front. What price security here? I hung up my clothes anyway, got onto the bed, lay back with a cigarette and reflected on the day's events – bloody hell! It had been less than two hours since I got off that train but it seemed like forever – and there was still lunch to look forward to. I wondered what sort of place I had ended up in. I had a real feeling of foreboding. Was this an RAF base or a lunatic asylum?

Destiny, helped by the RAF drafting office, had deposited me here. I had the power to change these circumstances, but would I? Would this place suit my temperament, would my family like it here? We would be a long way from friends and family at home in Yorkshire and Scotland and if they wanted to visit they would be in for one hell of a journey. I had the feeling that I had made a big mistake and I should make plans for the exit as soon as possible, especially now knowing that I was not even expected here in the first place. This accommodation was crap and should have been replaced years before. Was Ballykelly actually part of the air force? With the surreal incidents I had experienced so far this was in serious doubt, as it was different from anything that I had experienced in my service career thus far. However, I also knew that I would not thwart my destiny, not for a while. I owed it a settling-in period at least.

As for Chic McGurk, God knows what state he was in when he finally woke up. It was not until several weeks later that I came across him again at work. He now sported a very ugly bright red scar over his left eye but it somehow seemed to complement all the other nicks, creases and holes around his face. To my eternal relief he never mentioned the incident and although he seemed to recognise me he was very distant – perhaps he could only remember people when he was drunk, or perhaps he thought I had beaten him up on that fateful day and was scared of me?

2

The Social Vipers

I must have fallen asleep for a while – I could sleep anywhere at any time – and was woken by someone moving about in the room. It was a guy getting himself ready for bed. He was in his pyjamas. I got up and went over to him. He was in his late twenties, of medium build and he had a long, oval, open face with two doleful-looking eyes almost hidden beneath very bushy eyebrows. He sported a mop of dark curly and wiry hair that stood out in all directions on his head and made him look like he had just experienced an electric shock. He somehow reminded me of a cocker spaniel.

'Hi, I'm Gordon Blair – just been posted in and will be staying here for a while. Have you just come off night shift?'

'How's about ye, I'm Winston Finlay – Doc to my friends,' he said in a quiet lilting Irish accent. 'No, I've not been on night shift but I always come back to the room for a bit of shut eye after lunch.' At that he hopped into bed, pulled the covers over his head and was snoring within thirty seconds. Now it was not unusual for guys to go back to their rooms for a lie down after lunch – but I had never seen anyone putting on their pyjamas and getting fully into bed before!

I looked at my watch – it was half past eleven. I must have been asleep for only about twenty minutes. I was about to get back on my bed to light up another cigarette when the door opened once again and in walked a dark swarthy-looking character of medium build, turning slightly to fat. He had a round, open and pleasant face with a well-groomed head of wavy black hair. He eyed me with suspicion so I jumped in first. 'Gordon Blair, just been posted in and I've been allocated a bed in here until my family arrives later on.'

'James Curry, Esquire,' he gave out a strange *hee, hee, hee* and his shoulders shook slightly. 'I'm the corporal in charge of this dump and I stay in this wee hovel at the end here.' He pointed to the door of a room that I had not previously noticed. He had a strong west-coast Scottish accent. 'I see Doc's back in his scratcher – he's never oot o' the bloody thing. Be sure yi get a bed where nobody's stayin' – some of the guys are away on detachment. Have yi eaten' yet?'

'Right, I thought the place looked a bit deserted. No, I haven't eaten yet.'

'C'mon then, let's go.'

So this was my introduction to my future soul-mate, friend and oft-times my nemesis. He was one of the most colourful characters in Ballykelly at that time and we were destined to share some memorable experiences in the future. He was not the only one who fell into this category, but he was the best.

The lunch menu and the food were of a very high standard so with food in my belly and a new acquaintance who was neither drunk nor stupid – at least not at that time – I began to feel somewhat more relaxed.

The catering in the airmen's mess at Ballykelly remained second to none all the time I was there. The mess itself was modern and set up to give the impression of a restaurant instead of the normal 'school dinner' type table and seating arrangement. The catering staff was always first class and always accommodating which was not normally the case on an operational base.

This was probably because of the competition from Ma Hassin's café, situated on the main road outside the main gates. Ma served up the most prodigious plateful of cholesterol in the shape of an 'Ulster Fry' – in any combination of the ingredients. Her fried soda bread was the best dough in town! More important though, she also gave tick when airmen arrived back at the base pissed out of their skulls, having spent all their money, and were in dire need of a grease injection to settle the gut. She never refused to cook for them, and none reneged on their debts – but then she probably had some heavy protection policy, enforced from among the local community.

After lunch we went back to the room to while away the rest of the lunch break. Doc was still fast asleep, snoring his head off, and he remained comatose until he was rudely awakened by a very loud alarm clock at about quarter to one. He got out of bed and pulled on his uniform over his pyjamas. I wondered if he wore his pyjamas all the time, as I had not seen him take off his uniform when he first came in. He and Jimmy left to catch the bus that would take them back to work at H&R. I spent the afternoon going round the various departments to 'check in' – which was mandatory on any new base. I went first to the general office and they confirmed that I was indeed posted to Ballykelly and that I was not therefore an IRA insurgent. Then I did the rounds of the SWO's office and the stores, where I had to buy a new 'working blue' uniform, and then to the station tailors to get the bloody thing altered. It was always a mystery who the uniforms had been made for – the original models obviously gave lie to the belief that no aliens from outer space had ever visited earth! I went to the families office and was told that it would be about six weeks before a house was available. I phoned my wife from this office and told her of the day's events. I never got down to H&R flight that day as it was a bloody long way and there was no transport available – at least that was my excuse.

I went to tea with Corporal James Curry Esq. and when we came back to the room some of the other guys were there. Jimmy Buckley, Rex McCartney, and of course Doc, who was back in bed again! Jimmy Buckley was a very handsome Irish lad with dark hair and dark Spanish-looking eyes. He resembled George Best but he was better looking as his features were more refined. He was always quite unassuming and even remote until drink had been taken and then he usually caused mayhem. After about six pints of Guinness he began to have difficulty focusing with two eyes, so one eye would partially close while the other looked out of its socket across his nose, giving the impression that he was leering at all around him. If you were a woman this was a signal that he was about to home in and start his 'chat up' mode. If you were a man and no women were present it was a signal that you better be prepared to join in some outrageous stunt or get out of the room! Sometimes he was even known to ignore the ladies in favour of making a fool of himself. It all depended on how much drink had been taken.

Rex McCartney was a tall and very slim Irishman with a common Irish feature of a long, slim, hook nose. He had a very soft high-pitched and melodious voice giving forth a Northern Irish accent. He was a very good singer of the Irish ballads and he loved nothing better than to entertain an audience – especially a female audience!

At that time I did not of course appreciate the fact that this little band of brothers was a nest of 'social vipers'. Mad, bad and dangerous to know.

After the introductions and some chit chat it was suggested that we all went together to the cinema. The film ended at about nine and we were walking back to the room, hands thrust deep in our pockets for protection against the biting wind. With the dismal prospect of doing little else with the rest of the evening other than going to bed, I asked if they wanted to go for a drink.

'Nae money!' came the reply. 'An we dinna get paid 'til Thursday.'

'I've got some money,' I said, 'so I'll stand you a drink if you like.'

At this there was a general rising of the spirit. I had brought about twenty pounds with me which was a small fortune in those days – I had five pounds in my pocket as we trundled over to the bar in The Crossed Keys Club.

We went upstairs into the pigs' bar and I took the order – four pints of Guinness – and went up to the counter. I had never been a great lover of Guinness but was weaned on the tale that Guinness was better in Ireland than it was on the mainland, so I had to give it a try.

'Four pints of Guinness, please,' I said to the barmaid.

The face on this woman would have stopped a stampede of horses dead in their tracks. Her features were completely unemotional and unmoving. They obviously couldn't move because of the make-up plastered all over them. The panstick foundation was so thick it would have immobilised a broken leg. The face powder on top of this was obviously applied by someone standing at the other side of the room and throwing it at her. It was blotchy and allowed the pink, cracked, panstick to show through in places, giving the impression that she was suffering from some incurable skin disease. Her lips were cherry red and shaped like cupid's bow well outside the limits of the lip itself – in fact the arches of the bow nearly disappeared up her nostrils! The bottom lip was as bad since the lipstick line extended down to the middle of her chin. There were two large splodges of rouge on her cheeks with no pretence of blending them into the surrounding make-up to give a more natural look. Her eyebrows had been completely plucked out and pretend eyebrows drawn in with a thin pencil at an extremely exaggerated position up on her forehead. But the most alarming feature of all was the fact that all this was applied only to the bits of face that could be seen by looking directly into a mirror. In other words this was a full frontal onslaught, again without blending around the ears, under her chin, or down her neck. This was evidenced by the fact that her hair was pulled back off her face in some sort of French roll. Her eyes continually rolled in their sockets but she never focused on anything or anyone, however I got the impression that by the rolling of the eyes and occasional lift of an eyebrow and a slight imperceptible lip pout she thought herself as being very sexy. She owed more to Coco the Clown than to Coco Chanel!

I was mesmerised for a few seconds but did not want to appear to be staring too much, so I turned round from the bar and gave a wry smile to my drinking companions. They in turn were gesticulating that I might be getting an erection and might be in with a chance – if I really fancied it! I looked heavenwards and gave them a surreptitious V sign.

'Who the hell is that?' I asked when I finally got the drinks back to the table. It takes a considerable amount of time to pour four Guinnesses from one pump and I had to endure the occasional doe-eyed glance from the barmaid. She never spoke once and I was scared to start a conversation in case her face cracked further, like some Victorian china doll.

'That's Molly – commonly known as Molly the Mask,' came the reply.

'Christ, I wouldn't want her to take me up a dark alley! Is she local or was she shipped in with the last circus to hit town?'

'Don't think you'll ever get the chance of taking her up an alley because it might spoil her make-up. Nobody seems to know where she comes from as she never speaks to anyone. We think she might be a man,' was the reply.

The round had come to eight shillings – two bob a pint, that's ten pence if you were born after decimalisation. Two other guys dressed in civvies came into the bar, sat at the table and looked longingly at the beer. When asked if they wanted a pint they enthusiastically did not refuse. They did venture to introduce themselves but there was so much noise I didn't catch their names.

After we had drunk about four pints each, someone started to sing and the others joined in. These boys had a prodigious repertoire of songs. There was some singing attempted at Kinloss, especially on the bus when returning from a dance in Buckie or Elgin or wherever, but nobody knew all the words to any song so it was merely done to make a noise akin to football chants. But here was something different, songs were sung with a passion and all due respect was given to the singers of individual songs. Most of the songs I had never heard before – 'The Wild Rover', 'Jug of Punch', 'Leaving of Liverpool', 'The Juice of the Barley', 'Shackletons Don't Bother Me', and many more.

Davey Hughes, one of the late comers, was a particularly good singer and he gave it all the gusto he could muster. So much so that his neck bulged to twice its normal size and went a deep scarlet – as did his face. He reminded me of a cock turkey in heat – it really was quite alarming because if his head had burst there would have been blood and snot all over the place.

24

Another guy dressed in uniform came in and sat in the corner next to our table. He was obviously on duty. He was tall, thin and gaunt with a pimply pockmarked face that resembled the surface of the moon, and his hair was long, fair and looked as if it had just been washed – about two years ago! As he sat there watching the proceedings with sunken eyes and listening to the music he was shaking, and his hand continually cupped his mouth and his fingers played with his lips as if he was trying to wipe away some non-existent spittle. By this time all cares had left me and while taking the order for the next round I included him.

'What're you drinking mate?' I said.

'I don't know – you haven't fuckin' bought it yet!' This man was Tommy Craigden – and Guinness and any other liquid libation was his staple diet.

When my fiver had run out we bid Molly goodnight, but she surprisingly did not respond, and we left. I had bought about fifty pints and, having drunk six pints myself, I had had a bountiful introduction to the Black Nectar and acquired a determination to learn the songs. More importantly I had been accepted into the vipers' nest.

3

Aircraft Handling and Rectification Flight

Oh, my bloody head! It felt like someone was inside my skull and trying to kick his way out of it. I had never been much of a beer drinker and the six pints of Guinness were taking their toll.

It was six o'clock in the morning and I had been woken by the noise of some of the guys getting up and preparing for the early shift. I turned over and tried to get back to sleep. Hopeless – my head hurt too much. I got up and had a shower.

After breakfast I boarded the bus that would take me down Dukes Lane – the main road on the base – to my assigned place of work, Shackleton Handling and Rectification Flight.

In the interests of greater economies and efficiencies, a bright spark had decided some time ago that it would be best to eliminate the individual squadron structure for the groundcrews and to amalgamate them into one happy band of brothers. On reflection, I suppose that the system did work to a degree but it destroyed the intense competitiveness that prevailed between squadrons and the familiarity that was built up between aircrew and groundcrew as part of the same group. Under the H&R regime, the aircrew did loosely remain within their squadron groups but they shared the larger pool of aircraft made available from H&R flight. However, unlike a real squadron, very little social interaction took place between aircrew and groundcrew and this led to the groundcrew regarding the aircrew as an inconvenience, people who took out perfectly serviceable aircraft and broke them! This would not have been too bad, but ninety per cent of the flying hours were spent within the boundaries of the base, as the aircrew went round and round doing circuits and bumps in order that the pilots maintained their required flying hours. The rest of the aircrew were only on board as ballast, but it also ensured that they got their share of the lucrative 'flying pay' – lucky bastards!

However, the formation of H&R dragged together all the characters from the various squadrons and it was this increased family – living, working, travelling, drinking together and all the while taking the piss out of each other – that gave the unique blend of humour that was to prevail throughout life at Ballykelly. Also there was fierce competition between the various shifts, with each of them blaming the others for not having done their share of the workload.

I went into the crewroom that was so filled with smoke that I had difficulty breathing – and I was a smoker. There was a blackboard that proclaimed what was thought of Handling and Rectification flight – 'H&R SUX'! A few guys were lolling around on armchairs talking and reading but the main source of the smoke was a table in the corner where a game of brag was taking place. There were a few coins on the table, therefore no serious gambling, but the atmosphere was obviously intense and demanded all the attention of the participants – it was eight o'clock.

I went up to one of the guys in an armchair.

'Any officers or chiefs around at the moment?' I enquired.

'What trade are you mate?' he replied.

'Engines.'

'Right, you'll want to see Gordon Mendes. He'll be next door, c'mon.' I followed him up to the door of the 700 office where all the NCOs hid in case someone gave them a job. It never failed to amaze me how many NCOs it took to write out a few job cards and look after the Form 700s, which were the maintenance record books of the individual aircraft.

'Gordon, someone here to see you.'

Flight Sergeant Gordon Mendes came out of the office and I was pointed out to him. He came forward in a stooped sort of gait, offering me his hand. He was medium build, slim, thin faced and had a full head of black hair.

'Hello mate, what can I do for you?' he said in a mild west-coast Scottish accent.

'JT Blair, Engine Fitter, Flight. Just arrived – I was posted to 203 Squadron so I suppose that I have been assigned here? No one up at the general office could tell me for sure where I would be assigned but they suggested that I should start here.'

'Stupid bastards! The right hand doesn't know what the left is doing around here at the moment. I don't think you are part of our complement so you might have to go to the hangar on Minor Servicing Flight. I'll find out.' He disappeared into his office.

At 'the hangar' the aircraft were taken in after 250 flying hours for inspection and servicing. This was a real cushy number and my heart soared at the thought of it.

'Nope, they've never heard of you either. Are you sure you are posted here?'

'Christ, Flight, I went all through that yesterday with those bloody Snoops in the guardroom and then the SWO who wasn't goin' to let me on the station at all!' I produced my transfer papers once again. My head hurt!

'Okey-dokey. I'll check a bit further and get back to you. Go and have a cuppa.'

I went over to the water boiler and made myself a cup of tea, and sat down on an armchair thinking of my rotten luck in not being assigned to 'the hangar'. I thought I would push this a bit further when the Flight came back. Just then the outside door opened and a sergeant came in.

'Starter crew for Bravo,' he shouted.

At this every last mother's son in the crewroom got up and started producing tools, spare parts and excuses as to why they could not be part of the starter crew. Some who had no tools to hand just ran out the back door and no doubt hid in the toilets. I had seen this before at Kinloss – and confess that I had been part of the process there – but there it was done in protest that the bloody fairies on the squadron would not pull their weight with all the odd jobs that had to be done. I could have bet that most of those evading work now were the self-same type – Fairies!

The last two guys heading out the front door were blocked by the sergeant.

'Right, you two will do!'

'Ah, bloody hell – we need to change a fuse on Golf, Roy. Can't you get someone else?'

'There is no one else – you'll have to do it. Hey you – have you got nothing to do?'

This remark was shouted in my direction and I looked around to see whom he was talking to. There was nobody else there.

'Eh, who me? Just been posted in. I'm waiting for Flight Sergeant Mendes to come back to me. He told me to wait here.'

'What trade are you?'

'Engines.'

'Same as me – you must be able to handle a set of CO_2 fire extinguishers – c'mon, give us a hand, will you?'

'But what about the flight sergeant – he told me to wait here,' I protested.

'While you are out, I'll see Gordon and tell him where you are – OK? I'll get you a pair of overalls.' He went into the 700 office.

I was trapped. I couldn't see any way out of this, but standing beside a Shackleton on a starter crew on a cold winter morning was the last thing I wanted to do – with my head! I put on the overalls that had Sergeant Wilstead written on the label sewn on the front – I detected that they had never been exposed to engine oil in their long life.

The starter crew were responsible for the safety of the aircraft and the surrounding area during the start up of the four engines and the removal of the external power supply – a Ford six-cylinder engine driving an electrical generator commonly known as a Houchin set. The last thing was to remove the heavy chocks from in front of the wheels and then marshal the aircraft off the pan – ensuring that it did not hit anything in the process.

The Houchins were heavy beasts with a thick power cable that connected into the aircraft socket. They were towed to the aircraft by tractor. However, as every tractor in the RAF belonged to whichever lazy bastard had booked it out of the MT section, and these could be any trade, the Houchin was merely deposited by them as they seldom hung around to share the fun. This then meant that after the engines were started the Houchin had to be manhandled to a safe position at the side of the pan, in the presence of the engines churning over their lethal propellers. Unless of course the tractor driver had been collared for starter duty – then the tractor was hooked up to the Houchin and flamboyantly driven away into the blue yonder, as the tractor driver escaped any further involvement in the proceedings. However, this was an extremely unusual thing to happen, as the tractor drivers rarely came back to the crewroom because they had the means of cadging their tea and wads elsewhere and were only contactable by radio – sometimes.

I did not really mind doing the job as I had done this hundreds of times before at Kinloss, but I cursed my luck and vowed never to be caught so easily again. However, I was very concerned about my head, and my stomach was beginning to churn over alarmingly.

We walked onto the pan where the aircraft was surrounded by all manner of aircrew. The pilots were going round the aircraft looking in every orifice, peering into the undercarriage bays as if they were looking for stowaways, kicking tyres, pulling themselves up to peer into the air intakes and the radiators of the engines, pushing and pulling at the propeller blades, feeling for 'blade rock' – as if they would recognise it if it was there. They turned the propellers, testing each one in succession.

They pulled at the access panels, they got their backs against the tail fins and tried to wrench them out of their mountings. They also went around checking for oil leaks, coolant leaks, methanol leaks, fuel leaks. If they could not identify the leak by feel or smell, they had this habit of tasting it – I have often wondered since how many of them have succumbed to some nasty or fatal disease as a result of this practice. I am sure that some of these fluids must have been carcinogenic.

One pilot I know found a substance on a wheel – did all of the usual things, feel, smell and finally taste. He turned to one of the groundcrew and asked what the substance was. 'Piss!' came the reply. 'How do you know?' he asked. 'Because I just did it!'

After the captain and the co-pilot came the engineer, navigators, signallers in abundance all peering, poking, shaking, smelling, tasting – each one trying to be the genius that would find something to stop the aircraft flying, thereby saving them the inconvenience of actually earning their flying pay.

I can guarantee that the activities of this roving band of marauders used up more fatigue life of the aircraft than flying ever did. Only when the mission was to, say, Key West in Florida for two weeks for a 'training exercise' did the practice cease. Then every last one of them would have overlooked a missing wing!

We plugged in and started the Houchin and powered up the aircraft. This gave the engineer some more toys to play with – fuel booster pumps, fuel priming pumps, fuel tank gauges, all of which were operated and peered at with relish inside the aircraft at the engineer's control panel. This gave another opportunity for the aircraft to be grounded if any fuel leaks were found by the still marauding gang outside.

When nothing was found that would stop the sortie, the disgruntled band loaded up their rations for the day – nearly breaking their backs in the process. The rations were the only other thing that would entice them on board. There was always an abundance of food piled onto the kite and some of the signallers were passable cooks as the Shackleton had a fairly good galley on board. 'Honkers stew' was a favourite – anything in a tin that could be thrown into the one pan and heated up. An amazing combination of favours that has forever been kept secret from the outside world.

Loaded on next was the aircrew's most treasured possession – the crew box. This contained all the galley equipment and cooking accessories that had been cobbled together over many years by each individual crew. The boxes and their contents were jealously guarded and if one had been lost there would have been serious repercussions for someone – probably the most junior signaller.

This day nothing was amiss and the aircrew took up their positions on board.

Each engine was started in turn, normally starting with the number three engine – starboard inboard as this engine drove all the hydraulic and pneumatic services. If this engine did not start immediately, another engine was selected in sequence and that engine would be tried again later. Normally, if the engineer had not been too heavy handed on the priming button and the pilot was judicious with the use of the throttle, the engine would turn over several times while belching out a non-combusted fuel vapour that resembled smoke. Eventually it would give a cough, fire and burst into life with one hell of a roar. Oh, my poor head!

The sequence was repeated until all four engines were happily ticking over at minimum revs and you could not hear yourself think. Oh, my bloody head!

Next the signal was given to disconnect the Houchin. I went forward and pulled the cable from the plug as a colleague stopped the generator engine. Together we stowed the heavy cable on top of the set. My companion let off the brake and picked up the heavy towing arm, and we collectively began to pull and shove the thing to the side of the pan. There were some frozen ruts on the pan that affected where the bloody thing wanted to go – and that was straight for the propellers of the numbers three and four engines. I stopped pushing and went round the front to help with pulling and steering the thing away from the props. This required considerable effort but we got it moving. But the effort had affected my guts. I used every effort to stop myself from spewing up on the pan and I only just made it to the grass verge when up it came. My colleagues didn't look too impressed!

I managed to spit the residue out of my mouth, wiped my nose on the nice clean overalls and cleared the tears away from my eyes before being given the signal to go in to remove the chocks. Big, heavy wooden bastards at the best of times with a thick piece of rope attached, but mine had become stuck as the wheel had run up against it.

'Bastard thing!' I thought. I pulled on the rope until I was fit to burst again – nothing. It would not budge!

I went round the back of the wheel to the other side of the chock, lay down on the ground and tried to kick the thing loose with the heel and sole of my boot – nothing!

'Bastard thing!' I thought again 'Why me? Why now?' Just then the guy who had successfully removed his chock from the port wheel came running in and started to pull on the rope, as I did the kicking act on my back. Eventually the bloody thing came loose – it had been stuck to the concrete by frost. Bastard!

The pilot was given the signal that the chocks were clear by one of our number who had picked up the marshalling bats, and the engines were revved up with a sustained growl to start the aircraft moving. Oh, my bloody head. Oh, my bloody guts! Once the propellers had a hold of the air, the aircraft gave up its inertia and started to move smoothly forward. The thing had barely picked up some momentum when the pilot slammed on the brakes to test them. The kite came to a rapid stop with a high pitch squeal. Oh, my bloody head! The pneumatic brakes were released once again with a hiss and the engines revved to propel the thing in the right direction as directed by the marshaller – the Mark 2 Shackleton with the tail wheel was steered by a combination of revving the engines on the appropriate side and applying the brakes normally on the opposite side. The aircraft swung round to port and blasted the two of us with icy air and some small accumulations of hoar frost, ice and sand. Bastaaaard!

At last the bloody thing was trundling down the perimeter track out of my sight. 'Hope their piles don't take a pounding while flying round on circuit and bumps – up and down – for the next six hours,' I thought. I also wondered what I was doing here after the sunshine of Singapore.

We went back to the crewroom. Funnily enough my head felt a bit better.

4

The Introduction

Back at the crewroom, I quickly took off the overalls in case someone else decided to give me a job and went to seek out the flight sergeant.

'Where the bloody hell have you been?' he asked. 'I thought you had buggered off home.'

'I got caught sitting still while every one else stampeded for the door. I had to help out in a starter crew.'

'Good man! Look, we have been right through to the postings office and they have confirmed that you have been posted to 203 Squadron – there is no place for you in the hangar so I suppose you will just have to stay with us here. We don't have your records through yet but we will team you up with someone who will show you the ropes. Davy! Come here a minute will you?' he shouted at a slim, slightly built, fair-haired, good-looking guy who came ambling over with a smile on his face. He was one of my drinking companions from the night before but I still hadn't known his name. Such was the poor drunk's charter – take the drink but don't introduce yourself in case there is any pay-back.

'Davy, this is Gordon Blair – just been posted here from Singapore. I want you to take him round with you for the next few days and show him the ropes. Gordon, this is Davy Hamilton.'

We shook hands and he asked if I wanted a cup of coffee. We got the coffee and sat down to talk.

At this time I was a little bit pissed off as I had been through all this work before. First-line servicing of Shackletons was not an easy job for the engine fitters. The engine trade was responsible for refuelling, re-oiling, topping up coolants and methanol. This doesn't sound too bad but all of these, apart from the refuelling, had to be carried out on each individual engine, which made it very labour intensive. Then there were the spark plug changes, which were very frequent, the fuel and oil leaks that had to be sourced and mended, the starter motor changes,

33

the propeller changes and then the engine changes. Christ, the list was endless!

Refuelling was carried out by filling each tank individually to a predetermined level, three tanks per wing, to give the right fuel load required for the particular sortie to which the aircraft had been assigned. The level in the tanks was measured by using dipsticks of varying lengths, one for each tank. The dipstick had to be covered in chalk so the fuel level was obvious, therefore sticks of chalk were part of the engine fitter's toolkit. The Shackleton did not succumb to modern technologies in any way shape or form – not for them the central pressurised refuelling which is normal on modern aircraft – no! The Shackleton was thirties technology and would remain so until its final demise in the nineties.

Fuel tank dipsticks were used as the aircraft fuel gauges were not only deemed to be unreliable but they were more accurate when the aircraft was flying as opposed to reposing in the 'sit up and beg' attitude on the ground. However, the Mark 3 Shackleton with the nose wheel was always in the flying attitude – and their gauges were also inaccurate.

If your luck was in, you could get someone to help with the refuelling, so two ancient bowsers – also thirties technology – ordered by telephone from the MT section, would come trundling out to the aircraft and position themselves square on to the outer engines. This was the position that allowed the boom on the inside of the bowser to be deployed over the inboard propellers – all very scientific.

The tank filler caps were accessed by using a screwdriver to unlock 'Dzus' bayonet fasteners on the small covers on the wing – easy! Unfortunately, the slots in the Dzus fasteners were so worn that you were lucky to get them open at all. It took a superhuman effort at times and this was no joke in the wind, wet or snow, further exacerbated when you were holding a torch in the dark! The problem was that you had to put so much downward pressure with the screwdriver on the almost non-existent slots, to try to turn the fastener, that your footing was lost on the slippery oil-covered wing surface. Because of this, gravity took over and it was not unusual to see guys ejected off the rear of the wing, which was some ten feet from the ground at the outer tanks. Health and Safety were still things of the future! In fact, Davy my assigned mentor had broken both his wrists during one such incident. It made it very difficult for him to lift a beer glass for several weeks – but he managed it.

The re-oiling was a particularly heavy and dirty job. The Griffon engines could use, by either burning or leaking, in excess of a gallon of oil per hour. In fact it was a popular conception that the twenty-five-gallon oil tank was the limiting factor in how long the Shackleton could remain airborne. The re-oiling was done by an ancient, cumbersome oil bowser, towed by a tractor under the wing adjacent to the outer side of the outboard engines. The oil was pumped by an old waterjacket-cooled diesel engine situated at the back of the bowser. Of course, as the engine heated up the water in the jacket would boil, so as the bowser was towed around the aircraft it looked like some travelling steam circus had come to town.

One man would stand on an oil-covered running board on the bowser and open up a small access panel – worn Dzus fastener again – on the cupola to the rear of the outboard engine. Inside was the oil filler cap – a knurled nut, which was prevented from vibrating loose by a twisted length of wire. In common parlance this was known as 'wire locking'. However, depending on the age of the aircraft, the knurled nut was invariably as smooth as the proverbial baby's bottom through the successive use of pliers on the nut to loosen it.

The task was hopefully to be able to untangle the locking wire and pull it through the hole in the nut without breaking the wire. This saved having to renew the wire, thereby saving some time. If the wire could not be untangled then it had to be snipped off. The 'knurled' nut had then to be unscrewed either by hand or by the use of pliers. This was not easy as everything, including your gloves or hands, was covered in oil.

Once the cap was opened, after much cursing and swearing, a large nozzle was inserted into the neck. Again this was not easy as the hose attached to the nozzle could have refuelled a battleship. It was heavy, uncompromising and did not always want to accommodate the bends that were necessary in the cramped space between bowser and wing to get the nozzle into the tank neck.

The nozzle was inserted and opened up. The engine on the pump would strain under the pressure of pumping very high viscosity oil. This was worse in the winter when the cold weather turned the oil nearly solid. The bowsers were fitted with oil heaters but they seldom worked. The oil would be injected into the tank in a heavy stream or huge globs that would quite often backfire, covering the operator in oil or an oil emulsion from the tank. The worst situation was when the diesel engine stalled under the strain, as they tended not to start when they were hot.

Once the tank was full, and you were never quite sure whether it was or not, the nozzle and hose were passed up to another guy on the wing and he would carry out the same operation on the oil tank of the inboard engine which was accessed from the wing behind the engine. This tended to be an easier operation unless there was a wind or frost or snow, which caused the guy to slide off the wing at a great rate of knots. If you were lucky enough to get someone to help with the re-oiling, they always opted for the wing tanks as it was slightly easier.

The tank cap was closed and the knurled nut was tightened either by hand or by pliers. Then came the tricky bit when the locking wire had to be threaded through the little hole in the nut. If you had managed to undo the wire before, it might break when trying to re-thread it through the hole or, even worse, break when twisting up after you had successfully threaded it through the hole.

This meant that all of the effort that had gone into saving the wire in the first place was to no avail after all, and the bloody stuff had to be cut off and a new piece of wire produced from the pocket, threaded through the anchor point then twisted, threaded through the nut and twisted again.

There was no way that this wire-locking operation could be carried out while wearing gloves so, while your hands were covered in oil, they were also getting bloody cold. After this, because your hands were covered in oil, it was not worth putting gloves on, therefore your hands got even colder on the way to the next aircraft.

After this operation – re-oiling up to eight or nine aircraft – you knew you had been working! I have been covered in oil and I have seen guys that have been literally drenched from the top of their heads to their toes in the brown/blue treacle-like substance. So this was to be my lot for the foreseeable future.

Junior Technician Davy Hamilton was very talkative and told me all about life on Shackletons and life in general around Ballykelly. He wasn't very dirty looking for an engine man! Funnily enough, he never asked where I had worked before or what I had been doing in Singapore – and I never told him.

'Right, let's go and I'll take you across to the stores to get kitted out.'

Outside we went and then I realised why he wasn't very dirty – Davy was a tractor 'owner' with his very own shiny blue and yellow machine! Now I had the measure of the man.

I went with him to the store for the standard working kit for Shackletons. Overalls, waterproof overalls, parka-type anorak, sea-boot socks, Wellington boots and the inevitable 'trog' boots. The trog boots were the favoured footwear as they were similar to hiking boots, were thick soled and therefore gave good insulation against the elements. They were often seen being worn at the NAAFI dance so they must also have been the height of fashion! In fact I know for sure that they were the only decent footwear that some of the guys possessed.

However, some of the older and more fashion-conscious guys preferred to wear the Wellington boots 'seadog fashion'. This required that the tops of the boots were turned over and down so the boot came halfway up the calf, the long sea-boot socks were then folded down over the top of the Wellingtons with the uniform trousers tucked inside the socks. Normally the exposed areas of the thick white socks were filthy, having been covered in soot and oil that had emanated from the engines and pervaded the whole of the aircraft. The degree of filthiness was a direct indication of how long it had been since the socks were last washed. A squadron of groundcrew on Shackletons did not exude sartorial elegance in any way but looked a rag-tag lot not dissimilar to a gang of Irish navvies, which of course in Ballykelly they were! Some of the guys were in such a state of dishevelment that when they were up in the accommodation area they had sight like radar, keeping a constant lookout for the SWO or one of his cohorts who would have taken a fit of apoplexy if they had caught them disgracing the Queen's uniform.

I accompanied Davy for four days and I didn't do very much work, as his ego took over as the experienced man – and I let him. He probably worked harder than at any other time in his life as he showed me the ropes. Then I met Charlie Hendle, whom I knew from Kinloss, and Charlie had mentioned that he had not seen me since those days. After Charlie had gone Davy said, 'You never told me you had worked on Shackletons before – how long did you work on them?'

'You never asked – three years at Kinloss and one year in the Griffon engine bay at Changi.'

'You bastard!' he said, grinning, as he realised the biter had been bitten.

5

The Bigot

My first working week on the base had been completed and it was Saturday – day off! I had gone into the NAAFI after lunch, just for a couple of pints. But, as in all these things, 'The best laid plans of mice and men gang aft agley'. Someone suggested going down to the Droppin Well pub for a 'few' – so off we trotted.

Jimmy Curry was already there and we had several pints of the 'velvet nectar'. We went back to the mess for supper. Jimmy suggested that we should go down to Limavady for a few more so we caught the bus outside the gates.

Limavady was not a very exciting place at the best of times but on this dark winter's night in late January there was hardly anyone around on the streets.

We went into Vera's bar.

Vera was a homely lady and she was kindness itself. She was dumpy with a round face that always supported a wee smile. She used to wear one of those wrap-around aprons whenever she served behind the bar. Clem, her husband, was also a very affable character and always had a new joke to tell – mind you, you could hear it about fifty times a night as he told it to each one in succession as they came into the bar. 'Here boy – have ye heard this one?' To be honest, I don't think I ever heard him tell a really funny joke but you had to laugh anyway.

In those days the Guinness was served in half-pint stone-coloured bottles with a cork in the neck. The Guinness was delivered to the publican in barrels and was decanted by him into the bottles and the cork inserted. The bottles were kept on a stone shelf behind the bar to keep them cool. If the temperature around the shelf went over 55 degrees Fahrenheit, the complete shelf of Guinness was gathered up and taken through into the back parlour to keep it cold.

This exercise was carried out due to experience, because if the Guinness got too warm the corks would explode out of the bottles and there would be one hell of a mess of not only beer, but brown adrenalin running down people's legs – especially in this neck of the woods where IRA gunmen were not unknown!

As only a certain amount of Guinness was available in bottles, when a crowd went into the bar we would buy 'the shelf' of Guinness. This meant that more Guinness had to be decanted and the call would go out for Clem to come and do his stuff – just when he was settling down to watch 'Z Cars' or something.

'Jeeze boys, ye must hiv a terrible thirst the night,' he would declare as he shuffled through the back.

'Naw, it's just that we've come in tae ogle at the beautiful Vera an' mebe get her tae dae a striptease the night.'

'Jeeze, ye must be hard up.'

This particular night a crowd gathered and the 'shelf' was bought. In reality this meant that there were only about four pints per person, not a great deal unless mixed with something else.

By this time Jimmy was on the something else – double whiskies – and with the amount that we had consumed in the afternoon he was well on the way to being stottin' drunk. When he had too much to drink he became a bit maudlin and wanted to phone his girlfriend who lived in Scotland – none of us ever met her. He asked Vera if he could use her telephone. He had done this before. The phone was located at the top of the stairs off a corridor at the back of the bar. This was the entrance to Vera's private accommodation.

Vera gave her permission and lifted the flap in the bar to let Jimmy through. He bounced off the counter a few times like a steel ball in a pinball machine but eventually made it to the bottom of the stairs; however, the climbing of them defeated him. Vera shouted for someone to come and give him a hand up the stairs. Somebody went and steadied him while he climbed. The phone was on a table on the top landing and there was a little stool for sitting on. Jimmy was placed on the stool and left in private to make the call.

We got on with the task of drinking and forgot all about Jimmy until there was this enormous crash from the stairwell and Jimmy came tumbling down the steps, landing sprawled on the floor still clutching the phone in one hand. The apparatus had been ripped off the wall and the bare wires were evidence of this.

'Are you all right, Jimmy?' cried Vera.

'Aye – but I've been cut off!'

No other harm was done and he subsequently paid for the damage.

Jimmy and I stayed at the pub until well after closing time. All the others had departed the scene long ago – probably across to the dance in the Agricultural Hall know locally as the 'Aggy Hall'. Clem stepped out of the doorway, checked that the coast was clear of Royal Ulster Constabulary, and ushered us out into a cold and wet Limavady High Street.

We stood around looking for a taxi to take us back to Ballykelly but as usual they are never around when you want one. With all the beer that I had consumed and the effects of the cold air I was soon desperate for a piss, so I left Jimmy hanging onto a lamp-post and went up an alleyway to relieve myself of the terrible burden. Why is it that you only ever get a loan of alcohol – you never get to keep it and you have paid enough for it.

I was gone for no more than three minutes. When I returned to the lamp-post – no Jimmy!

Where in hell was he? I began to scour the street for any sign of him but he was nowhere to be seen. I stopped a guy who was eating a fish supper and asked if he had seen anyone on the street recently.

'There was a lad that was picked up by the police a few minutes ago – do you think that was him?' he asked.

'Christ, anything is possible. Where would they have taken him?'

'The police station is just down the road aways – turn to the right and it's on your left.'

'Thanks mate.' I started to walk down the road.

I eventually arrived at the police station and dithered whether to go in or not. It looked a pretty foreboding place surrounded by a high fence topped by razor wire and I was not too sober. I didn't want to end up in the cells for the night for being drunk. However, I plucked up the courage and entered.

There was a small outer reception area separated from the main office by a counter that was sealed off to the ceiling by very thick and what looked like bulletproof glass. The RUC were very intimidating-looking characters as they were invariably tall and well built. However, the main reason for their intimidation was the heavy belt that they wore around their waists that supported a very large gun holster – something that was never seen worn by the police on the mainland. The belts were worn over a normal tunic jacket and this gave an old-fashioned military air to the perception of these men in black. While they were professional in their outlook towards the use and handling of the weapons, the guns were there as a constant reminder of the delicacy of the situation caused by the 'Troubles' in Northern Ireland.

As I heard the heavy wooden door, covered on the inside by a metal lining, slam behind me I could hear a familiar voice shouting out at full volume from somewhere within the bowels of this place.

'Yer nothin' but a bunch of Fenian bastards! If ye dinae let me oot o' here I'll report ye tae the Pope! Let me oot or I'll get ye excommunicated!' It was my old pal Jimmy.

Now Jimmy was a hardened Rangers supporter and a staunch Protestant 'Blue Nose'. He would have known that this tirade of abuse would hit a raw nerve as everyone in the RUC at that time was as 'blue nosed' as himself and they would not have taken kindly to being referred to as the former arch enemy – Fenians – nor have any allegiance to the Pope.

I staggered up to the counter where a constable was busy writing in a book.

'Aye – whit can I do for you, sur?' he enquired.

'Eh – I think you have a friend of mine in here. I think that is him I can hear shouting from out the back there – Jimmy Curry's his name and we are stationed along at Ballykelly. Any chance of getting him released, so I can take him home?'

'My advice to you sur, is to fuck off home on your own and leave Mr Curry to us. We'll see that he is returned to Ballykelly.'

'Why? We were only out for few pints and on our way back to the base in any case. What has he done to deserve getting picked up and brought in here?'

'That's none of your business, sur! Away home wi ye and we'll say no more about it!'

From the bowels once again came the cry, 'Youse is nothin' but a bunch of Fenian bastards! Let me oot o' here!'

'Ah c'mon – be reasonable. I can easily take him back and I'll say no more about it.'

'Sur, I've told you to fuck off out of it, so unless you want to join your mate through the back you should take my advice!'

'Charming,' I thought – but discretion being the better part of valour I decided to take his advice 'Thanks a bunch,' I said to the constable and struggled to open the door before going out into the cold night air. Now what – how do I get back to Ballykelly?

I was just about to walk back up to the main street when a RAF Land Rover arrived. It was obviously a 'paddy wagon' as the back was covered in with a stout cabin and the rear door had bars on the window.

The Land Rover was backed into a short alleyway at the side of the police station. The driver got out and knocked at a door somewhere up the alley. A sliding panel in the door was opened which released a shaft of light into the darkness. Some conversation took place and the door was opened.

Within a minute, two RUC came out frogmarching Jimmy between them. I heard him before I saw him as he was singing the good old 'Sash my father wore' at the top of his voice, interspersed with 'Goodnight Fenians' sung to the tune of 'Goodnight Ladies'.

Jimmy was roughly manhandled into the Land Rover and the door was closed. As soon as the door closed there was silence. The driver came round to the front of the vehicle and made to get in.

'Any chance of a lift back to Ballykelly mate?' I enquired.

'Got any ID on you?' I produced the plastic card, which he took and scrutinised for a couple of seconds. 'OK, get in.' I jumped up into the front seat and we set off.

I shouted into the back of the vehicle 'Are you all right, Jimmy?' There was no reply. 'That's my mate in the back. Have you got any idea what he has done to get lifted in the first place?'

'I haven't seen a charge sheet but the RUC mentioned something about indecent exposure and religious bigotry.'

Whether these were separate incidents like having a piss on the main street while singing the 'Sash' or whether the two were connected – like simulating sex with the Virgin Mary outside the Catholic church – I will never know.

Jimmy spent the night in the cells at Ballykelly and was released the next day without charge. He came into the room with a hang-dog look. However, he looked more like a hound dog because he was sporting two black eyes. He could not remember anything of the previous night's events so how he acquired these 'keekers', again we will never know.

'Ah, blessed is the dawn that brings no troubles!'

I was back to nursing a sore head – again!

Back to the NAAFI after lunch for a 'hair of the dog'.

6

Bodo Bound

Two weeks later, on my first long weekend off within the working rota, I went home. I got a lift in a Hastings aircraft that was going from Ballykelly to Finningly in Yorkshire not many miles from Doncaster. Great! I was home within two and a half hours, as my father-in-law had come to pick me up to take me to Doncaster.

I had a good time with my wife and the kids, however my wife was complaining about the length of time it was taking to get a married quarter. She was getting a bit fed up staying with her mum. I had been informed that a house would become available in Eglinton within two weeks. I had not had the opportunity to visit the Eglinton houses but I understood that they were to be taken over as redundant navy housing stock.

Due to the fact that a house was imminent, I elected to drive the Zodiac back to Ballykelly. I had acquired all the necessary paperwork from the Ministry of Agriculture, required because of the continuing foot and mouth disease on the mainland. The RAF would pay for the costs of the travel on a mileage basis and also the cost of the ferry from Heysham to Belfast.

I arrived at Belfast but had no real idea of the direction or the road that I should take to get to Ballykelly, as my last journey there had been by train – I remembered it well! I stopped for petrol – which was not unusual with the Zodiac – and after the petrol was pumped in I followed the pump attendant into the wee shop on the forecourt. He had been very friendly and talkative as he pumped the petrol into the tank – we had discussed the weather. His wife or some other woman was behind the counter.

While paying for the petrol I enquired, 'Would you have a map?'

'Now where would you want a map of?' she asked

'Of Northern Ireland, of course!' I replied.

'Now why would anyone want a map of this wee place – ye could hardly get lost, could ye?' came a smiling retort from the man.

'Ach I'm not to sure about that,' said the woman. 'There's a few strange wee corners to be goin' round an' ye'd want tae know about them for sure.'

I got my map and came out of the shop scratching my head. I was not sure whether I had been in that conversation or not. This happened a lot in Ireland. I found the 'few wee strange corners' and drove up the road.

During that week it was confirmed that we would be allocated a house in Eglinton and that it would be ready at the end of the following week, after redecorating. I phoned my wife to tell her the news and during that week I made all the necessary arrangements for her to catch the Heysham to Belfast ferry. I would drive down to pick her and the kids up. Her journey was set for the Saturday following next.

During the week, Gordon Mendes came to me. 'Gordon, you would be doing me a big favour if you could take on the detachment to Bodo next week.'

'No can do, Gordon, I have my wife and kids coming over a week on Saturday and I need to be here for them and get the house in order before they come – we're moving into a house up in Eglinton.'

'That's all right then, this is just a short trip up and down to Bodo – leaving on Tuesday and back on Thursday – you really would be doing me a favour as I am short of experienced engine men capable of going,' he continued.

'Well, if you are sure that it will only be a short trip, I suppose I could do it although it will be a bit tight for time.'

'I'll make it up to you – give you a couple of days off to be with your wife when she arrives,' he promised.

'It's a deal – but I would rather have the Friday off before she arrives to get the place sorted for her.'

'OK – it's a deal.'

Bodo – Norway. Thirty-two miles north of the Arctic circle so at that time of the year there would be no sunshine at all and it would be very cold. I had been there before and in summer it is an extremely beautiful place set in the Saltenfjord among high mountains with sheer cliffs falling right to the sea. The town of Bodo is typically Norwegian, pristine clean and colourful because all the houses are painted bright colours. It was formerly a big fishing town until they fished all the cod out of their seas and it was hard to see what industry now supported the town although it looked very prosperous.

However, at this time of year I did not relish sitting in a Shackleton for some twelve hours while it flew around the North Sea in ever-decreasing circles pursuing a submarine on some exercise or other, landing at Bodo, then having to work in freezing conditions to get the aircraft ready for the homeward leg.

Bodo was a regular sortie for the aircraft at Ballykelly. Norway had limited submarine reconnaissance capability and relied on the RAF Coastal Command, through the auspices of NATO, to keep the Atlantic, North and Arctic Seas scanned for the deadly enemy in the Cold War.

I don't know whether any Shackleton ever deliberately found a Russian submarine, but of course the aircrew had to be honed to perfection through very expensive exercises that involved finding friendly submarines – but only because they knew roughly where they were in the first place. This type of exercise went on all over the world, but obviously friendly subs were easier to find in the warm Caribbean or Gulf of Mexico seas, which were visited frequently. Nobody wanted to go to Bodo in the winter!

For these sorties the groundcrew flew with the aircraft. The normal complement was engine fitter, airframe fitter, electrician, armourer and possibly a fairy – radar or wireless technician or such.

There was no set list of spares that had to be taken on any of these trips, each man just took what he thought was necessary or by experience would be needed. On the Monday morning I compiled my spares kit in preparation for an early start the next day.

On Tuesday morning, we breakfasted early and then drove down to the aircraft at six to get kit loaded on board. For long haul flights or when there were a lot of people on board, the luggage and spares etc. (including parachutes) were stored in panniers that were winched up into the bomb bay. These were of course inaccessible during flight. On sorties like Bodo, the luggage was stored on the bunk beds inside the aircraft.

I joined the throng going round the aircraft – peering, poking, knocking, lifting, pushing, but definitely not tasting. I hoped that I could find something to stop the thing from going – but then there were more aircraft – not many serviceable though. I should have sabotaged the lot of them the day before!

We eventually got in and for safety reasons during take-off and landing the groundcrew had to sit on the floor around the main spar.

Someone once compared the Shackleton to an elephant's arse – grey and wrinkled on the outside, brown and smelly on the inside. This odour was a combination of the worn brown leather seats mingled with the smell of hundreds of sweaty bodies that had sat on them and were currently sitting on them, mixed with the hot electronic equipment, the aroma of long-ago cooked food from the galley, a faint smell of petrol, all mixed with the throat-grabbing aroma of 'Racasan' disinfectant fluid from the Elsan chemical toilet. This gave the Shackleton its distinctive ambience.

However, the comparison to an elephant's arse missed the part about the noise that came from the bowels. The noise insulation on the Mark 2 and 3 Shackletons was supposed to be superior to that of the Mark 1 – which had no insulation at all. I think the MoD had been cheated out of a lot of money by some clever company contracted to carry out the soundproofing. The fuselage of the aircraft had been decorated with a flock material covered with a very nice brown leather-look material that passed as soundproofing, but this in effect did little more than stop you seeing the rivets vibrating on the panels. Additionally the insulation had been removed from the area aft of the main cabin door to restore the centre of gravity of the aircraft after a couple of them had crashed.

The engines were started up, and from that moment onwards all possibility of normal speech communication was lost. The noise was even louder if you opened your mouth to yawn or to try to clear your ears. Only twelve hours to go!

The aircraft was taxied to the holding area near the end of the runway. By this time the engines were sufficiently warmed to allow pre-flight engine runs to be performed. Each engine in turn went through a set routine of being revved up to maximum revs at 2750 RPM to ensure that full power was attainable. The engine RPM were then reduced to 2000 and the magneto was tested. Each engine had two sets of spark plugs – inlet and exhaust. These plugs were sparked by the single-dual magneto on the engine with the exhaust plugs sparking a couple of degrees after the inlet plugs to ensure efficient burning of the fuel in the cylinder.

In turn, the side of the magneto powering the inlet plugs was switched off and any major drop in engine revs indicated that not all the exhaust plugs were firing. After switching the inlet plugs on again, the exhaust plugs were switched off and any drop in engine revs indicated that not all the inlet plugs were firing. This test was known as a 'mag drop'. This test was always a bone of contention between pilots and groundcrew as some pilots could not remember which magneto switch had been activated to give the 'drop' or would confuse the bank of plugs that were faulty. This meant that the engine had to be run up again before the plugs were changed, resulting in a hot engine and burnt fingers when finally changing the plugs. It was worse if a set of plugs were changed only to find that the mag drop was still there on the other set of plugs, again because the pilot had become confused.

Next the constant speed unit was tested. This unit altered the pitch of the propeller to keep the engine revs at a constant speed while the engine throttle was adjusted to give more or less power output. The throttles could be pushed 'through the gate' which meant that the engine high-speed supercharger was brought into operation and water methanol was injected into the intake manifold to cool the fuel mixture. This resulted in a positive inlet manifold pressure of plus 25 pounds boost which increased the power from 1960 to 2455 horsepower – awesome! Normally this higher power output was only used for take-off under heavy load conditions as the increased strain tended to knacker the engines pretty quickly.

These series of tests on all four engines took about ten minutes. Once again I prayed that the engines would not pass, but once more God ignored me. I promised myself that I would start going to church.

The aircraft was taxied to the end of the runway and clearance for take-off was given by the control tower. All engines were revved up to max power, the brakes released and we surged forward with a jolt. On this trip the aircraft was fairly light so we were soon airborne and slowly climbing away from the ground.

Once the plane had been checked for fumes, the groundcrew were released from the floor and took whichever seat was available. Smoking commenced. This was not a passenger aircraft therefore there were limited seats for the passengers on board. Most groundcrew had been on detachments or sorties and each had a favourite seat or bed. My favourites were either of the two swivel armchairs at the beam at the rear of the plane adjacent to the door. These seats had domed windows that gave an all-round vision of the relevant side during flight. It also tended to be warmer down at the rear as any warmth up front permeated rearwards, however it was noisier due to the lack of insulation. I grabbed one of these seats. It was still cold but I hoped it would soon begin to heat up – sometimes it didn't as the petrol-fuelled dragon heaters were very temperamental.

In spite of the noise from the engines, which had by now been throttled back to cruising power, I slept for a while only to be awakened by one of the crew members kicking my foot and proffering a plateful of bacon butties. I took one but was offered the plate again so I took another. A tray of tea arrived shortly afterwards. This could be heaven! All this was done without speech as there was little use trying to shout over the noise of the engines.

Without the use of intercom, which meant plugging and unplugging the lead from one socket to another when walking around the plane, all communications were carried out by facial expressions, shoulder shrugs, hand and arm movements – pointing, thumbs up, thumbs down. You had to be pretty determined to try shouting at each other and if this was done, there was always the possibility of causing ear damage.

The engines droned on and on, their exhausts glowing cherry red, reassuringly indicating that they were each firing on all twelve cylinders or as near to that number that made no material difference. There was a gauge on the pilot's console that had three little propellers mounted in it, one propeller per number two, three and four engines. The RPM on the number one engine was the standard by which the others could be set. If the little propeller rotated anticlockwise, this engine RPM was slower than number one and conversely if it rotated clockwise it was going faster. This indicator allowed the pilot, by use of the constant pitch levers, to try to synchronise the three other engines in loose harmony to the revolutions of the number one engine. If all four engines were in sound modular harmony, then there was a constant pitch of noise. However, as the constant speed units on each separate engine were mechanical devices, there wasn't a hope in hell of the engines remaining in perfect harmony so there was a constant rise and fall in the pitch of the sound, which reverberated throughout the plane. The small synchronising propellers were evidence of this, as they would rotate clockwise and anticlockwise in complete conflict with each other and by default in conflict with number one engine.

It was said that if a human being could be strapped tightly enough to the engines while they were running, their teeth would have been vibrated out of their head and their internal organs turned to jelly. Thank the Lord for the thick-soled trog boots, as they insulated these vibrations from the floor into the body.

And so it went on – hour after hour. I read a book. Lunch next – curry made from anything that was ever tinned, including fruit! Very nice. I cleaned up in the galley after lunch, which was appreciated by the chef. Afternoon tea and then into Bodo.

As the Shackletons were regular and frequent visitors to Bodo, the re-fuel and re-oiling bowsers were always there to meet the aircraft. This day was no different. Once the plane came to a halt on the hard-standing outside a hangar and the engines were stopped, the two fuel bowsers took up position in front of the outer engines. Bloody good service, didn't get this treatment back at base. Up here the tanks were normally filled to the top for the trip home.

Got out of the plane – Christ it was cold, and pitch black apart from the areas that were artificially lit. There were a few inches of snow on the ground which was frozen solid. I talked to the captain who had no faults to report – great! I didn't want to be working in this temperature. Although we were all well wrapped up in heavy arctic anoraks and down-filled trousers, we had been sitting in a warm aeroplane for the last twelve hours and getting outside was a bit of a shock to the system. The aircrew soon departed the scene to the warmth of the Narona hotel down in Bodo town.

As there were no faults for any trade, the rest of the guys volunteered to help with the refuelling and re-oiling so we could depart as quickly as possible – Christ it was cold!

I got onto the starboard wing and started to refuel two of the three tanks. I leapt over the fuselage and opened up the tanks on the port side. Bob 'Bumbly' Barfly, the armourer, was on this wing and would look after the filling of the tanks over here. I left him to it – he had done it before. The hard-standing was well enough lit so there was no need for torches. The re-oiling was done by two of the other guys.

All three tanks on either wing were filled. I closed the tank caps on my side and then leapt over the fuselage to check that the fuel tank caps had been replaced properly by Bumbly on the others – they had.

As the engines were still hot I would need to come back in the morning to check out the coolant levels and around the various other systems but we were all glad to be getting out of the cold so soon. It felt like it was getting colder by the minute.

A Volkswagen minibus had arrived and was ready to take us down to the hotel so we closed the door on the aircraft and stowed the access ladder in the undercarriage bay. Even back then security was paramount.

The Volkswagen was loaded up with our gear and the driver took off at a rate of knots. Up here, after the snow arrived in October the roads were never entirely cleared of snow until spring arrived. The philosophy was to leave about four inches of snow lying on the road at all times, unless it thawed which it never seemed to do. Having this snow on the road necessitated every vehicle having spiked snow tyres fitted to the wheels and the snow ensured that the spikes would cause no damage to the road surface. This resulted in the drivers becoming very experienced in driving in these conditions.

It also resulted in them becoming very blasé about the conditions and they took great delight in doing skid turns around corners at one hell of a speed. Sideways stops were another favourite. All reminiscent of the slalom skiers that every Norwegian had aspirations of becoming. This is quite disconcerting when you are not used to it but in all honesty I never felt unsafe with them. In the town there was a law that you could be fined for splashing pedestrians with slush or snow, so they tended to be very careful in built-up areas.

We made it safely to the front door of the hotel in a flourish of snow. Signed in at reception and then up to the room, showered, letting the hot water permeate through to the bones, changed and then went down to the hotel restaurant for dinner.

7

The Gourmet

The dinner menu was written in Norwegian and French – very snobbish. One of the young guys – an electrician by the name of Colin Smutch from Stirling – was not impressed. He was obviously very picky about his food and therefore was very reticent to order in case he got anything green on his plate or any rice or pasta or fish or tomatoes or mushrooms. I asked him what he really wanted and he said egg and chips. He said that if he had known that we were going to have to stay in a hotel where he couldn't choose his own food from a hot plate then he wouldn't have come. He was told that there was the smorgasbord that he could choose from. He went up to the groaning table to have a look and came back with a very wry look on his face.

'Ugh, I'm no eatin' that shite!' was his comment. 'It's aw fish eggs an at. I widna pit tha in ma mooth. There's coo's tongue there an' aw, I widna eat oonythin' that's bin in an animal's mooth – just imagin' tha – ugh!'

I don't suppose he had ever thought of how eggs arrived in this world.

The rest of us were becoming pissed off at his rantings over the lack of choice on the menu – though I had to agree with him as there was only about five choices and three of them were fish. The prices were also extortionate.

'Dae we's hiv tae eat here? Cud we's no go oot an' get a black puddin' supper or at?'

'For Christ's sake shut up will ye? Look, they've got steak tartare on the menu. Why don't you have that – but ask for it well done,' I said.

'Whit is it?'

'It's like a hamburger,' I replied and gave the rest a wink.

He reluctantly agreed to order the steak tartare and the waiters gave him a look of disdain when he asked for it 'well done'. However, the waiter obviously thought that he had misheard or that there was something missing in the translation and gave a shrug.

Colin sat and watched the rest of us eating our starters. The smorgasbord was great with all sorts of meats and pickles and cheeses. Obviously none of this was to his taste, as he just sat there and contorted his face into grimaces of disgust as each of us relished the various delicacies that we had chosen.

'I don' know how youse can eat that shite,' was his constant banter.

'Shut the fuck up Colin, or we'll hold you down and stuff it up your arse,' somebody whispered. It didn't shut him up though. He obviously felt very smug about the fact that he had the superior tastes and would not expose them to the stuff that we were eating.

Finally the main course arrived.

'What the fuck is that?' Colin shouted. 'That meat is fuckin' raw an they've pit fuckin' green slugs an grass on ma plate. An whur's ma chips?'

The green slugs were asparagus and the 'grass' was cress.

The other few diners in the room looked round to see what all the fuss was about.

'Shut up, Colin – keep your voice down,' he was counselled, but he had obviously lost the plot by this time. The rest of us were falling about laughing.

'Did youse ken that this meat wid be raw? Ye dirty bastards! Ah canny eat that shite an' 'am starvin', ye bastards!' He was near to tears by this time and so were we.

'A'm goin' tae report youse tae the captain – this is no fair, it's like stealin' anither man's rations,' he wailed.

'Calm down for Christ's sake,' I said. 'Look if it will make you feel any better we'll ask the waiter to get the steak cooked for you. Do you want to do that?'

'Ah jist wish that ma mither wis here, she'd ken whit ah'd want tae eat!'

I called the waiter over and he sidled up with that smarmy look down the nose that waiters in posh restaurants have. As if they have just smelled something that has been brought in on someone's shoe – and you are it.

'Would it be possible to have this minced beef grilled as the young man does not want to eat it raw?' I asked.

'But sir, this tartare is made from the very finest meat and herbs – it is famous throughout Norway – the chef will go mad if I ask him to cook it.'

'I've no doubt that the chef will go mad but we have a guy here that has already gone mad. Perhaps if the chef does not want to cook the tartare then he could cook him something else – a steak perhaps?'

'Or just egg an' chips!' said Colin, 'an' nae green stuff!'

The waiter did not acknowledge this desperate plea. He lifted the plate with a flourish and flounced off into the kitchen. Some shouting could be heard from that direction as the chef learned that not everyone in Norway that night relished his renowned tartare. The waiter came back into the dining room and gave a slight nod of the head to show that all was in order.

The food eventually arrived back out of the kitchen. Imagine Colin's delight when he saw that the tartare had indeed been fried up into a beef burger with chips, and even better, there was an egg on top of the burger.

A smug grin came to his face as if to say that he was once more in charge of his taste buds and didn't have to eat the stuff that we were subjecting ourselves to. He tucked in to the chips and egg but was not about to tackle the burger as he had seen the green herbs mixed in its raw state. There was no evidence of green in the cooked state.

'What's wrong with the burger, Colin?' he was asked.

'It hud awe that green shite in it – ah'm no eatin' that!'

'I'm sure that the chef would have taken all the herbs out of the tartare before he cooked it.'

'Di yi think sae?' He sounded surprised. 'Well ah suppose ah cud try a wee bit.'

He cut a tiny morsel off the corner, gingerly put it to his lips and reluctantly took it into the very front of his mouth but was ready to gag it out in a nanosecond. He nibbled on the morsel.

'Hey that's fuckin' great,' he said and started to cut huge chunks off the burger, dip it in his egg, pile up his fork with chips, squeeze the whole lot in his mouth and demolish it. Once he had cut away the outer, better-cooked part of the burger, the herbs were once again in evidence but at this moment Colin was colour blind as starvation was the driving force.

We were all very unimpressed with the restaurant and we did not venture there again. Instead we went downtown to a café to eat reindeer balls, which was minced reindeer meat rolled into balls and stewed and tasted delicious. Colin could not be convinced to eat this and would therefore satisfy his hunger with the crisps that he had bought in a local supermarket, declaring that they were the best he had ever tasted. However, we were staying at the hotel on bed and breakfast basis and after the first morning Colin never appeared at breakfast again – they only served Continental breakfast without fried eggs. Colin would satisfy himself with more crisps.

8

Snow Storm

The next morning, Wednesday, I looked out of the window and it was snowing. About six inches had fallen overnight and it made the whole of the town look very fresh and clean – as it does.

After breakfast, 'Bumbly' Barfly phoned the airfield for them to send a wagon to pick us up and take us to the aircraft to carry out the rest of the maintenance work. He was told that because of the snow the Shackleton was isolated until the snowploughs had cleared that part of the airfield – it was not a priority.

This was no real problem as it was still early in the morning and very dark. However, only when it was a very clear day was there a faint glow of the sun in the south and even then the sun never came above the horizon. This was not a clear day.

I met the captain in the hotel foyer and informed him of the situation and said we would try again later.

The snow kept falling.

We tried the airfield again at about eleven but were once again informed that the Shackleton was unreachable as they were concentrating on keeping the runway clear. Bugger!

We phoned yet again at two but nothing had changed.

The snow kept falling.

A couple of us went around the town looking at the shops to see if there was anything we could buy as souvenirs. Bloody hell it was cold. We had to keep diving into the shops to get a warm before darting to the next. We ended up in all sorts of establishments – women's lingerie, women's frocks, greengrocer, paper shop but this was OK as there was plenty of porn on the shelves to browse around. We were in there for so long that we almost thawed out. Remember that this was 1968 – there was little access to porn in the UK and wouldn't be for another twenty years or so.

I couldn't afford to buy anything as the prices were prohibitive, but my single mate did – three copies of *Spic and Span*. Good man! We went back to the hotel.

The snow kept falling. Christ, we will never get out of here.

We phoned the airfield again, but nothing had changed – it was four pm.

I went looking for the captain and found him in the bar. I informed him of the situation once again. He said that he would have to check up on the situation for flying in the morning and get back to us.

'The sortie has been cancelled for tomorrow morning. We are trying to set something up for Friday now – depending on the weather situation,' we were informed some time later.

Shit! This meant that I could not now get to the house on Friday to tidy up for my wife and kids coming on Saturday. Still, no real panic as yet.

We went out to the Phoenix Restaurant that night as in those days in Norway, in order to get a drink, you had to eat. However, the cost of the food and drink was so high that there was no drunkenness among us. The place was fairly well deserted but a few aircrew came in and bought us a couple of rounds of beer.

Back to the hotel – it had stopped snowing.

Next morning, we phoned the base once again and were told that a wagon would be down within the hour to pick us up – great!

The transport arrived and off we set on the new layer of snow, skidding around the corners, which was even more fun when we got on the airfield roads – for the driver.

It was still very dark but it felt warmer than it had been – or perhaps we were just getting used to it. We got to the Shackleton.

The snowploughs had certainly cleared the peri-track and the hard-standing, but in so doing they had piled the snow up under the wings to about four feet, and in front of the wheels. In fact the whole of the aircraft was surrounded by this wall of snow so that it looked like a shadow of itself lying on the ground. Unfortunately the shadow had this four-foot dam all around it.

How in hell's name were we going to extricate the kite from this?

We asked the bus driver to order a power set for the aircraft but as he spoke little English we were not sure that he understood. We also gestured for him to order some sort of mechanical shovel to come to shift the snow wall from around the aircraft. Again we were not sure that he understood.

The first priority was to get the snow off the wings as it was very thick and obviously very heavy. The undercarriage 'oleo' struts were very compressed. Why hadn't we put the bloody thing in a hangar when we arrived? Bugger!

We went into the hangar near the hard-standing and someone produced a couple of brushes and shovels. We cleared a way up to the door of the aircraft, retrieved the steps from the undercarriage bay then tried to open the door – it was stuck solid with ice. What a pain!

We went into the hangar and phoned the 'ops' room and told them of the predicaments of the snow, the stuck door and the need for power. Could they send down a power set, a mechanical shovel and a de-icing machine? We would have to wait.

In the meantime we started to clear the snow off the wings and the fuselage. I was walking round checking the methanol tanks and ensuring that the oil tanks had been properly wire-locked. They had.

Where was the smell of fuel coming from? There was fuel coming from the port number two tank overflow. Obviously the tank cap had not been screwed down properly. The rise in temperature had expanded the fuel in the tank and it was leaking through the tank cap.

I asked the guys who were clearing the snow from the wing if they could clear the tank cap – however, there was no way that they could do this safely without clearing the snow from the wing root outwards. Even there the snow had frozen solid on the wing surface making it impossible to get into the tank without damaging the tank flap. I had to wait.

Half an hour later we had two power units and two mechanical shovels turn up almost simultaneously. The driver had understood more than we thought. We had finished clearing the wings and now only awaited the de-icer.

The boys had managed to get the door open as it was not as badly frozen as the wings. I think they must have pissed on it.

The power unit was fired up – thank the Lord that it worked – plugged in and the galley was fired up. Coffee – wonderful! The galley store was raided for any leftovers and cheese sandwiches were made for lunch along with tomato soup – luxury. Colin had some crisps.

Things were looking better all the time.

The de-icer eventually arrived and the wings and fuselage were sprayed with the sticky viscous fluid. This was a terrible job in the wind as you got covered in the bloody stuff and it felt like you had had a bath in syrup. Today there was no wind – however, this is all that it had going for it, as I was to soon find out.

Once I had access to the leaking tank cap, I opened up the flap and could see that the fuel was indeed coming from the cap. I tried to screw down on the star nut but it was already tight – I could get no further turns on it. Christ, these armourers are strong bastards, I couldn't even undo the screw. I got a pair of pliers out of my pocket but I still had trouble turning the bloody thing. Eventually it started to turn. I lifted up the cap and lo and behold, there was no seal on the rim of the cap.

The seal was a simple neoprene ring that sat in the recess of the tank cap. In all my time on Shackletons I had never known one to leak or for that matter go missing. Where the hell was it? I racked my brain but I was certain that it was not there when I opened the cap a few minutes ago. The only conclusion was that it had been lost during the refuelling exercise. Fantastic!

Where was it now? I got the guys together and told them what had happened and that we should start to search the remaining snow under the wing for the missing seal. This was tackled with enthusiasm but in the darkness of midday it was like looking for the proverbial needle in a haystack, especially since the mechanical shovel had removed most of the snow from that area.

While this was going on, I knew that I had not brought a seal with me in my spares kit, but I got the spares out just in case one had jumped in when I wasn't looking. I searched frantically through the stuff that I had brought. Nothing.

The only other hope was the airframe fitter – Jimmy Asore – perhaps he would have a seal that would fit. We searched his kit. Nothing.

Still they were almost bound to have something up in the base stores – Shackletons had been going in and out of here since forever, somebody must have left a tank seal behind at some time.

I removed a seal from another tank and Jimmy and I walked up towards the base building complex to find the stores. The other guys continued with the search in the snow. We eventually found the store and asked the storeman if he had any Shackleton spares that might have been left as we were looking for a seal like this one here.

'Ja, we hif some stoof down inside that you might vant to look at.'

My heart soared. There had to be something that would do the job.

Nothing! There were some bits and pieces of equipment, mainly stuff that should have been scrapped, but no bloody tank seal.

'Have you got any other seals that we could have a look at to see if they would fit?'

'Ja, come mit my.' My heart soared once again.

He took us round to a board that was covered in O rings, mainly for hydraulic systems, but none of them were anything like big enough. Bastard!

'Do you not have anything else – a seal-making kit or anything – it only has to last one trip?'

He shrugged his shoulders and shook his head. I had forgotten that they probably ran a real air force up here and did not have to rely on made-up spares like we sometimes did on Shackletons.

We thanked him for his efforts and began the trek back to the aircraft. It was getting cold again. I did not relish the thought of having to put in an Aircraft on Ground (AOG) requisition for a bloody tank cap seal. An AOG was the highest priority placed on a spare to get the aircraft back into service.

On the way back Jimmy said, 'We'll just have to make one from something.'

'What can we make it from?' I asked. I thought he might have a sheet of something in his spares kit. No such luck.

'We'll have to look around when we get back to the Shack.' He had an idea.

We looked all over the aircraft for something that could be modified into a seal but there was nothing.

'Thought not,' said Jimmy. 'We will just have to take a tread off the access ladder and make that into a seal.'

'Piss off,' I said, going up to the steps. 'The treads are knobbly on one side, that would never seal the cap.'

'Well, we could take one of the more worn treads and try to smooth it down a bit before we cut it into the seal shape.'

I thought this was worth a try so we ripped a rubber tread off the steps. It was a sorry-looking piece of material with the glue hanging off the back and the front was dirty and knobbly.

We took it across to the hangar along with our tool kits. Jimmy cut the tread in half, which was still big enough to cut a seal out of. We then put the thing on a bench and tried to file down the knobbly treads. This worked after a fashion but we could not file it really flat.

We then marked out the tread with the other seal as a template. Jimmy had a set of tinsmith's cutting shears in his kit and he started to cut round the periphery of the mark. This was surprisingly hard to do, as the neoprene was very resilient. He completed the task but the thing did not look very circular. The inside circle was even worse. The 'seal' ended up looking like a multi-sided aberration.

I suggested that we should try again with the other piece but this time cut the inner circle first, as the tread would be easier to hold for the inside track. We tried to file the knobbly bits off again and this time rub it down with an emery cloth. It worked to a degree but still did not look very impressive.

We marked it out and drilled a hole in the centre to get the shears started and work out towards the inner mark. This was a bit better but was not easy, so the circle was by no means round. After cutting the outer edge, which was marginally better than the last, we had to be satisfied. We could have pulled another tread off the steps to try again. This was a possibility and was discussed, however we decided that we could not do much better and this exercise had taken the best part of two hours. Bollocks!

It was now late afternoon and I still had all the coolant tanks on the engines to check. I took the seal up to the fuel tank, which was still leaking. I put the seal into the cap recess – it didn't fit all that well – forced the cap down until I could lever the star nut over the prong on the cap and started to screw down on the star nut.

It worked! The tank stopped leaking and the whole thing seemed to be a snug fit. Thank goodness that was finished. My trepidation had diminished with one last turn of the screw. I replaced the other cap seal, checked the coolants, which required only a minimal top-up, signed the temporary F700, called the transport and we were on our way back to the hotel. We went along to the Phoenix again for supper and then an early bed.

Next morning, Friday, the weather was fair but it was still very dark and cold when the transport picked us up at six-thirty. The aircrew would follow on when we had prepared the Shack. We arrived at the aircraft and I was very relieved to see that the tank was not leaking. The aircraft was again covered in a thick frost but no snow.

Why do people live in these conditions year after year? Bodo is a beautiful place but only when you can see it.

We called for the de-icer once again and a couple of the guys did the necessary on the wings, the fuselage, engines and propellers. Jimmy had to get up and polish the pilot's windscreen as we thought they should be able to see where we were going – home!

The main body of the aircrew arrived but the pilots and navigators were still up at Operations, getting the instructions for the day's sortie. Hope it was straight home.

While we were waiting for the jockeys, the rest of the crew were milling around. I just hoped that they would not notice that there was a tread missing from the steps, and that no one would slip on the steps as they climbed up.

The pilots arrived with the duty-free goods and the customs officer who would see us off the premises and ensure that we did not return to scoff the duty-free anywhere near Norway. I think that if we had crash-landed anywhere in Norwegian territory there would have been a customs officer there, making sure that the duty-frees were not consumed – or even used as an anaesthetic for emergency operations.

All was loaded on board. We carried out the starter crew operations, stowed the equipment, pulled the chocks, ran round to the door, climbed aboard and the door was closed. Thank goodness we were on our way. I would still make the deadline of getting down to Belfast to meet my wife tomorrow. Whew!

We took off and slowly lumbered into the sky. Sortie for the day was to arrive at a pre-determined area to search for a submarine that was hiding behind a rock somewhere in the vicinity. Same old thing.

Breakfast had just been eaten so we had been in the air for nearly two hours. I was just settling down in one of the little bunk seats on the port side of the kite. Jimmy Asore was next to me. We each had a cup of coffee. I was feeling kind of smug, as things had turned out not too bad after all. The farther south we flew, the lighter it got and it was a very clear morning. I must have dozed off.

The next thing I knew was a sharp dig in the ribs. I came to with a jolt. Jimmy was standing over me and looked like he was nearly apoplectic. He was saying something and pointing out the window. I could not hear what he was saying but I turned my head in the direction of his finger.

Fucking hell! There was fuel coming out of the port number two tank at a tremendous rate. It was cascading away from the wing obviously caught in the partial vacuum of the airflow. How long it had been doing this was anyone's guess. It had been dark up to now.

I stared at the fuel for several minutes – it seemed like hours – wishing it would just disappear. I had to do something. How could I get out of this – all sorts of things were racing through my head. At last I had a plan – I knew what to do.

I steeled myself. I went through the galley door, climbed over the main spar and went up to the engineer who was sitting at the panel intently studying nothing.

I put my hand on his shoulder, trying to look very relaxed and nonchalant. I attracted his attention. At the top of my voice I hollered, 'Would it cause too much inconvenience to use the fuel out of the number two tanks first?' I think he thought that this might be a trick question or perhaps he thought I was swotting up to become an engineer.

He gave a shrug of his shoulders combined with an open hand gesture and mouthed, 'Why?' I wished he hadn't asked that!

He lifted the flap on his earphones and I got my mouth as close to his ear as possible.

'We have a slight leak from the fuel cap on the number two port tank. It needs to be used up first if you can manage it.'

He looked at me with some disbelief and shouted very deliberately in my ear, 'How do you know?'

I signalled for him to follow me. He unplugged himself from the intercom and followed on. Once we reached the small window at the bunk seats, I pointed out of the window. He looked for quite a while. Turning back to me he shrugged his shoulders as much as to say that he couldn't see anything unusual.

In that instant I thought I was saved and that all the fuel that was going to leak had indeed leaked. However, I think we must have been passing through a cloud when he looked, for when I looked again there was a plume of fuel coming from the tank flap.

I pointed once again and this time he saw what I was pointing at – he turned back and I could see a certain amount of panic in his face. He searched round for the nearest intercom socket and plugged himself in, lifted his mask to his face and started to talk to the captain.

The captain came down the back to see for himself. He turned to me and shouted in my ear, 'What do you think it is?'

I shouted back, 'A leaking tank cap seal.'

He gave me a thumb up and disappeared up the front.

Within five minutes there was fuel spray coming from both wings. The captain was jettisoning the fuel from the number two tanks on both sides. I wondered why he was doing this as even with the leak it was safer to just start using the fuel from the number twos instead of pouring it all over the North Sea.

One of the signallers came back for a piss in the Elsan and shouted that the captain was abandoning the sortie and we were diverting into Kinloss – about two hours away.

For the rest of the journey down to Kinloss all smoking was banned so it made it seem like a very long time before we were asked to take our positions for landing. Due to the fuel leak and the abandonment of the sortie, the airfield was treating the landing as an emergency even though the cause of the emergency had long since disappeared over the North Sea.

After touching down, the aircraft was chased along the runway by four fire engines all with blue lights flashing. The captain brought the aircraft to a halt on the intersection of the cross runway and shut down the engines. By this time, Jimmy Asore was up and busy around the interior carrying out part of his after-flight servicing. I moved down towards the rear door and opened it.

We were completely surrounded by fire engines and the crews were busy reeling out their hoses in the vain hope that the aircraft would suddenly burst into flames so they could justify their existence. This was probably the most exciting thing that had happened to them in years.

Jimmy – for reasons best known to himself – opened up the drain tap for the galley waste tank and all the gunge and gore that had been collected during the flight came pouring out of the side onto the runway.

Eureka, the firemen had been justified in reeling out their hoses as here at last was the leak that caused the emergency and it was all hands to the pumps.

The charge was led by a big flight sergeant who was coordinating the response. He was waving his arms around in the effort to get his lads to bring the might of the Fire Service to bear on this potentially dangerous fluid.

I was leaning out of the door and saw what was about to happen. We were about to be covered in ten million gallons of foam that would not have done the aircraft any good at all.

I shouted to the flight sergeant, 'That is not a dangerous leak – it's only a drain!'

At hearing this, he bounded forward towards the offending stream of gunge – he stuck his hand into the flow, caught some in his cupped hand, lifted this to his nose and smelled it and then stuck his tongue in it to taste it. All this had taken about two seconds.

'What the fuck is it then?' he shouted.

'Galley waste and shit,' I replied.

'Bastard, I thought it tasted like that,' he muttered and I saw him turn slightly pale. He turned to his troops and broke the news that the emergency was over and that they should pack up the gear. This was done without much enthusiasm.

This was another example of the tasting philosophy that prevailed throughout Coastal Command – they were all at it. Bless them! I often wondered how he knew it tasted like shit.

Once we had unloaded all of our personal gear from the aircraft my moment of reckoning arrived. The captain and the engineer took me aside and asked what had happened with the tank cap seal. I told them the whole sad story and apologised for having put the aircraft at risk.

'All right then – let's have a look at your handicraft,' said the captain.

I was done for – I'll get ten years in Colchester for this, I thought. With shaking legs and a fast-beating heart I went back into the aircraft, up to the over-wing hatch, opened the hatch, crawled out onto the wing, over the fuselage and out towards the offending fuel tank. I was followed by the captain and the engineer. At this moment, I was cursing every armourer that ever lived and vowed never to speak to one again as long as I had a hole in my arse. Bastards!

With shaking hands I opened up the wing flap and unscrewed the star nut on the tank flap. I got it opened, extracted the offending piece of material and handed it to the captain. He showed it to the engineer.

'Where did you say you got this from?' he asked.

'From the aircraft steps,' I had to admit – now feeling like a complete prat.

'Not a bad effort – what do you think, Flight?' he asked the engineer.

'Don't suppose there was much more that could have been done in the circumstances,' he replied.

'Look,' said the captain, 'I should probably take this further but you were obviously working in difficult circumstances up there – so we will say no more about it.'

At that he hurled the 'seal' into the long grass at the side of the runway. I could have kissed them both on their rusty rosettes!

We departed the scene. We were not going back to Ballykelly today.

I was not out of the woods yet, however. The captain had to report that the sortie had been aborted because of a fuel leak from the tank cap and that the decision was made to jettison the fuel and hence the landing here at Kinloss.

I was 'collared' by the baby-faced flight engineering officer in the H&R crewroom, who demanded to know why the tank cap had leaked, as he would have to submit a report on the incident.

I had not reckoned on this interrogation and was caught off-guard, and had to think fast to protect my self and my co-conspirators. I told him that the cap seal had a split because it had obviously got stretched and widened when the cap star nut was screwed down on it. The split was undetectable under normal eyeball inspection and would not have been noticed during refuelling.

He asked to see the this seal but I told him that I had disposed of it as I did not want it to become mixed up with any new seal that would be fitted. He threatened to charge me with neglect and disposing of valuable investigative material that could affect the manufacture and supply of future seals. Little prick!

I knew that neoprene from the entrance ladder was unlikely to ever be used again to manufacture a cap seal – so I was more confident and knowledgeable than he was on the subject but I refrained from telling him this.

I told him that he must do as he saw fit. He turned on his heel and went off muttering something about Ballykelly incompetence. Bastard! After all, I had been trained at Kinloss.

We flew back to Ballykelly the next day. My wife and kids had been picked up at Belfast by a couple of mates organised by Gordon Mendes after I had phoned him to tell him of my predicament. I got home to a reception that was colder than it had been in Bodo, but the frost soon melted. The house was still very cold though, as the only heating available was a coal fire in the living room and we had no coal. We put the electric oven on and sat round that for a while before going to bed.

We talked about Penang with some nostalgia and wished we were still there.

9

The First Party

The next few weeks were a settling in period for all the family and for me at work. I was making new friends and acquaintances so we decided to hold a party up at the house in order to get to know some of them a bit better.

It was the end of February and we had received all our deep-sea container shipment from Singapore – the goods and chattels that we had amassed while abroad. All the standard stuff that seemed very exotic in those days. There was the intricately carved standard lamp and matching coffee table that had developed a crack due to the change in weather conditions between Singapore and Ballykelly. Ballykelly had more monsoons.

The camphor wood chest – rumour would have it that you came back from Singapore with either a camphor wood chest or a baby. We bought our chest within the first month of arriving there.

Then there was the carved wooden fish that got broken one night when it was thrown at me during an argument. There was the bronze cutlery set – which was a bugger to clean – and the Chinese hardwood table lamp that was nearly too heavy to lift.

There was the hi-fi amplifier that was powered by valves, as transistors had not been invented yet and the hi-fi turntable with the bent stylus.

There was my record collection that consisted of four LPs and a couple of singles. The LPs were Dean Martin, Herb Alpert, Slavonic Folk Dances and Tom Jones. The Tom Jones LP I bought because I misread the title – I thought the title was LIVE. As it turned out it was Tom Jones 'live' at some crappy stadium where the sound system was not all that it should have been and he was hardly discernible among the sounds of knickers being ripped off and thrown at him – ugh! One of the singles was by Cliff Richard – my wife loved Cliff but I could not stand him so I never bought an LP of him – that would have been purgatory. I think the other single was Bing Crosby singing 'White Christmas'. I don't think I ever bought another record until CDs came out in the 1980s.

Then there was the pram that was bought by my mother-in-law for our first child. This was a coach-built 'Osnath' pram that could have substituted for the coach used for the state opening of parliament. It had cream coachwork and a brown hood and cover. It was coach-sprung from two large and two smaller wheels and the whole ensemble glided along like a Rolls-Royce. It was great to take shopping as it had a huge compartment hidden in the bowels. The only problem was that it could not be fitted into a car, so the only journeys it ever undertook were to the local shop and walks around the houses.

As we had lived in a residential caravan near Elgin when we first got married, it seemed like the pram was almost as big as our accommodation. There was no way that we could get it through the door of the caravan so it had to stay in the site owner's shed that was full of pigeons. Great care was taken covering the pram over with a dustsheet every night.

We then moved to a caravan site in St Andrews when I was posted to Leuchars and the pram came too. Again we had to keep it in the farmer's shed that doubled up as a toilet.

When I was posted to Butterworth in Malaya, I thought that I had seen the last of the pram – no such luck! As I had left four months before my wife, the pram had duly been packed up and sent out with the rest of our clobber. It did not serve much purpose in the heat of Penang, as it was too claustrophobic and hot for the kids to lie in. When we moved from Penang to Singapore I thought we would get rid of the damn thing then – but no, it came to Changi with us, and here was the bloody thing in Northern Ireland.

This then was our total worldly worth and we were very proud of it – apart from the bloody pram!

The party was organised for the Saturday evening. We had invited some of our neighbours and I had invited about six single lads out to the house for a bite of supper and a few beers. The lads were mainly those that I had met initially and had shared the accommodation with down at the base – Davy Hamilton, Jimmy Curry and Jimmy Buckley included.

 Of the characters in this group there were two in particular that are worthy of individual mention – Jock Turnkey and Ozzy Quant.

Jock Turnkey, to no one's surprise, was a Scot. He was quite diminutive, very slim and sported a large moustache. He was a corporal engine fitter but I think the examination board must have had a bad day when they passed him. His sole purpose in this life was to consume alcohol.

Ozzy Quant was a strange racial mixture of an Irish father and a Philippine mother. This mating would normally result in a quite exotic, good-looking individual but in the case of Ozzy something must have gone badly wrong. He was extremely small with a swarthy skin and a great hooked nose. His lack of height was exaggerated by the way he was perpetually bent over as if he was permanently in pain. In pain he deserved to be, as he had a stomach full of ulcers. He had so many that he occasionally had to go and have them counted. Eleven at the last assessment.

The presence of these ulcers gave rise to the fact that Oz had to continually suck Horlicks tablets to calm them down and give him a modicum of sustenance. The other thing that Oz liked to consume was neat Bacardi so he was the only guy I have ever known who almost lived on Bacardi and Horlicks, as nobody ever saw him in the airmen's mess.

The Saturday evening turned out to be one of those brilliantly clear starlit nights, as cold as the Arctic. One of those nights when it hurts to breathe and your breath seems to solidify as it hits the air.

The guys started to arrive at about seven and they were all very generous and thoughtful with the presents that they brought for my wife. There were flowers, chocolates and plant pots. Their mothers must have brought them up well. On reflection I realise that most of them probably had not been inside a house, except for a public house, for months or even years.

More important though was the amount of alcohol that they had brought. There were spirits of every kind, beer in abundance and a demijohn of Emva Cream sherry from Cyprus. All of this had been brought into the country duty-free from the various detachments that were continually going on. I had never seen so much booze in one place outside a pub. Although my wife and I enjoyed a drink, we were not into it in a big way – in those days.

Apart from my wife and a couple of neighbours' wives, there were no other women there. None of the guys had a girlfriend that they would have wanted to bring along. I thought this a bit strange at the time but then they probably spent most of their time in a bar and if they could not meet a woman there, they were not going to meet a woman at all. In those days in Ireland single women did not frequent public bars and there was no way that any of our heroes were going to drink in a lounge bar. Lounge bars were for poofs!

The party started to liven up a bit after a few drinks. My record collection added nothing to the proceedings so one of the neighbours fetched some records from her place. This helped the drink go down a bit better and there was the occasional bit of dancing, if you could call it that. I could see that a couple of the guys were becoming a bit fruity as they danced and that they were being egged on by the women who were aware of the situation and were exploiting it for fun. They actually thought it was funny to dance close to a guy, just to see him trying to hide his embarrassment when they separated and he was left standing in the middle of the room with a hard-on he had difficulty hiding from the rest of us. The problem for those guys was the fact that they had nothing more than their right hand to go home to, and no doubt some of them were great exponents of the art. Some of them had declared that if their right hand could cook, they would have married it.

The party was in full swing after about three hours when Davy Hamilton came up to me and asked if it was all right for his mate to come in.

'Where's your mate?' I asked.

'He's in the car.'

'You mean he's been in the car since you arrived three hours ago?'

'Well, he was pissed then and was sound asleep. I didn't want to wake him up because he would have been in a terrible state and obnoxious.'

'For Christ sake, Davy, it has to be minus ten out there, you had better get him in before he gets hypothermic.'

We went out to the car, which was a Ford Anglia, and had difficulty opening the door as the locks had become frozen. I went back into the house and got a kettle of boiling water to pour on the passenger door lock. I wondered what would happen to the occupant of the car if we could not get him out. I could see him through the bit of window that I had de-iced by using the heat from the palm of my hand. I was not sure even now that he was not a dead duck, as there was no movement from him when we banged on the door – he was gone to the world. Or gone from this world?

The hot water worked and we got the door open but there was something very funny about it. Unless locked, the door was only kept shut by a bungee cord that was attached to the door handle, went across the prone body of the passenger and was tied to the handbrake. Of course as we had the door open to try to extract the body, the bungee cord was stretched to its limit and we could not undo the bloody thing to release him. The cord was also digging into his legs in an alarming fashion.

The occupant was still comatose, lying back in the seat with his mouth open. Davy trying to shake him awake and actually became quite rough with him but there was no response.

'Norman, Norman, for Christ sake wake up!' Davy shouted, but there was no movement.

'We'd better get him out of the car quickly and carry him into the house,' I said.

I climbed into the car across our patient. With the door closed, it was an easy matter to undo the bungee cord and open the door properly. I swung his head round into the car as Davy swung his feet over the door sill. He had had to chop him behind the knees with his fist to get him to bend his knees before he could dig his legs out of the foot well. It was like rigor mortis had set in.

We eventually got him out of the car and with me at the head and Davy at the feet we started off towards the house some fifty yards away. This guy was as light as a feather. He could not have weighed much more than eight stones so we were not struggling under his weight.

About halfway to the house, our hero gave a retch and spewed up what seemed to be half the daily allocation of Guinness for the whole of Northern Ireland and half the contents of Ma Hassin's café. As I had the head end, I dropped this as quickly as I could. I had no desire to be covered in whatever it was that was escaping from this guy's stomach.

His head hit grass that was as hard as iron due to the frost, and Davy dropped the other end. I think these actions were the saviour of him as he gave out a groan and started to take some control of his actions. The first of these actions was to roll over onto all fours and deposit the other half of his stomach contents onto the grass. This done, he rolled into a sitting position with his head between his legs and started to spit and clean out his mouth of all the detritus that remained. Every now and then he would look up to the heavens in some sort of effort to focus in on where he was. He looked dreadful! His eyes were boggling out of their sockets and were streaming with tears.

He put his head between his legs once more in an effort to wipe away the phlegm so he could breathe more easily. The next thing he was trying to lie flat out on the grass, apparently in an effort to get back to sleep I thought.

'For Christ sake Norman, get up will ya,' said Davy and gave him a jab in the ribs with his foot. Lifting one foot off the ground sent Davy careering away from the scene in a convulsive drunken dance and he ended up sprawled out on the frost-covered grass some twenty feet away.

He rolled over onto his back and started laughing in that inane fashion that drunks have. This started Norman off laughing and the pair of them could not stop. Norman started to cough and I thought that I was going to have to send for an ambulance as the cough went back to a retch and even more stomach contents made themselves visible. This guy is going to die, I thought.

Eventually they both managed to get themselves onto their knees and crawled towards each other. Supporting themselves they eventually got to their feet.

'How's about ye, wee fella?' enquired Davy.

'Fuck, do I need a drink!' replied Norman.

These were the first words that I ever heard coming out of the mouth of Norman Lindsay. It wasn't the first thing that I had seen though.

We carried the wee fella into the house, much to the consternation of the womenfolk who gathered round to administer some first aid to this utterly dishevelled person.

'Who the hell is that? Where did he come from? What on earth have you done to him?' my wife asked.

'Nothing, we only went out and brought him in from the car. He's Davy's mate Norman. He got himself in that state. He's had too much to drink and has been sick outside.'

'He looks like he should be in hospital. How much have you had to drink, Norman?'

This question was directed at the total wreck who was barely standing on his own two feet. Now that we had got him into the light he looked worse than I had imagined outside. He was as white as snow with a touch of green around the gills. He pulled himself up to his full five foot two inch height and declared through a very dry mouth that would hardly let him form the words, 'Not enough, what have you got?'

'Would you like a cup of coffee or something?'

'Would I feck – I need a drink – have you got any?'

'I don't think you should have any more drink until you've had something in your stomach. Have a coffee and maybe something to eat. What do you say – I've got some nice soup that only needs heating up.'

'Are you tryin' to make me ill or somethin'? I need a drink to get me going again, I don't need any food at this time of night. Have you got any whisky?'

'All right, you go into the bathroom and get yourself cleaned up a bit and I'll pour you a whisky. What do you take with the whisky?'

'More friggin' whisky,' came the reply.

He went into the bathroom and we heard some more retching and cursing before he reappeared. There did not seem to be much improvement in his appearance as my wife handed him his glass of whisky.

He took the whisky with a nod of thanks and staggered off into the sitting room to join the party. He found himself a chair and sat down cradling his drink in both hands. He did not do much more for the rest of the evening, just sat in the chair with his body swaying, his head bowed and lolling from side to side. Occasionally he would lift his head and look round the room suspiciously as he tried to focus on the other people there. This he failed to do with both eyes open, so one eye would be closed to aid the process. At this time he would give out what passed as a mocking laughing grunt. He could not hold this effort for too long so the head would loll back down again. The whisky was still un-drunk but the glass was carefully cradled.

During the evening, several people had asked, 'Who's your friend?' I just shrugged my shoulders.

After the incident with Norman I thought my trials and tribulations were over for the night – no chance! About an hour later, Jimmy Buckley came up to me and asked if it was all right if his father joined the party.

'Of course it is all right, where is he coming from?'

'He's in his car outside – he drove me here.'

'Oh no not again – why didn't you bring him in the first place? He'll be frozen stiff out there!'

'He'd had a few drinks and I didn't think I was going to enjoy the party so I wasn't goin' to stay all that long so I didn't think it was worth asking you if my dad could come in. I forgot all about him.'

We went out to the car and by this time the temperature had dropped considerably. The insides of the windows had steamed up with the man's breath and this had frozen, so there were Jack Frost patterns all over. We could not make out if there was anybody inside or not. We tried the doors but they were either frozen solid like the Anglia's or they were locked from the inside.

Both Jimmy and I banged on the windows to try to wake his dad up but there was no movement from the inside. Christ, maybe he'd frozen to death!

I went back into the house to get another kettle of hot water. I was beginning to feel like an expectant father being asked by a midwife to keep the hot water coming. I poured the water over the door lock and handle and tried the door to no avail. I went in to get another kettle full and repeated the exercise. By this time, the first lot of water had frozen on the doors as a reminder of just how cold it was. Again there was no movement of the doors. Bastard! We kept knocking and knocking at the windows but there was no response from inside.

'We'll need to get the police to come and try to get him out,' I said.

'Christ, we can't do that,' said Jim. 'If they come they might suspect that my dad was driving with a wee drink in him and that would not do at all.'

'Well, we can't leave him here all night in this weather, he is bound to die of hypothermia before the dawn – what are we going to do?'

'We'll just have to break into the car somehow,' said Jim. 'What's the best way of doing that?'

'I suppose we could do it with a hammer or an axe. I'll go and get something from the house.'

I went into the house. The party was in full swing with the Clancy Brothers belting forth the 'Wild Rover' and every one else joining in. I fetched a hammer from the utility room where the pram stayed. I went back outside. Jimmy was still hammering on the window with his fist but nothing was stirring inside. I gave him the hammer.

'Better break the passenger window. Be sure to cover your eyes when you hit it, just in case any shrapnel comes back at you,' I said.

'Don't you worry about that,' he said and gave an almighty smack at the window. The bloody thing shattered in a thousand pieces.

'Here – youse boys! What the feck di ye think yer doin' tae my car!' This cry was followed by the sound of running feet coming down the street. Jim and I were about to take off at a high rate of knots until we realised who was doing the shouting.

'Da, it's me, Jim. We thought you wiz holed up in the car and in danger of catching hypothermia. Where the frig have you been?'

'Feckin' hypothermia is it? I'll gie ye feckin' hypothermia, more like I'll lay youse out on a friggin' slab, ye bastards. Look fit yiv din tae ma car, ye couple o' buck egits ye!'

'Christ, I'm sorry da but we thought you were still in the car and had gone into a coma from the cold. We wiz only tryin' to get you out. Where the friggin' hell have you been all this time?'

'I got fed up waitin' and went down tae the pub in the village for a couple o' pints. I met some friends o' mine down there – they were the right sort – if ye know whit I mean?'

'Oh aye – I ken whit ye mean all right but ye might have come and told us ye were goin'. We'd never have had tae break the window if we'd known where ye were at. Now look whit you've made us do. This is Gordon whose house I'm at for the party.'

'Hallo Mr Buckley,' I said. 'I'm sorry about the window but we were really worried about you – I'm glad to see that you are all right. I think you should come into the house and I'll get some plastic sheeting to put over the window to get you home.'

'Aye, thanks laddie. Don't feel guilty aboot the window – it'll fix. I'll take ye up in yer offer tae come intae the hoose though. Call me Bill,' he smiled.

We all three went into the house. Jimmy and I were frozen stupid but Bill, who only minutes ago we thought was near death's door, had a nice warm glow from what was no doubt several drams in a nice warm pub. There seemed to be no justice.

The Clancy Brothers were now belting out the 'Irish Rover' accompanied by the assembled mass. These Irish do a lot of roving I thought to myself. I got some plastic and went out to cover up the window by trapping it with the door. Walking back to the house I realised that I had hardly had a drink all night and definitely none within the last couple of hours. I hoped there would be something left – and no more people to be rescued from cars!

I went into the living room and the Clancy Brothers were belting out 'The Jug of Punch' – accompanied by the assembled mass.

Norman Lindsay was still sitting on his chair looking round the room with one eye closed and the untouched whisky grasped in his mitt – God bless him!

Bill Buckley had produced a bottle of Scotch from his coat pocket when he had come into the house. This was greeted with a cheer and was immediately snatched from his grasp. I managed to get a couple of glasses before even this ran out.

Bill and Jimmy Buckley departed the scene at about one in the morning. We thought that they should stay, but Bill was adamant that he was fit to drive – he wasn't. The RUC picked him up a couple of miles down the road and they both ended up in the clink for the rest of the night. Bill was charged next day with 'Drunk in Charge of a Motor Vehicle'. Not even his friends of the 'right sort' could save him – if ye know whit I mean?

The rest of the night passed without incident, apart from Norman falling off his chair and spilling a perfectly good drink in the process. He remained there, comatose once again, for the rest of the night.

The next morning the place looked like a bomb had been dropped and had killed all the people. There were bodies, empty glasses, beer bottles everywhere and the whole place stank of bodies, drink and cigarette smoke. In amongst all of this devastation my two daughters were playing with their toys quite unaware of the mess. I wished that I felt like they did.

The boys helped to clear up and were given breakfast as their reward. After breakfast, we all went down to Vera's in Limavady for a hair of the dog.

10

Gnashers in Gibraltar

We were off to Gibraltar for a quick mid-week trip. Gibraltar was one of the places most often visited by the Shackleton squadrons as it was reasonably close and had duty-free goods for sale. I had been there several times in the past so I knew it quite well and I liked the place.

On this particular detachment we were to be in the air for some eighteen hours and the aircraft was to be full of all sorts of people. The essence of the trip was to conduct a navigational exercise, leaving Ballykelly and flying into mid-Atlantic beyond the Azores to find and rendezvous with weather ship *Kilo*, drop them some mail and then make the run into Gib. A very long and very boring journey.

Because of all the people on board and the length of the journey, the toilet requirements were subjected to detailed military planning and it was decided that two Elsan chemical toilets would be required to collect all the bodily waste. The duty Elsan mechanic – these people sometimes doubled up as airframe technicians – was duly dispatched to fit in and top up the extra toilet with Racasan fluid.

My groundcrew companions on this little sortie were Doug Morris, airframes, George (Dod) McHair, electrician, Sid Dyler, armourer, and Dave Dingle, fairy.

We were to take off at six in the evening so everyone was out at the aircraft at about five-thirty loading up their luggage in the bomb bay panniers and doing the usual kicking and licking of all things Shackleton. On these sorties, nobody wanted to find anything wrong so the kicking and licking was not carried out with any great enthusiasm.

After everyone was stowed on board, the engines were fired up and we were off on our journey. We settled down to the constant mildly unsynchronised drone of the engines and the bone-shattering vibrations combined with the gentle up and down and sideways movements of the craft caused by some inclement weather somewhere off the southern tip of Ireland.

We were served dinner around eight. Pre-prepared food trays heated up in the infra-red oven followed by canned fruit and condensed milk – excellent. I crawled down to the rear of the aircraft to the tail observer's position where there was a very comfortable leatherbound mattress. This was a favourite spot as the Perspex cupola gave an unfettered view of the surrounding sky and sea. On this evening there was not much sky and sea to observe so I soon fell asleep and woke up about an hour later feeling very refreshed. I crawled back up into the body of the craft and made George McHair and myself a cup of coffee.

The name George was commonly shortened to 'Dod' in Scotland – don't ask me why. He was about six feet tall with short curly hair and wore big round glasses. He came from Crail in Fife and he looked kind of gormless.

This was Dod's first flight in a Shackleton and he did not look too comfortable. I gave him the coffee and asked him if he wanted to play some cards. When I say 'asked' I really only imitated the dealing of cards and shouted at the top of my voice into the very bowl of his ear – 'Di ya want tae play a game o' cards?' A less than enthusiastic nod was his reply.

We sat down at the mess table and played a game or two of crib, writing the scores down on a bit of paper as we had no crib board. We had been there for about half an hour and I could see that Dod was not feeling too great. I don't know whether it was the effects of the dinner or the coffee, but I could guess it was a lot to do with the motion of the aircraft. He gestured to me that he was feeling a bit sick and I could see that he had lost the entire colour from his face. I gestured to him that perhaps he should go for a sleep down in the rear observer's 'bed'. He nodded his head and I showed him the way. He crawled onto the mattress.

I went up to the galley and helped out in the preparation of supper. This entailed opening multiple cans of meat and vegetables, potatoes and stuff to throw into a large pot to make the ubiquitous 'Honkers stew'. Once this brew was up to temperature I busied myself by doing the waiter bit and handed out the trays and eating irons to the rest of the crew.

I had completed the rounds of all the people in the main body of the craft and only had the groundcrew boys down the back to serve. I armed myself with a couple of trays and served a couple of the guys.

There was only Dod, myself and one other left to serve. I went back to the galley and got another couple of trays. Dod was the last apart from myself to get a tray. He was sitting in the starboard observer's beam seat with his head bowed into his chest. I went up and gave him a kick to indicate that I was here with his supper.

Dod looked up at me and he was not a pretty sight. I don't think I have ever seen anyone as green as he was at that moment. He looked like an unripe turnip.

I indicated the tray to him but he just took one look at the stew, bolted out of his chair and disappeared down the back of the aircraft. I shrugged my shoulders, sat down in the newly vacated armchair and ate my supper.

Dod came back into the compartment still looking terrible. I gestured to him about having a drink of water. He gave me a thumbs up sign and tried to smile at me. There was something wrong with his smile. He had a huge gap in his upper teeth which presented itself as a gaping black hole in his mouth.

I indicated this to him by motioning to my own teeth and then pointing to his and then pulling my open hand across my throat indicating the negative. It took him a full nanosecond to comprehend what I was trying to relay to him. He put his hand across his mouth and panic set in as he finally realised what I meant. He turned an even whiter shade of pale.

I shrugged my shoulders in an effort to ask what had happened to his teeth. He indicated back that he had been sick and motioned a gaping hole. Now it was my turn to take a nanosecond to realise what had happened.

Bloody hell, he had only gone and puked his teeth into one of the Elsans! Why had he done that – there were sick bags everywhere around the aircraft.

Poor bugger, I really felt sorry for him as he now looked very forlorn as well as very green. We were only some seven hours into the flight time so there was a long way to go and a lot of body fluids and waste material to be passed into the Elsans before we hit Gib.

Dod sat himself down in one of the observer's armchairs and veritably scowled at every passing body that went to use the toilet facilities. I am sure he was counting the numbers of pissers and shitters, hoping that the latter were not using 'his' Elsan; all the time imagining the effects that this would be having on his teeth. However, he did seem to perk up a little as time went by and was almost human by the time we reached Gib.

We arrived at eleven in the morning, an hour ahead of schedule, and it was a steaming hot day. As soon as the aircraft had been brought to a halt everyone evacuated as quickly as possible to try to get some relief from the heat and the stench that was building up inside. Everyone, that is, apart from Dod who was now the self-appointed guardian of the Elsans. He would not leave the aircraft until he had taken possession of the putrefying, foul-smelling things.

The aircrew departed in the crew bus. We had asked them to send out a 'honey bin'.

On Coastal Command, airframe technicians were paid the princely sum of one shilling and sixpence extra a day to empty the Elsans during the after-flight servicing of the aircraft. At Ballykelly and other mainland stations, this was easily earned as all the Elsans were emptied onto the grass surrounding the dispersal areas. This was biodegradability and eco-friendliness taken to the nth degree long before the words had been invented.

However, this quest to save the planet was not possible in Gib as the nearest green grass was somewhere in the foothills of the Pyrenees. No, in Gib the Elsans had to be emptied into what were known as 'honey bins'. These were merely storage tanks on wheels with a platform on the side and a lid on the top to accept the Elsan contents. They were towed around the dispersal by a tractor.

As was usual at Shackleton bases, the home base personnel serviced visiting aircraft – unless there were snags to be cleared. On this occasion there were no snags so we were able and anxious to leave as soon as the transport returned for us. The Gib guys were in no hurry to carry out the servicing, as we were to be there for two days. Sadly, no honey bins were hoving into view and we were parked a long way from the control centre.

By this time, Doug Morris had extracted the Elsans from the bowels of the aircraft and these were under the close scrutiny of our toothless wonder. Unfortunately for him, the Elsans had become mixed up in their extraction so he did not know which held his precious teeth. The day was getting hotter and the vapours that were oozing from the fetid things were clearly visible to the naked eye. Unfortunately, the smelly vapours were also clearly sensed by the naked nose. However, Dod stuck as close to them as a bluebottle would around a pile of shit – as this clearly was.

The bus arrived to take us to ops. Still no honey bin – what to do? We packed our luggage into the bus and were ready to depart. Dod indicated that we take the Elsans in the bus with us so he could empty them down at the squadron. He was told unanimously to 'Fuck off' in no uncertain manner.

In the end I elected to stay with Dod and the Elsans while the rest went down to the squadron and could hurry along the long awaited honey bin. The temperature got higher and the effects of a seventeen-hour flight in a flying 'road drill' were beginning to show. We were also dressed in our hairy blue uniforms while all the local lads were in khaki drill. We sat there in the shade of a wing for another half hour and this seemed like an eternity, then out of the heat haze we could see a tractor appearing like some mirage out in the desert. As it got nearer we could see that it was indeed towing the by now revered honey bin. The driver pulled the rig to a stop quite close to where we and the Elsans were waiting.

'Watch'er cock,' said the driver when the din of his tractor had died away. 'I hear you have an urgent need to empty your Elsans? I've never heard of that before. Has some aircrew bastard finally shit a golden egg?'

'Sorry to have got you out here but my mate's false teeth are in one of these bins so we need to get them out before we hit the town tonight. He wouldn't stand a chance without them.'

'Fuckin' right,' he said. 'Mind you, by the looks of him he could earn a bit of money givin' blow jobs to the fishheads around the docks. Come to think of it, he could earn a lot of money with those dirty old bum bandits,' he laughed. 'Do you fancy it mate? I could set you up wiv a few.' He gestured to Dod with his right arm, a thrust of his groin and a salacious look on his face.

I could see that Dod was mortified at the suggestion. I could have bet that he did not know such things were possible, as he had never been near the navy nor had come up against any shirt-lifters in his life – not in Fife anyway.

'Phruck off!' he said through his unsupported top lip. 'A'm no intae onyphrin' like phrat. Ah jist need tae get ma theeph back frae ane o' yon phrilphy bins.'

I realised that this was the first time that he had spoken since getting off the plane. Up to now he had merely nodded or shaken his head. It was quite a shock to hear him speak without his teeth.

'Only jokin', Jock. Let's get these bloody things emptied for you. I'm Tony by the way.'

'OK, but iphrr yi dinna mind I'll dae the emphtyin' sois'll no miph ma theeph.'

'Fair do's,' said the lad. He went over and picked up one of the Elsans and heaved it up on to the platform of the honey bin.

'Cor, it don't half pong. They're not normally as bad as this, it must be because you have had them sittin' in the sun for a while.'

Dod got himself up on the platform and I could see by the look on his face that he did not relish the job in hand. The mere smell had turned his pallor back to that of the turnip and his adam's apple was visibly bobbing up and down as he tried very hard to swallow the sickly saliva accumulating in copious quantities in his mouth.

The lid of the tank was opened and the toxicity level from this must now have been a lot worse but Dod could not delay the inevitable any longer. His head disappeared into the tank and his whole body shook with the gut-wrenching contortions of one who tries to be sick with nothing to be sick with, apart from a little foul-tasting bile – commonly known in Scotland as 'the dry boke'. His head came out of the tank and he looked absolutely ghastly and completely drained. Poor bugger. He wiped his nose, removed his glasses and dried his streaming eyes on a hanky that he produced from somewhere.

'Will I come up and empty it for you?' I said.

'Naw, I'll be awphright noo. I'll dae it. I need tae gat ma theeph.'

At this he lifted the bin up and started to slowly tip the contents into the tank – all the while scrutinising every single piece of waste that went over the rim. There was lots of solid floating stuff and eventually the whole stream got clogged up by wet toilet paper stubbornly clinging to the rim. He had to put the bin down on the platform to clear this paper dam by kicking it back into the bin with the toe of his shoe which was now left covered in wet shitty paper.

The draining process was resumed and as the bin became emptier and the angle had to be increased to continue draining, Dod's head almost disappeared into it. The liquids were finally drained out of the bin and all that was left was a thick sticky mass of indiscernible constitution.

'Ma theeph micht be in this shipht. Ah need somphrin' tae stir it up. Hiv we got onyphrin'?'

I went into the aircraft and came back out with a fuel tank dipstick. He started to stir at the mass with this and occasionally used it to stab at some solid piece of shit that had not yet become dissolved by the Racasan. How he thought his teeth would have become embedded in solid shit, I don't know. This procedure went on for some minutes until he realised that his teeth were not in this bin. Sod's Law!

Dod looked absolutely dejected as he eyed up the other bin. I took the drained bin from him and picked up the second one and carried it across to the honey bin. I thought that this one did not seem to smell as bad as the first. I handed it up to the poor bugger.

With Tony looking on, he started the draining process once again and this time there didn't seem to be any toilet paper in the stream to clog the flow, nor did there seem to be very many solids. The draining process went relatively quickly and the bin was tipped up to the acute angle with Dod's head stuck inside once more.

'I can see phrem!' an exultant cry echoed from inside the bin.

He held the bin at this angle and reached up inside to retrieve the errant teeth.

'Phruckin' hell! I've lost the buggers,' came his anguished cry.

Dod withdrew his head from the bin and hurled it across the concrete dispersal with an almighty 'Phruck!'

'What's happened?' I asked incredulously, but I already thought I knew.

'The phruckin' theeph have drophed into the phruckin' honey bin. I'll nephre get them back noo!' He sat down on the platform and tears of frustration started to swell up in his eyes. Poor bugger, he was the one that was totally drained now.

Tony and I looked at one another and little smiles were playing at the sides of our mouths. I had a twinge of conscience.

'Look, come with me and we will empty the honey bin somehow so's you can get your teeth back,' said the lad.

'Ah dinae care if ah nephre see the phruckin' phrings again!' came the dejected cry.

'Oh come on now,' I said. 'We still haven't missed lunch yet and you'll need your teeth for that.'

'Phruck ophrr – phrat' nae phrunny!'

'It wasn't meant to be funny. Come on, we need to make a move or we will be here all day.'

I retrieved the now dented bin and the other one and stowed them beside the aircraft wheel. I put the dipstick back inside and closed the door. We climbed on board the tractor and made our way to the squadron ops room. It was nice to be on the move and getting the benefit of the evaporating air. I was soaking wet and Dod looked like he was about to drown. He still looked like the unripe turnip and held his head in his hands all the way there. We arrived at the squadron, dismounted from the tractor and went into the cool shade of the line office.

81

'Hey chief, got any idea how we can empty a honey bin so's we can retrieve a set of false teeth out of it?' asked Tony of the Chief Tech in charge of the line.

'I've never heard of a honey bin having false teeth before. How'd they get in there?'

'These guys are on the aircraft from Ballykelly and this one was sick in the Elsan and lost his teeth in it. He tried to get them back but they have slipped into the honey bin. He needs them for his lunch.'

The chief looked at poor old Dod, who was by now beginning to regain some of his colour but being without a top set of teeth and with dried, used toilet paper wrapped around his right shoe made him look a bit of a prat. The chief smiled and turned away from us – I could see his shoulders heaving as he tried to suppress a gut-shuddering laugh. His hanky was evident as he fished it out of his pocket. Eventually he disappeared totally under the counter. Tony and I shrugged our shoulders, smiled and winked at each other – we were becoming used to the situation.

I must admit that I never actually heard any laughing so the chief's sides must have been splitting with the suppression. After several minutes he reappeared and his eyes were wet with tears. He had trouble keeping his composure and seemed ready to dive under the counter again at any minute.

'OK, let's see. The honey bin is normally coupled up to the sewage drain and then emptied. If we do that now, the teeth will be down the drain before we know it. We need to catch the solid stuff coming out of the bin. We need some sort of filter. Anyone got any ideas?' Funny thing this, the further up the ranks one went, the less they wanted to use their brains. I suppose they became atrophied after a while, with lack of use.

'We could use the friggin' Engineering Officer's hat. He's got a brain with more holes in it than a piece of friggin' Gruyere cheese so probably his hat is the same,' suggested Tony.

'OK, let's not go there. We need a piece of small-holed grating or something, anything lying about anywhere?'

'I've got just the thing in the car!' said Tony. 'Be back in a mo.' He ran out of the office.

He returned inside three minutes. 'There you are – these should do the trick'; he threw a pair of women's fishnet tights on the counter.

'I didn't know you were into wearing these,' said the chief.

'Naw, I screwed a Spanish bird in the back of my car the other night and she went home without these and her panties.'

'Lucky bastard!' said the chief woefully. 'OK, these should be OK to put over the drain – OK?'

I wondered how many OKs you could get into a sentence.

The three of us went out to the tractor once again and climbed aboard. Off we went with the honey bin like some treasure hunters to find the drain that would finally give up the sacred teeth.

We arrived at the drain point and Tony uncurled the hose from the back of the honey bin. He opened the drain cover and tied the fishnet tights loosely around the gaping hole. This drain point must have been a branch of a main sewer. The stench from it would have stripped varnish off wood. The smelly atmosphere kept drawing and puffing, no doubt in unison to the sea waves rising and falling at the drain exit point, somewhere offshore. Whew, what a stink! Trouble was that all the holidaymakers would be swimming around in this effluent – going through the motions, so to speak.

Dod was given no choice in that he had to take charge of the hose end and direct the contents of the honey bin down the drain through the tights. They were his teeth after all, so he could endure the stink.

Tony opened up the valve on the honey bin and the contents started to disgorge themselves onto the tights. The tights worked quite well but they soon became overwhelmed by all the solids coming out of the tank. God knows when the tank was last emptied. We certainly did not recognise any of the contents thus far.

We had to have some way of forcing the solids through the tights – but what? There was a stopcock spanner lying up against the perimeter fence wire netting. I went to fetch it. At at least three feet, it was long enough to keep me a reasonable distance from the stink while I stirred.

I tried to force the shit through the relatively close weave of the tights but this would have taken forever – if the material could have withstood the strain. Not unsurprisingly, the material gave way and we were left with a gaping hole once again.

'Bloody hell, we'll never be able to filter this shit this way,' I said. 'We need to offload it in batches into a bucket or something and then pour this down the drain without the filter. Any buckets nearby?'

'I'll nip back and get something,' said Tony.

We uncoupled the honey bin from the tractor and he scooted off. I was becoming pissed off with this exercise.

Tony came back with – guess what – an Elsan. We started the process once again, this time decanting the slurry into the bin and then allowing Dod to carefully pour this into the drain but never allowing the angle to go beyond the horizontal. Christ, this would take hours. I was starving. However, we persevered with the task.

Dod must have decanted about twenty or more bins when he let out a great shout.

'Ah've seen phrem! They're in the bin!'

With no further ado, Dod set down the bin, rolled up his sleeve and plunged his hand into the slurry that now contained his teeth. He was taking no chances about pouring any more of the stuff out before retrieval. He was groping around with extreme concentration up to his elbow in shit.

'Ya whore sir! Ah've got phrem!' He pulled his hand out of the bin and sure enough there were his teeth tightly held in his grip. They were almost unrecognisable, all covered in nasty-looking bits and pieces, but at least he had them.

Thank Christ for that, I thought, we can get the hell out of here. I looked at my watch – two hours had passed since we landed. The temperature had risen still further – we had no sun cream on and I was as thirsty and hungry as hell. I could have eaten a scabby-headed bairn! Dod carefully wrapped the teeth in his hanky and put them in his pocket. He ran his left hand down his right arm to get rid of the majority of the shit that was still clinging there. He didn't half pong!

'C'mon, I'll give you a run over to the other side of the runway so you can get down to the mess before it closes at one-thirty. Where's your luggage?' enquired Tony.

'The other lads took it with them so I think the best thing is for us to get back to where we will be staying before we go to the mess. Do you have any idea where we will be staying?' I asked.

'Probably in the transit block, I'll take you there.'

We jumped onto the tractor once again and it was good to get the wind in our faces and cool down a little. I felt very hot. We arrived at the block, thanked Tony for his help and arranged to see him in the NAAFI later on for a pint.

We went into the accommodation and found our bags had been deposited in a room. I stripped off and went for a quick shower. Dod came with me and I could hear him scrubbing away at his teeth while I enjoyed a cool spray. Dod used the shower after me.

Back in the room I changed into shorts and a shirt. Dod changed into slacks and shirt and we made off for the mess. He was grinning all over his face and I must admit that his teeth did look exceptionally white.

I told Dod that I thought of marketing Racasan as a tooth cleaner. I even made up an advertising slogan based on the old 'Pepsodent' advert.

'You'll make your teeth as white as you can, when you clean your teeth with Racasan.'

Dod was not amused!

11

The Stripper

After a little siesta in the early evening, we went across to the NAAFI with the rest of the gang and met up with Tony. We had a couple of pints then Tony scarpered off on his hot date. After all, he was in need of a new pair of fishnet tights. The rest of us opted to walk downtown instead of getting a taxi. We needed to stretch our legs and it was a beautiful evening.

I always liked Gib, as it was quintessentially British but with the tinge of the exoticism of Spain and this gave it a tremendous social atmosphere. This was especially true in those days as there were very few tourists around and the main trade came from the military presence on the Rock and the visiting British and foreign military personnel.

The one thing I did not like about Gib was that all the bars served bloody Toby beer. This tasted like diesel or cat's piss so I was always reduced to drinking double Scotch with lemonade and ice – a terrible burden to bear.

We had hit several bars, had a few drinks and a few packets of fresh prawns and were moving on through the town, ending up in Sugar's bar. Sugar, the owner, was well known in navy circles – he had been found in a few. He was blatantly homosexual, something that was not openly displayed in those days as poofs had a habit of getting beaten up quite regularly. This would normally be when they had come on quite strong with some macho character that they fancied who turned out not to be of the same persuasion. However, with so many navy personnel in Gib there was a fair chance that a lot of the 'right' persuasion were available. It was always asserted that only three things mattered in the navy – Rum, Bum and Baccy!

Why had five heterosexuals been persuaded to go into Sugar's when there were obviously so many dangers lurking inside? The answer was simple – there was a board outside advertising a STRIPPER on at 9.30.

It was now 9.15 – just in time! In poor old sex-starved Britain of this era authentic striptease was a very rare thing to see and something not to be missed whenever it was available. We could have gone across to Spain for some real erotica where there were rumours that there was a woman who did some very strange things with a donkey, but none of us felt like making the effort, so in we went.

The bar was not very full and we had no difficulty in getting a round of drinks. We sat there and 9.30 came and went. We had more drinks and 10.30 came and went. It was obvious that the lure of the stripper was a ploy to attract and then keep the lads in the bar without having to produce her.

'Hey Sugar, you bent bastard – when is this bloody stripper comin' on?' one wag enquired.

'In a minute, in a minute, have some more drinkies, darling!' he flustered.

'Fuck that, if she's not here in two minutes me and my mates are gonna take this place apart!'

'OK, OK I'll go and get her.' His arms flapped around limply in a dismissive manner. He rounded to the end of the bar and disappeared through a dirty curtain into some inner sanctum.

From behind the curtain there came 'Hey you!' from Sugar, followed by a high-pitched scream and then a lot of shouting in Spanish by a woman. Nobody in this world can shout and argue like a Spanish woman. It never fails to amaze how many words can be rattled off in so short a time and this seems to be achieved without ever drawing breath.

Sugar's voice. 'Well, if you don't wake her up and she is not ready to dance in five minutes then you and her can bloody well go back to where you came from!'

He came flouncing back into the bar still being harangued by the woman who now appeared from behind the curtain. Christ, what a sight, she was about four foot six and as wide as she was tall. She was dressed all in black with a headscarf on her head. Her face was small and round with a huge nose that had a large wart growing on one side. Her whole presence was grotesque. She had obviously just been woken up by Sugar as her eyes were very puffed and bleary – probably hence the initial scream. She was still haranguing Sugar and her arms were being thrown about with the occasional raised middle finger being shown in unison to one eye being closed, giving the 'evil eye' to the poor man, who was by now trying to ignore her presence. Little chance as she went on and on and on.

'Hey Sugar, hope that's not your stripper!' bellowed one spectator.

Sugar tried to ignore this remark but the woman stopped her ranting and smiled at the man. This was an awesome sight as she only had her two front teeth on the top, which made her look even more like a gargoyle. The smile was only fleeting as she started her tirade once again and turned back to the curtain whence she came.

Sugar took the opportunity and tapped a wine glass with a teaspoon to attract everyone's attention.

'The beautiful Sanita – tonight's stripper will be with us shortly so I would advise everyone to charge your glasses at the bar before this begins. Thank you.'

From behind the curtain came the most horrendous caterwauling of two Spanish females in hot argument. The caterwauling was interspersed by the odd slap of hand on cheek, which seemed to increase the crescendo for a while then it subsided to the normal of around a hundred and ten decibels.

Sugar went up and put his head through the curtain and shouted 'Stop it – Stop it!' The reply was a pan or some other metal container hurled at his head. The container hit the wall and then fell to the floor. He jumped back into the bar apparently unscathed.

The cacophony from the back room continued for ten minutes more then suddenly stopped. Everyone in the bar looked expectantly across to the curtain and there was the little woman smiling quite demurely at Sugar and nodding her head. It was still not a pretty sight!

The nodding from the woman galvanised Sugar into a state of fluster. He came round from behind the bar and started to shoo the lads away from the centre of the room. Some were reluctant to go as they had secured what they thought was the best vantage point to watch the stripper. We were among those. However, the floor was cleared with those on the stage area pushing those on the perimeter further back. This caused some altercations but it was done in reasonably good humour.

Once the area was cleared, Sugar looked around him with an air of satisfaction and clasped his hands together at the top of his chest in the effeminate way that some gay guys do.

'Gentlemen, I want you to take your hands out of your pockets and put them together for our lovely stripper for this evening – Sanita – and I don't want to see your hands go back in your pockets again while the show is on.'

At this he went across and put a shilling in the jukebox and selected three tunes.

The jukebox carousel trundled round and stopped, the pick-up arm went into the carousel but came back out again – empty!

'Oh shit, the bloody thing has let me down again – has anyone got another shilling?' said Sugar.

Nobody made a move to give the mean bastard a shilling so he minced his way back behind the bar to get another. He put this in the slot, selected another three tunes and again the machine kicked into life. This time the pick-up arm connected with a record and deposited it on the turntable. At this, Sugar gave a smile and shouted 'Gentlemen – the lovely Sanita!' He did a pirouette across the floor and disappeared behind the bar.

At this, the curtain was pulled back and into the room came the 'Lovely Sanita'. When I say she came into the room, she was actually pushed into the room and that was as fast as she moved all night.

The poor girl could not have been any more that fifteen or sixteen, she was not very tall and was as skinny as a rake. She had long dark hair that had obviously not seen a hairbrush for days so there was no telling when it had last been washed. It hung in long matted strands but was set off rather alluringly by an artificial rose that had been stuck indiscriminately into the side of her head. The head of the rose was pointing towards the ground and the rather long stalk was pointing skywards, however it had obviously been stuck through one of the selected matted areas to firmly secure it and this was a success.

She had quite a pretty face but her make-up was something to behold! Everything was in very vivid hues. She had sky-blue eye make-up that looked like it had been put on by a paint roller. She wore false eyelashes and her eyebrows were painted on in the most alarming fashion – black and very thick. The rouge on her cheeks was scarlet, looked like it had been applied with the same instrument and with no attempt to blend in with anything else. Her lipstick was so thick that most of it had deposited itself on her teeth, which were by now also red.

She wore a red dress that had obviously adorned the torso of some flamenco dancer twice her size, as she could dance around inside the thing without it moving. Her shoes were very pointed and very high heeled – they were also three sizes too big for her and the heels clumped on the floor with no regard to what she wanted her feet to do.

If it had been any other situation you would have thought that she was a little girl playing 'dressing up'. Also, if it had not been so funny it would have been tragic.

The comedy was complete when, just as she reached the middle of the floor to start her 'performance', the jukebox started to play Jimmy Shand's 'Bluebell Polka'.

'Who put that on?' shouted Sugar but he got no reply.

The place was in an uproar of laughing and clapping and the poor girl took this as appreciation of her talents – she was unaware of the irony of the music. The old woman was standing looking through the curtain smiling and nodding her approval of the proceedings so far.

The girl started to dance round the floor. When I say dance, it consisted of a few twirls, a very bad impersonation of a flamenco handclap and a few heel clacks that were unsuccessful due to the size of her shoes. Because of this, the shoes were the first things to be discarded. After that, she started to move more easily – not well but easily.

About halfway through the record, she started to remove her dress. Removal was done without 'tease' and merely consisted of her removing the straps from her shoulders – this was ironic as she had spent most of her time trying to keep them on her shoulders – and simply letting the dress drop to the floor. There were cries of 'Put it back on!' but she was oblivious to this.

What was now exposed was her vest. It was not a camisole nor a slinky silk top – but a plain common or garden cotton vest. I knew it was common or garden because that's where it looked like it had come from. It had obviously been worn while washing the dishes recently as there were suds stains down the front. I must say it was not particularly dirty but it was stained. There were great masses of hair sprouting from under her arms. Her knees were also dirty as were her feet.

She pranced around the floor in this apparel until the record stopped. While the jukebox was making up its mind what record to select next, the 'stripper' went up to the bar for a drink of water. Lads started to leave the bar shaking their heads in disbelief. Our excuse for staying was that we still had quite a lot of drink to finish off.

The jukebox sprang into life once more – Mario Lanza singing 'Granada'. Sugar's eyes went skywards.

Our girl came back onto the floor, obviously emboldened by her refreshment, and started her movements once more. She did a couple of rounds of the floor then lay down and removed her vest. This made it even dirtier than it had been! She got up and started to prance round the floor again this time alluringly holding her vest between her two hands across her chest and then occasionally trying to drape it over some poor unsuspecting bugger's head. Nobody was falling for it.

Now she was down to her bra and pants. I think it was a bra but it was not supporting anything inside. In fact the thing was as loose as her dress had been and jiggled up and down of its own volition as she pranced around the floor. Again when half the record was through she dropped the straps on the bra and let it fall to her feet. She stepped out of it and kicked it into the audience. It was soon returned with a mighty 'Ugh, fuckin' hell!'

Her chest was really flat – not quite pancake flat, just a couple of little rosebuds in sight.

'Sugar, you're a dirty bugger – you've got one of your little boys to strip for you!' the comedian shouted. 'We want our money back, you little shit.'

Sugar's eyes rolled and he looked very perturbed at the suggestion that he give money back. He shouted something in Spanish to the girl and she spat in his direction and shrugged her shoulders and gave him the finger.

She removed the Aertex pants she was wearing and it was obvious then that she was a girl. She supported the biggest and darkest bush of pubic hair that had ever been seen on a woman. The mass started at her belly button and continued down over her crotch and down the inside of her thighs – quite a way. She turned round and the hair was sprouting from between the cheeks of her arse up to her waist. Awesome! A cheer went up from the crowd and this brought a smile to her face. The record stopped.

While the jukebox whirred away, the lass sat down on one of the newly vacated seats and absentmindedly started to pick her nose. Not just a little scratch, her pinkie was thrust up to the knuckle in her nostril and there was a lot of searching going on. She had obviously been taught that the pinkie was the socially acceptable way to pick her nose in public. Something was finally caught and extracted but of course being naked she had nowhere to put it so it was deposited under the chair. 'I wish she would play with her fanny like that,' yelled the wag. She did not have any time left to evacuate the other nostril before the music started once again.

She got up from the chair and started to prance round the room again. Her bush was an awesome sight and the guys started to clap in some encouragement to get her to do something dirty. She did something dirty all right – she lay down on the floor, splayed her legs a couple of times – more hair, it had to be a pubic wig – and rolled over once or twice. She got up off the floor and she was filthy with all the dirt, grime and spilt drinks that had been deposited on the deck.

Ugh! What a sight – her make-up was now even worse than at the beginning, her flat chest, back and bum were covered in dust and gore, however her knees and feet were not any worse than when she started, her mass of pubic hair was all covered in dust and other things, the hair on her head looked like it had swept the floor, which it had – but surprisingly, the artificial rose was still in place.

She bowed to the audience, picked up her clothes and retreated to the sanctity of the place behind the curtain – God bless her!

There was a stunned silence in the bar.

'C'mon lads, give the young lady a clap – show your appreciation!' shouted Sugar.

'She looks like she has the clap already!' came back one punter. 'What's next on the programme – get the old dear to strip?'

'She'll do it for a fiver!' said Sugar.

'Piss off – we'll give her a fiver to keep her clothes on!'

Our group, which had become somewhat dispersed, congregated again around a table and gave each other wry looks about the proceedings.

'Ya whore sir, that wis fuckin' great. Ah've never seen a stripper afore!' exclaimed Dod, who was by now well pissed. He had a great big smile on his face, proudly showing off his white teeth.

'This boy needs to get out more,' I thought.

The stripper came back into the bar. An attempt had been made to remove the make-up but there were still streaks of it left around her ears. She was wearing the stained vest once again along with a short ill-fitting skirt. Her arms, legs and feet were still dirty. She went round the bar touting for money and she probably picked up a couple of quid – not bad for what she did. Last I saw of her she was leaving the bar with a hairy-arsed matelot who had probably become infatuated with her. Any port in a storm.

The old woman followed them to the door, haranguing her all the way, no doubt telling her how much to charge and to bring the proceeds home if she knew what was good for her. I hoped that the matelot would treat her kindly.

A couple more drinks then Gib was closing down for the night – British influence at its best!

We had another couple of days sightseeing and lazing around Gib. Dod wanted to go and see the stripper again but none of the rest of us had the stomach for it. In the end we went back home without further incident.

12

Love's Labours Lost

The working life on the base became very much a routine. The working shift rota was in a five-day cycle, something like this: First day working from midday to eight in the evening. Second day was working from eight in the morning to two in the afternoon. Third day was working a twelve-hour shift from eight in the evening to eight in the morning. Then there followed two days off. The weekends were two consecutive weeks on duty for twenty-four hours on either the Saturday or the Sunday with a long weekend off every third week.

This shift system meant that there was a fair amount of time off during the day, which could be spent with the kids, playing golf on the course at Castlerock, fixing the car or taking the dog for a walk. We had acquired an Irish Setter pup as an addition to the family and she was the bane of my life, always demanding walks and more walks, even after she had just finished yet another walk. I took her with me when I went to play golf and even after she had run around the course for three hours she still wanted more.

After we had been staying in Eglinton for about nine months, we were offered a house down in the main quarters close to the base. The reason for this was that the Eglinton house was all of a sudden considered to be sub-standard. We could have told them that, as there was hardy a window that would stop a draught and the place was freezing all the time. We were glad to get out before the real winter set in.

The house we were allocated was fairly new and was nicely situated looking down on Lough Foyle. There was a bit of waste ground across the road in front of the house so all the kids in the neighbourhood could play there in safety.

It was much better socially being in the heart of things, apart from the fact that we were now much more accessible to the 'singlies' who frequented our house. However, most times they were welcome, even when dropping in uninvited. They were mostly after one thing – food! My wife is a marvellous cook and she delighted in feeding these reprobates – in exchange for the booze that they proffered in a sort of barter arrangement. We had many impromptu parties when several singlies would arrive separately – they always declared that they were unaware of the others' intentions, but I was never convinced.

We had set up a babysitting service with the couples living on either side of us so, for the first time in our married life, we had some freedom to get out and about in the evenings.

We still had the Zodiac and this tended to be the minibus, transporting boozers around the countryside when we could afford the occasional gallon or two of petrol. Sometimes we were down to putting half a gallon into the tank. This would get us about ten miles along the road – if we were lucky.

When we could get enough people to share the cost of the petrol, a favourite run was across the border to Buncranna in North Donegal. Only in Ireland could you get to the south by driving north. The pub there was the Drift Inn where we used to go for the bar suppers. Not that we were averse to the Guinness of course! They always had a big roaring fire and a good Irish band belting out the folk music and nationalistic sectarian songs. Great stuff – even though there was not one Catholic in our group!

We got thrown out of there one night when, after about eight pints, we unwittingly started to sing a Scottish Nationalist anti-royalist song to the tune of 'The Sash' so we were told in no uncertain terms that 'There will be no party songs in here.' What? After all the stuff that the band had been playing all night? However, we thought it wise not to argue for these were 'funny' times and 'The Troubles' were brewing.

It seemed very funny that to get to Buncranna we had to go through a checkpoint at the border, however after eight in the evening the border guards were not in evidence so this gave us a free run home. And I needed it! After about ten pints of the black velvet, driving a car full of eight or ten drunks was not easy. The drunks themselves were not normally a problem as most times they went to sleep and that is what I wanted to do. In cases like this I had to have a co-driver charged with staying awake to ensure that I did not fall asleep at the wheel. My task was to drive over the cat's eyes in the centre of the road to show that I was still in control. If more than two cat's eyes were missed it was the co-driver's job to dig me in the ribs to ensure I was still awake. Simple but effective until the co-driver also fell asleep. Still we survived, but the car was beginning to show the effects of this philosophy, as we ended up in a few hedges over time.

The NAAFI was a central meeting and drinking point for the 'gang' and the NAAFI dance was nearly always well attended, depending on who was on detachment.

Busloads of ladies were ferried in from places like Coleraine and Londonderry. These buses were euphemistically known as 'fanny bowsers' with the sex-starved contents being for the delectation of the sex-starved inmates of the base. However, the ladies were more than likely expected to buy their own drinks all night and then buy drinks for the poor airman that would deign to pick them up sometime around the last dance. This was not surprising as the ladies were probably earning more money working in the factories than most of the ranks on the base.

It was a funny thing that the dance was frequented most by those guys that were on shift. It was probably a way to relieve the boredom for most of them. While these would-be Romeos were on the dance floor for the last dance, no doubt treading on the girls' feet with their trog boots, other vile forces were afoot. These were the asexual ghouls who on hearing the last dance being called transferred themselves from the pigs' bar into the dance hall. These were the 'mine sweepers'. These despicable creatures would scour the tables in the dance hall and sweep up and drink any half-finished and left-over drinks. On a good night they could get a fair old haul and get even more pissed than they already were. Inevitably, they would raid a table of drinks that were expected to be there when the owners returned from the final grope of the night on the dance floor. If the ghoulish sweepers were spotted scooping the drinks, a cry would go out 'Hey that's mine!' Hence the name mine sweeper.

However, not all of the ladies were delectable. There were a lot who had evidence of a lot of chips having been consumed and this delicacy had gone straight to their arses and legs. In fact there was a theory going about that these women had been granted a special dispensation from the Pope to wear their legs upside down. Fine big lumps of agricultural Irish girls – built like Mullingar heifers. This was a reference to a local TV advert about a native breed of cow having 'beef to the ankles'!

Many romances were struck up at the NAAFI dances and even the senior NCOs would come sniffing around the airmen's fodder.

Ron Kerns was a sergeant and he was in love, madly and passionately, and would continue to be so every week, at least and until his bodily cravings were satisfied with a shag. The object of his current obsession was one of the 'mountain women', a local belle who used to frequent the dance and lived with her parents in an isolated cottage high up in the hills behind Limavady. The place was not only isolated but lacked some very basic facilities taken for granted by most of us, hot running water, central heating and indoor toilets to mention but three.

There was no shortage of enthusiasm on the part of the young lady either, who if anything was probably even more eager than Ron to consummate what was becoming a long drawn-out and mutually frustrating affair, having met two hours before! So what was the problem? What exactly was preventing a mutual joining which would harm no one and might indeed save Ron's sight, which was deteriorating in inverse proportion to the muscle development in his right arm?

The answer, simply put, was a combination of the weather and Ron's physical stature. The seasonal temperatures were such as to rule out an open-air erection in any mammal other than a polar bear, so an outdoor match was out of the question, and Kerns' height of six feet six inches made copulation impossible in anything smaller than a double-decker bus. Ron only had a Mini and had tried it once before in this car. While his feet were hanging out of the window some bastard stole his shoes.

Ron had run the lady home and she was obviously very taken with the fact that she had trapped a sergeant, a man of some standing – and his standing was plainly evident – with a car. He was even Irish, tall and good looking. Romance was in the air.

They had arrived outside her door and had started to kiss and pet in the car but Ron was becoming very uncomfortable and his 'stiffy' was taking up extra room in the Mini. The young lady had offered to 'play' with this but Ron wanted more – and so did she!

'Can ah no come in tae the hoose for a wee while? We could get ourselves comfortable in there,' pleaded Ron.

'No! Ma mother and father's probably still up so ah'll get a row if a bring ye into the house,' she returned demurely. 'We'll just hiv to make the best of it here in the car.'

'Ach c'mon ah'd like tae meet yer dad an it's getting freezin' out here.'

'No, it'll just cause trouble. I'll sook it fur yi if yi want.'

'Christ, there's no even enough room in this thing for that! Can we no go in? Please?'

'OK, if you insist. What we'll dae is that you come tae the door wi me an ah'll open it an say goodnight tae yi. After that you nip intae the house, ah'll close the door from the inside an' that'll be yi inside wi me. OK?'

'OK!' said Ron, glad at last that there was some relief in sight. He was already counting the times that he could probably manage it. The first time would just be a bit of a blast.

They got out of the car and walked over to the door of the house. Christ it was cold, but Ron's shivering was caused more by the fever of anticipation than the sub-zero temperature.

She opened the door and after a chaste goodnight kiss or two she said in a loud stage whisper, 'Thank you Ron, that was a lovely night, I really enjoyed myself, I hope we can do it again soon?'

'Yeah, it was great, can I pick you up next Friday and we'll go to the pictures?'

'Yes please,' answered the girl, 'I'll see you then.'

With a few more utterances of 'goodnight then' loud enough to be heard by anybody in the house who cared to listen, the desire of Ron's life closed the door with both of them inside.

Big Ron and his sweetheart were ecstatic, they could hardly contain their delight, the plan had worked like a charm and if they were careful and reasonably quiet, it could be used again and again. Man and girl got comfortable on the big sofa in front of the dying embers and nature began to take its course. Kissing with tongues thrust down throats, followed by hands disappearing into blouse, bra unclipped, tits exposed, hand up skirt, knickers removed and to Ron's delight he found his belt unbuckled and his fly being unzipped with some eagerness. Warm fingers were wandering around in the darkness inside his Y-fronts, which he had changed this very evening in case of just this eventuality. They were getting to the end of the warm-up period and closer to the object of his desire with much moaning when her mother's voice called from upstairs, dampening their ardour more than a little.

'Hey Maggie, is that fella away home?

'Aye ma, he's away back to the camp,' she shouted back. She was mortified.

'Just as well too, will ye bring the bucket up? Yer father wants a *shite*.' Jesus Christ! What now?

'I'll just hiv tae get it frae the back door, Ma,' shouted the girl whose eyes were now twice their normal size but she was trying not to giggle as she realised the irony of the situation.

'You'll hiv tae go,' she mouthed at Ron.

'But what about this?' he whispered showing her his now exposed large protuberance emanating from his underpants, with his trousers down at his ankles.

'You'll jist hiv tae save it for next week,' she giggled. She bent down and gave it a kiss. 'C'mon, let's have that and you out the door.'

'Bloody hell!' he muttered as he pulled up his trousers, lifted his jacket and followed her to the back door. More kissing and trying to put his piece back in her hand. Anything would do now but she pushed him out the door and lifted a bucket with a fitted lid from the coal shed. She blew him a kiss and she was back in the house with the door locked before he could protest further.

Bastard! So near yet so far! Bent double, he went round to the front of the house and got into his car, let the hand brake off and rolled silently away into the night. He had to stop the car a few hundred yards down the road to relieve his heightened tension by using the five-fingered widow.

'Bugger – nothing new in this,' he thought.

13

Engine Change in Bodo

There had been a long tradition that Coastal Command would follow the Soviet fleet wherever it went, and in those days it went quite far. This action was probably required in case they were lost and could not be found again. In essence, the Soviet fleet had a problem in that their Arctic port of Murmansk became ice-bound in the winter so they could not remain in that part of the world, as the one thing that a fighting ship needs is open water. So each autumn, before the ice really blocked them in, they sailed out of Murmansk into the northern North Sea, out into the Atlantic, down through the Straits of Gibraltar into the Mediterranean, up through the Bosphorus and into the Black Sea. In the spring they did the reverse journey. All of this to-ing and fro-ing had to be kept under the constant and unswerving gaze of Coastal Command in the shape of the Shackletons.

Whilst the fleet was in Murmansk during the summer it would carry out various exercises and these also had to be kept under constant supervision. This meant that every summer a full detachment of aircraft and men were dispatched to Bodo for a six-week stint of twenty-four-hour daylight, expensive beer and a little fishing. When I asked a local Norwegian what there was to do in the area he replied, 'In the summer we fish and we fuck. In the winter we don't fish.' That seemed to be a fair summary of the situation.

The summer of 1969 was no different and a full complement of Ballykelly's finest were dispatched to the land of fish and exorbitant prices. I was not among the anointed on this occasion. However, about three weeks into the detachment period, myself and Davy Hamilton were approached by one of our superiors who asked if we would be kind enough to go up to Bodo to change an engine on one of the Shackletons. When I say 'asked' the conversation went something like this.

'Hey, you two, they need an engine changed up in Bodo, so go and get an engine ready for transportation tomorrow and bring your bags because you're going with it.'

'Hey, thanks a lot, this is another jolly away from the family. My wife thinks I've got a lover up there. This is the sixth time I've been there this year alone.'

'Well, with all that Local Overseas Allowance you must be a right rich bastard.'

'Hey, less of the rich.'

However, Davy got his tractor started and off we went to the engine bay to select our engine. Some hope of selection, they only ever seemed to have one ready to go at any one time. We towed it carefully round to the dispersal area in front of the hangar in preparation for loading in the morning. All Griffons had to be towed carefully as the wheels on the engine stands were small, made of steel and the whole thing was obviously war surplus material, probably last used by the Dambusters. Sometimes the wheels were even round but mostly they would not turn because of their flat bottoms or rusted bearings. With the steel wheels crunching over the tarmac even at a very sedate pace it meant that the engines were subjected to massive vibrations even before they were installed on the aircraft. So they had to be towed at the pace of a funeral cortege with the engine resembling an oversized bier.

We assembled the engine change kit that included all the propeller change gear and transported this round to the engine. That done we buggered off early in case we got another job.

The next morning we were down at H&R for six. We were expecting the transport aircraft to be there first thing as the Shackleton in Bodo was a top priority job. However, we needn't have bothered because the bloody Hercules from Brize Norton did not arrive until ten.

We went up to the dispatcher on the Herc and told him we thought they would have been here really early. 'This *is* early!' was his surprised reply. 'We don't start until eight and it's about an hour and a half flying to here.' Lazy sods!

The engine was loaded onto the Herc leaving very nasty scars on the slip-proof covering on the drop-down door.

'Don't you ever oil these bloody wheels? asked a very disgruntled loadmaster.

'If they were oiled they still wouldn't go round because they're designed to be flat at the bottom. Don't ask why, that's just the way things are.'

He frowned, shook his head and walked away inside the aircraft muttering something about Coastal Command in general and Shackletons in particular. As soon as the engine had been secured inside the aircraft and all the other bits and pieces had been loaded on, the door was closed and we were off.

Now the Shackleton was a very noisy aircraft indeed but it was nothing compared to the Hercules. This was like travelling in an oil drum that was being beaten by pickaxe handles. And what is more it was not even as comfortable as an oil drum. At least the Shackleton had its comforts in the deep leather seats, bunk beds and the pillows in the bomb aimer's position. The Hercules had thin canvas 'para' seats that made your arse cold and had a metal bar across the front that was just right for stopping the blood flow to the lower legs and feet. The whole aircraft vibrated so much that it felt like the teeth were loosening in the gums. All very miserable but there was only six hours to go, as we had to go to Stavanger first for some reason or other before going up to Bodo.

As ever, we were very expectant of some good nosh for lunch. It had been some six hours since breakfast so we were dying of hunger. Midday passed, then one o'clock passed, and there still was no sign of anything to eat. I went up to the flight deck area which was like a different world from the cargo deck. Here it was relatively quiet and warm and even the vibrations were less pronounced. Little wonder we had never seen any of the crew on the cargo deck.

'Any chance of something to eat mate?' I enquired of the loadmaster.

'What! Didn't you bring your own grub? We didn't ration for you at all. I'll have to see what I can rustle up for you.'

'Thanks a bunch, I'm sure.'

About ten minutes later he came down to the cargo deck with two polystyrene boxes and handed these over to us. By this time even the polystyrene looked good enough to eat. He muttered some sort of apology for not having considered us earlier and quickly departed.

It was no wonder he left quickly before we could open the boxes. Davy struck it lucky because he had a sandwich and half a bag of crisps in his box. I had half a sandwich and a half-eaten apple in mine. The apple had gone brown where it should have been white. I ate the sandwich but declined to eat the apple. Davy devoured his nosh and didn't even offer me a bloody crisp.

We droned on and on for what seemed an eternity, being vibrated enough to turn blood to jelly.

Eventually the noise from the propellers changed and we landed at Stavanger. The aircraft was taxied round to a dispersal area, the rear door was opened but the engines remained running. The loadmaster came back into the cargo hold and picked up a small package and handed this over to a man who was standing to the side of the door. Once this was done the door was closed and the aircraft started to roll once again.

'What was in the parcel, mate?' I asked of the dispatcher.

'Fucked if I know, something that had been ordered from the embassy I suspect,' he said with a shrug of his shoulders.

Must have been a bottle of malt whisky for an embassy party, I thought. It must have been bloody important to divert an aircraft that was going about the Queen's business.

Another three hours flying up to Bodo, landing and taxiing round to the hangar where the detachment was housed. At last the incessant noise was switched off but it took several minutes to regain all the normal senses as I am sure my body was still vibrating at the resonating pitch that we had endured for the past six hours.

The cargo door was lowered and we were confronted by a veritable sea of friendly faces as the boys from Ballykelly swarmed on board to help unload the engine. Davy and I didn't hang about as we needed to find some fodder soon or we would die of malnutrition. Bloody Hercules, I never wanted to fly in one ever again.

We went into the hangar where the sick Shackleton was residing and off to the side was a small office that served as the detachment HQ. In the office we were greeted by Gordon Mendes.

'Hi guys. Glad to see you here at last. It's the number two engine that needs changing.'

'Hey wait a minute, Flight. We haven't had anything to eat since breakfast and we're starving. You don't want us to start on the engine tonight, do you?'

'No, I don't want you to start on the engine tonight. I want you to start on it now. There's a real panic about getting the kite back in the air to monitor some big soviet naval exercise that's going on. However, go and find yourselves something to eat and get back here as quickly as possible.'

'Bollocks, if it's that important we can make a start now and grab some supper later on.'

'OK, thanks, but you had better get yourselves organised with a room first before this place closes down for the weekend.'

We were run up to the living accommodation, got a room from an orderly, dumped our stuff and went back to the hangar.

The engine had been towed into the hangar and left conveniently for lifting when required. The propeller change kit and the special tools required for the engine bulkhead connections were also placed where we could get at them. The aircraft had been logged as AOG the previous day and if this was such a rush job it was surprising to see that no preparation work had been done by the guys who were there. They had not even removed any of the panels. When we asked them about this there were mutterings of 'Been too busy.' Too busy doing what? There were only another two aircraft on the detachment.

Davy elected to disconnect the bulkhead and I would remove the props. I had the front prop ready for removal, the rope slings were looped around the top two blades and the lifting crane was steered into position. Like everything else surrounding the Shackleton aircraft the lifting crane was not exactly a piece of modern engineering. The whole thing was a collection of steel tubes cobbled together to make a frame that resembled an offset pyramid about fifteen feet high. It had three wheels, two stuck out in front and a single wheel at the sharp end for steering. The wire rope winch was merely a reel that was turned by a handle and a ratchet device stopped the reel unwinding under the lifted weight.

The slings on the propeller were hooked onto the crane and the reel was wound up until the weight of the prop was taken up. By some violent rocking on the bottom blade, the friction lock that normally stuck the propeller to the rear collet on the shaft was broken and the propeller was free to slide off the shaft. I had a hold of the propeller blade to steady it while it was to be transported to an area where it could be laid down. This meant that I was walking in the middle of the triangle formed by the cross struts on the crane. Davy was steering at the rear. For some reason he swung the steering wheel round at an acute angle and the cross strut on my right-hand side caught me behind my right heel. I went down as if I had been pole-axed and the last thing I remember was seeing the right-hand wheel of the crane physically lifted off the ground as my foot, by now bent double, took the full weight of the crane and propeller.

I came to in the hangar toilet where I had been taken so cold wet compresses could be applied to my foot, quick thinking by someone. After a while I tried to stand on the foot but there was no way I could stand the pain, so an ambulance was called and I was whisked up to sick quarters.

My foot was strapped with bandages and I was given some analgesics then put in a room for the night. Christ, the pain in that foot was excruciating, it got worse and worse and lasted all night. I lay there wishing that I could transfer the pain to the other foot so as the sore one could take a rest. However, the pain in my foot was not the only thing that was disturbing me, I had my stomach to consider as I had still had nothing to eat.

At long last a new day dawned, Saturday, and the orderly who had strapped my foot came in with breakfast and laid it on the bedside cabinet that was some inches above my head as I lay there on the pillow. I could see that there were the corners of some toast lapping over the edge of the plate. Food at last, I could hardly contain myself. The orderly messed around doing the usual things like taking pulse and temperature. He didn't speak English and I didn't speak Norwegian, so after saying 'Good morning' that was the end of our conversation. He gave me some more analgesics to dull the pain in my foot and then he departed.

I pulled myself up to devour breakfast. Christ, on top of the toast there were dollops of a foul-looking fish, most likely pickled herring. I was never a lover of fish and even in my state of starvation I could not bring myself to eat this fare. I tried the toast after removing the fish from it but the fishy taste had been infused into it. I drank the coffee and slunk solemnly back down under the covers. My foot was still hurting like hell.

The orderly came back into the room about an hour later and through sign language and watch pointing he indicated that the doctor would be in to see me at one in the afternoon. He indicated that they would probably take some X-rays of my foot. He saw that I had not eaten the breakfast and shrugged his shoulders before removing the plate.

Around twelve the orderly came back into the room carrying a tray with lunch thereon. This had obviously been brought from the mess as the plate was covered by a metal tureen which he lifted with a flourish to reveal – boiled fish and boiled potatoes. No, not again! I ate the potatoes but could not stomach the fish. The orderly came and lifted the tray and again made a wry face about the lack of fish-eating on my part.

The time round to one o'clock seemed like eternity but eventually the doctor did arrive. He came into the room and asked the orderly to remove the strapping from my foot. As he was doing this the doctor was conversing about the merits of the 'free' British National Health System. He was quite taken aback when I told him that we had to pay for the system through National Insurance Contributions. When we discussed the amounts paid for either medical system he rationalised that medical insurance was cheaper in Norway.

A strange thing was happening at the other end of my body. As the bandages were being removed, I had a violent attack of 'pins and needles' in my foot as blood flowed to that part of my anatomy once again. The bandage had obviously been applied too tightly and the lack of blood to my foot was what was causing most of the pain. Once the 'pins and needles' had abated the pain was not too bad. It's a good job that it was not left for another day because I could have lost my foot to gangrene.

The foot was X-rayed but nothing was broken, although I did have a nasty cut on the back of my heel. I was given some more strapping on my foot, not too tight, some more medication and sent on my way with a pair of crutches. I swung my way to the mess where I was able to buy a plateful of reindeer balls and chips.

After devouring this, and because there was none of the Ballykelly guys about, I went back to the room and got into bed. I was knackered as I had been awake all night. Before I went to sleep, however, I did notice that Davy had not been back in the room since we had dumped our stuff.

Sometime later I was wakened by someone trying to break into the room through the window. This was quite surprising as the room was on the first floor. I got out of bed and hobbled over to the window and pulled back the curtains to reveal our Davy clinging onto the adjacent waste water pipe for grim death. I opened the window, much to his surprise, and enquired, 'Would it not be easier to come in by the door?'

'You bastard, how long have you been here? You've got the bloody door key,' was his reply.

The poor bugger had worked all night and all day to get the engine changed on his own, with only sporadic help from some of the others in the morning. He was filthy and looked absolutely knackered.

After a clean up, a sleep and a few beers in the mess that evening with the other guys we both felt reasonably refreshed. The next day we were given a choice of transport home. Five hours in a Hercules or twelve in a Shackleton. No contest, Shackair won!

14

The Crock of Gibraltar

Back to Gib for yet another long detachment. Four weeks this time in May. May was traditionally the month that the personnel stationed in Gib changed out of their winter blue uniform and into their tropical khaki drill (KD). Personnel coming from other stations had to follow suit. I had my own KD brought back from Singapore so it fitted me reasonably well. Others were not so fortunate and had to rely on the KD booked out from the stores at their home base. The unfortunate thing about this was that the guys had no real say in what the KD looked like when they put it on, and because it was only booked out for the duration of the detachment, there was no chance of having it altered by the station tailor – not that this would have done much good.

When I was posted from Leuchars to Butterworth in Malaya I went to the stores to pick up my allocation of KD. At that time I was built like a racing snake. I had a figure that most female models would die for, 38 / 28 / 38, and I was of medium height. The stores had a peculiar way of measuring for uniforms – hat size, neck size, chest size and the length between waist and knees. I ended up with shorts that two of me, and a couple of acts out of Billy Smart's circus, could have got into. They must have been 48 or 50 inches round the waist with a 56-inch hip size. In those days I did not realise that people could be this size. No problem though as I could take them to the station tailor and have them altered free.

She measured me up for the alterations and I could see that she was scratching her head how to achieve this near-impossible feat of engineering. The problem was obviously too much for her because when I went back for the shorts all she had done was to reduce the waist size. So I was left with a pair of culottes with legs so wide that when I walked my legs touched neither the front nor the back of the leg apertures. It looked like the trousers were moving completely independently to me, the person who was transporting them, to the amusement of all who witnessed this wonderful sight.

This was bad enough when I tried them on at home and my wife and neighbours threw themselves on the floor laughing. However, I had to wear them when I got to Butterworth.

I reluctantly put them on and I realised that I had become even thinner than I had been, as I had enjoyed a dose of the runs on my way up from Singapore to Butterworth on the train and had not eaten properly for about three days. I could hardly keep the bloody shorts on my hips and was continuously having to pull them up.

I had to walk from the billet to the squadron inside these things. In those days, very few people in the UK went on holiday in the sunshine and therefore the skin of all Brits was snowy white. So much so that those expats that had been abroad for a while referred to the pallor as a 'moon tan' so the new guys on the station were 'moonies'.

This moony was whiter than most as I never liked the heat too much. I had never exposed the flesh to the 'current bun' – apart from my face, which had become a rosy red, having been the only part of me to see the sun in Malaya. Inside my KD I must have looked like a Swan Vesta match carrying my matchbox around with me!

I walked down the road and I knew that people were flocking in from all points to see this apparition recently arrived from the UK. There were catcalls and wolf whistles coming out of every building I passed – especially from the Ozzies based on the station. I spent more time giving the V sign as I walked along than I have ever done before or since. I cursed the tailor at Leuchars every step of the way – twats.

When I arrived at the squadron, I was the butt of even more derision as I stood around waiting for the warrant officer to see me. When he opened the door to his office he took one look and his eyes moved heavenwards.

'C'mon in, laddie, you look a real sight, are you comfortable in those things? I bet you've got plenty draught up your legs anyway, take a seat.'

I had never tried to sit in the bloody shorts before so when I did it was a complete surprise. The material was so stiff that the legs once again acted independently and stood straight up like two cavernous apertures with my legs poking out from the bottom. At this the WO let out the hearty laugh that he had been holding in since he first saw me.

'Sorry laddie, I just couldn't help myself. Christ, don't they turn out some shit and call it a uniform. Would you like a cold drink? I would send you out to the fridge to get it but I don't want you to go out there into that crewroom as I can see that there is quite a crowd gathered to get sight of you. I'll go!'

'I'd love a cold drink, thanks sir.'

After he had given me the squadron pep talk he said that he would take me in and introduce me to the squadron adjutant. He left the room and came back a few minutes later and beckoned for me to follow him. As I walked out of the door, several cameras flashed as my future comrades recorded the scene for posterity while I tried to look like I was enjoying it.

I was ushered into the adjutant's office. He looked up and gave out an almighty 'Fuckin' hell!'

'I've seen some sights in my life but you certainly take the biscuit. Where have you parachuted in from?' he said in his upper crust accent. 'Take a seat.'

Not wishing to add to his merriment I declined and asked if I could stand. I could see the WO nod and the officer acquiesced with a wave of his hand.

I stood there and listened to what he was saying but I certainly didn't take any of it in. He had to keep his head down as he did not want to look at me and his voice went up and down in trills as he tried to force back the giggles. Once or twice he turned away to face the wall and gripped the bridge of his nose in a stalwart effort to control himself. I must admit I was beginning to find it all a bit amusing myself.

'All right, Mr Ryan,' he said to the WO. 'First thing is to show Blair here where the station tailor is so he can get himself sorted out with proper clothing. They don't charge a lot,' he added to me.

'Excuse me sir, but I don't have enough money at present to get a new KD. I'm broke til payday.'

'Well, you're not fuckin' well going to disgrace this squadron by walking around like that for a moment longer than you have to. Mr Ryan, we'll pay for the KD out of squadron funds and he can pay it back a little at a time. Get him to the tailor pronto and give him the rest of the day off so he can change into civvies until his KD is ready.'

We left the office and were walking down the corridor to the exit door when another door opened. The door was marked Squadron CO. A wing commander poked his head round the door.

'Mr Ryan, can you bring that man in here?'

'Bloody hell,' I thought. 'What the hell have I done now?'

'It's just that I have heard about this poor chap's plight with his KD.

108

I think it's a bloody disgrace that people think they can get away with things like this. I intend to make an issue of this. Would you mind if I took some photos of you in that ridiculous get up to put in with my letter of complaint?'

'Not at all sir, if it will help' I muttered somewhat abashed.

'It might not help but it should give somebody a bloody good laugh and shake them up a bit. Stand over there will you.'

I had more of a suspicion that these photos would be shown around the wing commander's dinner table at his next dinner party. Still, anything for a laugh. As they say, if you can't take a joke, you shouldn't have joined.

The photos were taken and I was escorted outside to some more wolf whistles from my new workmates who had assembled in the crewroom to catch sight of the apparition – the word had obviously spread like wildfire – bastards! The WO drove me up to the station tailors.

I walked into the room, which was occupied by about six Chinese men and women.

'Mr Chan can you sort this chap out with new KD and send the bill down to 60 Squadron? Thanks. We'll see you tomorrow when you are better dressed. Cheerio.'

I was left in the tailors, standing in front of a counter. Mr Chan asked for my name and number and he wrote this in an order book. He came round the end of the counter removing his measuring tape from around his neck. Once he caught sight of me in my shorts he let out this high pitched squeal and started jabbering away in Chinese. At this all the others in the shop came tumbling forward from where they were sitting at machines or on the floor to take a look.

There was much laughing and merriment, as I thought to hell with it, and did a couple of twirls to let them see the full effect of the haute couture achieved by good old British tailoring. The little Chinese girls were the most amused and ran about the room giggling behind their hands, as it would not have been good manners for them to laugh outright. However, laugh they did.

Mr Chan shook his head in disbelief at the sight as he began to take my measurements.

'You come back six o'clock – KD ready then,' he said

'What, six o'clock today?' I asked incredulously.

'Yes, six o'clock dis evening, we do not want for you be seen in dis KD again. Too velly bad for anyone to be seen dlessed like dis. Bloody stinking.' He went behind the counter still shaking his head.

I dodged my way back to my room taking advantage of every bit of cover that I could find. Thankfully the room was not too far and I did not suffer any more harassment. However, I was feeling a lot better at the prospect of not having to go to work in that bloody outfit in the morning and suffering the derision of my new colleagues.

I went back to the tailors at six and sure enough the two sets of KD were ready. I tried it on and it fitted perfectly. It also felt like the material had been caressed by angels compared with the galvanised iron-like substance that I had been issued with. I felt comfortable and could be one of the lads in the morning.

So I had my KD that I bought in Butterworth and I was very smart compared with some of the others that were with me on this Gib detachment. However, smart or not, it did none of us any good to be in tropical dress as here we were in Gib in the middle of May and it was bloody freezing cold. So cold in fact that on a couple of occasions there was sleet, and on one other there was a fair covering of snow. It was worse than the weather that we had left behind at Ballykelly.

Still, the show of getting the mighty Shackletons into the air had to go on in order to save the Empire for Queen and country. This was not easy in the near-freezing conditions and with the skimpy clothing that we had to wear.

With us on this trip was one Bill Michael, a sergeant engine fitter, and he was as mad as a plateful of scrambled eggs. Bill was also a veteran of Butterworth and I had known him there. I did not know him very well though, as he lasted only two days on the squadron. Bill suffered from an extreme form of acne that flared up in the strong Malayan sunshine. Flared up was the operative word as the poor soul went bright red and these huge suppurating pustules erupted all over his exposed face and body. It was so bad on his face that he could not wear his bottle-bottom specs and this rendered him virtually blind. The doc tried pumping him full of antibiotics for a couple of days but the condition did not subside so he had to pack up his family and get out of there fast, as it was feared that he would end up with septicaemia or something else just as nasty which could have been fatal.

He certainly was not in danger of losing his life on this trip as we hardly saw the sun and we were freezing as we went about our business of servicing the aircraft. Bill started to wear one of the Shackleton wheel covers as a raincoat.

The tyres on the Mark 2 Shack were over four feet in diameter and two feet in cross section and were very costly to manufacture. In order to preserve these expensive commodities from the possibility of oil or fuel dripping onto them from the inboard engines, they had to be covered by large, heavy, preformed neoprene covers. Oil or fuel dripping from the engines was a certainty and therefore the wheel covers were filthy and smelly. This of course did not deter our Bill who cut a dashing figure in this tyre attire. He wore the cover very elegantly with his head, decorated with his large specs, and legs protruding out of the holes that went round the wheel hubs. He looked like a giant Mediterranean snail crabbing its way between the crewroom and the aircraft. There were people falling around with laughter when they first came across this apparition. Still, he was warm and safe in his little portable house as we went about the routine of fixing and maintaining.

The worst part of the exercise for Bill was when he removed the cover: he was covered in horrible sticky black oil and rubber tyre dust. This accumulation could not be removed by normal washing so he had to resort to smothering his neck, shoulders and knees, where the cover had come in contact with his skin, in Swarfega and scrubbing this off with a nail brush. There was only one thing wrong with this operation that Bill did not know before – he was allergic to Swarfega when applied near his face. The inevitable happened and his whole face erupted once more just as it had in Butterworth. Still, as there was no sun in Gib at this time, he did not have to be evacuated back home. He did however have to go to the doc who filled him so full of antibiotics that Bill declared that he could visit every brothel in Gibraltar to shag every prostitute and cure them through his ejaculations of whatever diseases ailed them – including leprosy. He therefore became known as Captain Spunk – The Ejaculating Saviour and Prostitute's Friend.

After a few days of Mediterranean winter, the weather started to improve and the temperatures climbed to such a degree that we were able to go swimming. We went to the beach at the eastern end of the runway as it was closest to the place that we were staying.

We had been down at the beach for a couple of hours and were just getting ready to set off back to work to meet one of the Shackletons returning from a sortie. I took one more run into the sea. This was to be a spectacular running dive to impress all the other people on the beach. I ran down the beach and jumped into the sea and dived forward. It seemed pretty spectacular to me!

I was swimming around for a few minutes when one of the other guys said, 'What's all this red stuff coming from the bottom?'

I looked around and the 'stuff' seemed to be following me around. I could not think where it was coming from. I decided to get out of the water and as I climbed out I could feel a sensation on the sole of my right foot. I sat down to examine it and got the shock of my life. The whole of the sole was covered in small and large lacerations and the blood was pouring out at an alarming rate. I must have jumped onto a sharp stone or piece of coral in the water.

I was in a state of shock all right, in fact I felt a bit sick as the pain started to make its presence felt. I put my hand over the cuts in an effort to stem the flow of blood but this did little to help. I then grabbed my towel and wrapped this around my foot and tried to stand up. As soon as I put any weight on the foot I collapsed in a heap on the sand writhing in agony. This put the rest of the guys into fits of laughter but I had trouble seeing the funny side.

Once they had finished with their laughing, some compassion came over them and they decided that I was not putting on an act. A couple of them helped me to my feet and tried to support me as I hopped up the beach, fearful of the consequences if I put my foot on the ground. It was a very hot day and I was soon knackered from the hopping so they decided that I would need to be carried to the sick quarters which were about a quarter of a mile away. They cradled their arms together and I was hoisted up between them and we made good progress along the road. There were several changes of carriers along the way as the guys tired in the hot sun.

At last we reached sick quarters and I hopped in, supported by one of the guys, and was deposited in a chair in the waiting room.

The duty orderly was called and he came along to see what needed to be done. He was a big guy with thick hairy arms and a bald head. It was obvious by the way that he minced into the room that he was as bent as a nine-bob note. In an effeminate lisping voice he asked what had happened and once I had explained he bent down and removed the blood-soaked towel from my foot. The blood was still pouring out of my foot at the same alarming rate.

'Oh my goodness, this looks serious, I fink I'll have to get the doc to look at this,' he lisped. 'I wouldn't be surprised if he has to operate on this. I'll give you a tetanus jab in the mean time. You had better come into the surgery.'

He helped me along the corridor into the surgery and helped me onto the examination trolley. He disappeared for a few minutes and then minced back into the room carrying a kidney bowl with the necessary injection equipment and a clean towel to wrap round my foot.

'Take down your swimming trunks and I'll give you an injection,' he lisped.

I thought I would rather get tetanus than have him fumbling around my rear end.

'Only joking,' he said, 'I'll give you one in the arm.' I gave a sigh of relief.

Once he had completed his task he said, 'The doc will be along in a moment and he will sort you out.'

'Thanks, mate,' I said and he gave me a pouted lip wink and minced out of the room.

I lay there for several minutes waiting. The door opened and into the surgery came this tall, rather elegant, balding, spec-wearing gentleman. A wing commander no less!

'I say,' he said in his upper crust, cut-glass accent, 'I've been told you have a bit of a problem, old boy, must have a look, eh what?'

He unwrapped the towel from my foot and I could see him physically wince at the sight of the blood flowing freely from the numerous lacerations. He did not proceed any further and just wrapped the foot back up with the towel.

He looked up at me and said, 'That looks like a bit of a mess, old boy. I don't think I would want to do anything with this, you see it is rather the wrong end of the body for me. I am a psychiatrist and I am standing in as a locum while the real doctor is away on holiday. I would like Captain McSporran from the Black Watch to come and have a look at this. After all he is a real doctor and not a mind bender like me. Be back in a mo, toodle pip.' He left the room.

After having met the medical orderly I didn't want to know any more about benders!

I lay there for several more minutes and the throbbing pain in my foot was becoming more intense as the moments passed. At last I heard voices coming down the corridor.

'As I was explaining captain, just my little joke about his foot being the wrong end of the body. Thought it was rather good myself, eh what.'

The only reply to this was, 'Aye sir, so you said.'

The door burst open and I was confronted by a small dapper man with slicked back black hair, a thin manicured moustache balanced on his top lip. He had a slight squint in his left eye and I could see that he was wearing contact lenses. He was dressed in a khaki shirt with the insignia of a captain on his shoulders and he wore a Black Watch kilt.

The whole effect was one of authority and efficiency. No nonsense here then, I thought. He leant on the examination trolley.

'They tell me you've had a wee accident to yer foot laddie, what's yer name?'

'Aye sir, I cut the sole of my right foot when I jumped into the sea this afternoon. My name's Blair sir.'

'Ah, you'll be a Scot then, where do you work?'

'I'm RAF here on detachment from Ballykelly in Northern Ireland.'

'I bloody well know where Ballykelly is. I was drinking in the mess with a bunch of your guys last night. Got a bloody thick head today.'

Christ, that's all I need – a Black Watch doctor with a thick head in attendance to my very painful foot. I was not a 'happy chappie'.

'Right, let's have a look at this foot of yours.' As he began unravelling the towel, blood started to soak through and was now forming a pool on the floor.

He picked up the foot and examined the sole. 'Christ, laddie, that's quite an injury that you have here. I think I'll have to put a couple of stitches in this for you.' He turned to the orderly and said, 'Go upstairs and get my two orderlies to come down here with you.'

I thought I was in for the full treatment of full anaesthetic and the orderlies would be needed in the operation. How wrong I was.

The other two orderlies arrived, also dressed in khaki shirts and Black Watch kilts. Tough-looking buggers, the both of them prised straight out of the Lochee council estate in Dundee, without a doubt.

Once all were assembled in the room the captain started to take charge of the situation.

'Right, you,' as he pointed to one of the orderlies, 'once we have him lying down I want you to get to the top of the table and lean over his chest and keep his upper body down. If he gets free and bites me I'll hold you directly responsible.' He pointed to another of the orderlies and said, 'You lean over his hips and keep them pinned to the table. He can shit himself but I don't want him to raise an inch from the table – OK?' He pointed to the RAF orderly and said, 'You get a hold of both of his feet and keep them as still as possible, if one of them gets free and kicks me I'll give you a good kickin' in return – understand?'

The orderly looked at him in a surly sort of way but it was obvious that he understood the instruction.

To the wing commander he said, 'Sir, if you would be kind enough to stand over there beside his head perhaps you could use some of your psychiatry to calm him down when the party starts.'

I still felt reasonably comfortable at this time, as I thought these were instructions for the coming general anaesthetic. How wrong could I be.

The captain turned to me and said, 'Look laddie, I need to put a couple of stitches in the worst of the cuts in your foot. Because the sole of the foot is very tough it will not take a local anaesthetic very well and will not dull the pain of the sutures. I dinna want tae gie you a general anaesthetic as the stitching will only take a few minutes. That's why I want the orderlies to constrain you and keep you still while I put the stitches in – OK?'

I think I kind of half nodded in agreement as I could understand the reasoning behind the requirement, but my foot was already in considerable pain and I could not begin to contemplate the extra pain that the needle would cause by going through the toughened skin on the sole. I somehow thought that there would be little or no pain at all.

The captain busied himself at the stainless steel medicine cabinet threading up several needles for the task ahead.

'Right you lot, get a hold of him as I told you and don't let go no matter what he does or says.'

At this I found myself grappled into complete and utter submission due to the weight of the three orderlies lying across my body. I tried to see if there was any way I could move but there was none. I just hoped that none of the queens was getting a cheap thrill at my expense.

The captain came up to the foot of the table and proceeded to use an antiseptic liquid on the injured area, obviously getting into all the nooks and crannies that required cleaning. Christ, this was bad enough as the liquid stung like hell and the unsympathetic intrusions of the cotton wad being wielded by a sadistic kilted Jock made my body try to jerk involuntarily but without success because of the human restraints pinning me down.

The captain stopped his probing to my relief for a few seconds. He then turned towards the medical counter once again and picked up a suture the size of a small knitting needle. This he tried to insert through the skin adjacent to the first of the cuts he would attack.

'Ahhhh! You fucking bastard!' I cried out as the excruciating pain shot up my leg and nearly blew the top of my head apart.

'I told you it would be tough going,' said the sadistic little bastard, as he continued to force the needle through the skin. 'You can scream all you want. I won't mind.' I think he was relishing the thought of it.

He then proceeded to force the needle through the other side of the cut. This time it was from the fleshy side out to the sole. This seemed even more painful than the last puncture.

'Ahhh for fuck's sake – that's even worse – stop it! Stop it! Stop it!'

I could feel the blood draining from my face and felt the bile rising in my throat and I was certain that I was going to be sick. Just at this point there was a loud clatter from just beside me. The noise instinctively made me look round, just in time to see the wing commander collapse onto the floor – the bugger had gone and fainted. He hit his head on a chair on his way down and blood started to flow from the resulting gash on his forehead. Nobody rushed to his aid as they were too scared to let go of me. I was now so mad I would have killed them all.

The first stitch was in place and was drawn tight and tied off. This was followed by a few more dabs of the cotton wad just to help matters along.

'Do you think that stupid bugger is all right down there?' said the captain to the assembled masses.

One of the orderlies looked across at him and muttered uncaringly, 'He'll survive.'

'Right, let's move on while we've got this one constrained.'

He proceeded to thrust another stitch into the same cut and this was just as painful as the last, bringing more cursing and blinding from me. There were beads of perspiration on the captain's forehead with the effort that he had exerted to get the bloody needle through the skin.

'Right then, that'll do for that cut. I think there's only one more cut that will need a couple of stitches as the rest are all much smaller and will heal perfectly well on their own.'

Unfortunately the cut he was talking about was up nearer the heel. Much tougher skin here in comparison with what had been tackled before. The sadist started his work once again. He tried to force the needle through and he was cursing about how hard it was. I was also cursing at the top of my voice as the pain was unbearable. He could not get the needle through so he tried to pierce a smaller hole with a smaller needle as a pilot for the bigger needle to follow. This worked for him but it was double the agony for me. I was also becoming very claustrophobic and cramped with the weight of the orderlies bearing down on me. How long had this lasted? It was probably no more than five minutes but it seemed like forever.

At last the operation was over and I was released from captivity. My foot felt like it was twice its normal size and was throbbing like hell. I was soaking with sweat, my body felt very clammy and cold. I was in a state of shock and lay on the table unable to galvanise myself into action.

The captain's shirt was also soaked in sweat and his whole face was red and dripping.

'Right, let's get that daft bugger up off the floor and have a look at him.'

At this the orderlies went over and eased the wing commander into a sitting position with his head between his legs. He started to come round. His cut was still bleeding slightly and he had a slick of blood running down his right cheek. He was as white as a sheet.

'I say, what happened? Must have lost the place – eh what?' he said groggily as he felt at his forehead and realised that there was blood there.

'We had better have a look at that,' said the captain. 'It looks like it could be a fairly deep cut.' He moved over to the wing commander and knelt down to examine the cut.

'As I thought, it'll need a couple of stitches. Orderlies get him up on to a chair, please.'

The orderlies lifted the pathetic figure onto a chair and the captain busied himself back at the medicine cabinet once again. He turned to the wing commander with the needle and thread in his right hand and the inevitable antiseptic cotton wad in his other hand, ready to attack the cut. I could see the wing commander physically trying to recoil from the kilted sadist's planned onslaught.

The captain started to clean up the blood from around the cut in an unceremonious way. I could see that he was relishing the task in hand. He had just finished cleaning up and was about to start his needlework when the wing commander slumped into a dead faint once again. The poor bugger must have been scared witless with the pain that he was about to experience.

'That will make things easier for me,' said the captain. 'I knew he would jump around a bit once I had started in any case.'

He attacked the cut with energy and had the stitches in place within thirty seconds.

'Try and bring the silly sod round now,' he said to the orderlies.

One of the orderlies soaked a towel in cold water and applied this to the wing commander's forehead and brought his head between his legs once more. The man started to come round once again. He looked terrible – poor bugger!

During this time, one of the orderlies had been bandaging my foot and the whole thing felt a little more comfortable now.

'Right then, that seems to be you sorted. How are you feeling? I know that it must have been painful for you for a while there.'

I could hardly believe what I had just experienced and blew out through clenched teeth. 'Christ, it was agony, I am not convinced that that was the only way that it could have been done but it feels OK now.'

The wing commander was now on his feet and still looked a little pasty faced and groggy.

'I say, took a bit of a turn there, eh what? What are we going to do about this fellow's work, he can't possibly go to work with that foot, eh what?'

'Naw, I would agree with you there sir,' said the captain. 'We would not even want one of our laddies in the Black Watch to go to war with a foot like that. You need to write out an excused duty chit for him sir. Right laddie, you look after yourself.' He turned on his heel and with a swish of the kilt, he went out the door.

I was duly issued with the chit, a rubber sole protector that looked like it had been cut from a Dunlop tyre for my injured foot and a pair of crutches. I swung myself out of the medical centre door while the wing commander held it open.

'Come back and have those stitches out in about seven days time. See you then.'

I thought to myself that I would not be in Gib in seven days time so would be well out of this circus or theatre – but definitely not the medical kind.

I never knew it was so hard and tiring to use 'half arm' crutches. After I had gone about a hundred yards on my way back to the accommodation, I was knackered and I still had about three hundred more to go. It was the difficulty of keeping the forward motion in a straight line for more than just a couple of swings as the crutches got out of synchronisation and once or twice I was left with no option but to take some weight on my injured foot to regain balance. The whole perambulation must have looked like a drunken tripod lurching about with comments like 'You bastard!' whenever my foot came in contact with the ground.

After what seemed another eternity I eventually made it to my room and collapsed on the bed absolutely and utterly drained of energy and emotion. What we have to suffer for the Queen!

I could not even make it down town that evening for a pre-arranged free drinking session with the Canadian guys who were on the same exercise as us. This was a demonstration of how knackered I really was.

I went down to the squadron the next day to see what was happening. George Blackley, the flight sergeant in charge of the detachment, said that one of the Shackletons was returning to Ballykelly the next day and as I was of little use in Gib did I want to go home on it?

I accepted, as I felt that there would be little point in staying there on my own all day for the next five days or so.

The following morning, the Shack was duly loaded up and I managed to hop up the steps and sat in one of the navigator's seats. Several other groundcrew were returning as there was no need for them with one less aircraft to look after.

We had been in the air for about four hours when the engineer came down to me and asked me to go and look at the oil pressure gauge on the number two engine. I struggled up to his panel and the oil gauge was swinging around erratically from zero up to normal pressure. I looked at the engine RPM and boost gauges on the pilot's panel and there were no indications that the engine was in distress.

'It's probably only the pressure transmitter that is playing up since there are no indications of anything else being wrong. Have you had a look out the window to see if there is any sign of the engine losing oil?'

He shook his head and departed down to the rear of the aircraft. He returned in a few minutes and shook his head once more. 'Nothing evident back there, do you think it'll be OK?

'I'm sure that it will be OK and there is nothing we can do about it up here anyway so we are as well to let it be.'

'I'll just let the captain know the situation then.' And he switched on his voice mike and started talking to the captain.

The captain jumped out of his seat and was with us in a jiffy and was staring at the oil gauge while shaking his head.

'How do you know it's OK?' he asked me

'Well there are no other indications that there is anything wrong as the RPM and boost gauges are steady, there is no oil leaking from the engine so it is most probably the oil pressure transmitter that is playing up but there is no way we can test this in the air.'

'Well, it was OK yesterday, why should it go wrong just like that?'

I didn't think this was worth answering so I just shrugged my shoulders.

'I can't take a chance on it just being the transmitter. What if it is something else?'

'In that case, if it is something physically wrong with the engine, it could eventually seize but I don't think it is anything more serious.'

He looked at me with a raised eyebrow and returned to his seat. The engineer shrugged his shoulders in an effort to convey 'what next'.

We were soon to learn the 'what next' as the captain came over the intercom and said.

'Due a severe malfunction of the oil pressure on the number two engine I have contacted command base and they have advised me to divert to Shannon in southern Ireland. I will shut down the number two engine and therefore it will take about an hour to get there.'

I looked at the engineer and screwed my temple with my middle finger in an effort to signify that I thought the decision was loony. To travel all the way to Ballykelly would only take another hour and a bit and what were we going to do to fix the oil pressure in Shannon in any case? And what about my crippled foot?

We duly arrived at Shannon airport and we were marshalled onto the main airport concourse next to Russian Illyushin and Boeing 747 airliners. The Shackleton looked very out of place. The engines were shut down and everyone disembarked from the aircraft. I had real difficulty getting down the steps and was eventually lifted off the lower rungs by Sid Platter the armourer – a gentle giant of a man in every respect. I was soon reconnected to my crutches and hobbled around getting in everyone's way.

The captain came up to me and said, 'You had better come to Ops with me to tell them there what you will need to fix this thing.'

I presented him with my crutches and said, 'A new foot would be the first thing. I can't see myself climbing ladders to get at the problem. I am supposed to be a casevac!'

'Well, come with me anyway, they may have mechanics that can fix it and you can supervise.'

I thought that this would be one way of starting an international incident by allowing Irish nationals to work on a RAF aircraft – but it was his prerogative.

So off to the operations centre we went. The captain, the engineer and me, swinging behind like some latter-day Long John Silver. With the comedy that was about to unfold, I should have had his parrot on my shoulder as well.

We got into the room and we looked very out of place in our military flying gear against all the civilian uniforms that occupied the place. We went up to this large counter and were given some very odd looks as we presented ourselves.

'I don't suppose we need to say who we are?' said the captain to a man who had presented himself at the other side of the counter.

'No sur, dat you don't. I am the duty Operations Officer – Michael O'Shea. How can I help you?'

'We need some assistance in fixing one of our engines. As you can see this man here has had an accident and won't be able to climb a ladder but he could supervise one of your chaps, if you have someone to spare?'

'Ah now sur, dere would be a problem wid dat. You see we've been discussin de probability of dis afore you landed and de problem is one of insurance. Our union tells us dat our mechanics cannot work on any military aircraft no matter what they are. Dey would not even be allowed to work on Irish military aircraft – if we had any.'

Good Irish logic, I thought.

'So you see, sur, there is nuttin' we can do to help you.'

'But I was told that you would be able to cooperate if we landed here,' responded the captain.

'Dat we have sur, we've given you a parkin' space an' dat's another thing, we'd like you to move your aircraft off the main concourse as we think it will give our customers de wrong impression. We will give you a space down by our maintenance hangar. In the mean time if there is anytin' else we can help you wid then don't hesitate to tell us.'

'Well, we will need an electric power set and a fire extinguisher to get the aircraft started.'

'Jeez sur, de yi have to start a fire to get that ting goin'? The wonders of modern science – who would have thought it? We'll see what we can arrange but do you think the electrical coupling will fit?'

Nobody had thought of this. In all probability the coupling would not fit in the Shackleton socket and therefore the engines would have to be started on internal battery power.

The captain and a couple of the lads went back to the aircraft to start it up and taxi it round to the allotted hangar where it would be out of sight. There must have been about five hundred people watching the procedure for starting the Shackleton. They came from every corner of the airport and none of them would ever have seen anything like this in their lives. I was propped up on my crutches standing next to O'Shea looking out of the large terminal window.

Once the captain and the co-pilot were in their seats, the signal to turn over the number three engine was given by the guys operating the fire extinguisher. The engine turned over slowly and seemed to grind on and on without any response. The engineer must have been sweating over the fact that it might never fire and that the internal batteries would therefore run down very quickly. The engine kept on turning and the counter rotation of the propellers mesmerised the watching crowd. There was much pointing and laughing at the very sight of it.

All of a sudden the engine fired. It had obviously been over fuelled, as great long streaks of flames came blasting out of the exhausts followed by great clouds of grey black smoke that seemed to engulf the whole of Shannon airport. With this momentous event, the whole of the terminal building went mad and there was clapping and cheering from everyone.

'Jeeze boy, I thought I wiz only jokin' about settin' the bloody ting on fire. That was very impressive!' cried O'Shea.

The other two available engines were started in the same fashion, again to cheers from the assembled masses. The Shackleton started to roll forward when power was applied to the engines and the squeal of the brakes once again brought forth merriment from the crowd. In this setting, never had I seen the Shackleton look so anachronistic. It crabbed away from the terminal.

O'Shea then transported me across the airfield to where the aircraft was to be parked. We arrived just as it was being marshalled down a very narrow track into the mouth of the hangar. I could foresee trouble ahead as there were other aircraft lining the edges of the track, there was no way that the Shackleton could turn round to make an exit. It was trapped!

The engines were shut down and silence prevailed once more. The captain, co-pilot and the engineer came out of the Shack and the captain looked pretty pleased with himself.

'OK, you can get on with what you want to do now. What exactly will you have to do?'

'I'll have to climb up friggin' ladders with my sore foot for a start. All I am going to do is to swap over two of the oil pressure transmitters to prove that that is all that is wrong with the engine. It will only take about half an hour. I think you should try to make the arrangements for us to leave here right after the job is done, otherwise we are going to have to start and stop the engines a couple of times and the batteries might not stand that. By the way, do you know that we are trapped in this space without a tow-bar to pull us out?'

'Crikey, I never thought of that. How are we going to get out?'

I shrugged my shoulders. Apart from wanting to get home quickly it was not my problem. We could have been in Ballykelly on one bloody engine by this time. God knows what this guy was thinking about.

The other groundcrew guys went off and found a ladder. They got my tool kit from the bomb-bay pannier. I swung myself around on my crutches and managed to lug myself up the ladder to open up the panel that would give me access to the pressure transmitter. This I removed and the guys transported the ladder round to another engine for me. I swung after them. I removed the transmitter from this engine and fitted the one removed from the first engine. I then fitted the other transmitter to the faulty engine. The job was done in thirty-five minutes, even with a dickey foot.

Another half hour passed before the captain came back.

'All done, we can leave as soon as we are ready but how are we going to get this bloody thing out of here?'

I shrugged my shoulders once more. Just then the lads from the airfield fire department came rolling up in a Land Rover fire appliance. They were there to give us fire cover when we started up as they did not think a portable fire extinguisher would put out any fire, if what they had witnessed up at the terminal concourse was anything to go by. Cheeky buggers!

I told them that we would not be going anywhere fast as we were blocked in without a tow-bar.

'Jeez boys, what are you goin' to do about dat? Is dere anythin' that we could help you wid?'

'Well, if you could come up with some strong hawser-type rope and a tractor, we could certainly try to move the old bugger.'

'Certainly we could do dat, we'll be back in a mo.' And off they went.

They came back in about twenty minutes and in the meantime I had told the captain what we had organised to try to get us out. He looked a little more relieved now that some action was taking place.

'I'm sorry, we couldn't find any tick rope but we've got this here strong webbing strap dat should do di trick. It has a one hundred thousand pound breaking strain.'

'That should do OK.' Just then the tractor arrived. The tractor driver got down and started talking to the fireman.

'Dis here fellow says that he has no autority to tow any military aircraft so he wont do di job!' said the man. 'I tink myself dat he's one of di IRA and just doesn't want to do it — is dat right, Mick?' he shouted at the tractor driver.

'Go fuck yourself!' was the tractor driver's cheerful reply.

'See, I told you dat was di truth of the matter!' said the fireman, good-naturedly. 'Now who's goin' to drive the bloody tractor?'

'I'll drive the bloody thing.' This came from Sid Platter the armourer who had been within hearing range. 'We've got to get out of here soon as I am on a promise from the missus if I get home tonight. This is my once a year day.'

Sid got on the tractor and backed it up to the webbing strap that had been slung round the tail wheel oleo and the ends were connected together by the rather large buckle that was attached to one end. The webbing was hooked onto the tractor's towing hook and Sid took up the strain on the improvised towing arrangement. Someone was dispatched to the aircraft cockpit to sit on the brakes. The brakes were duly released and Sid urged the tractor forward in a low gear.

The aircraft started to roll but unfortunately the tail wheels were offset to castor when the aircraft was travelling forward. They did not therefore want to castor in the right direction when it was being towed backwards. Once the wheels had taken one revolution, they took a violent lurch to the side and the aircraft started to run off at an angle. This sidewise lurch meant that the aircraft and tractor were going in different directions and this put an extra strain on the webbing belt. The buckle on the belt gave way with a tremendous THWANG and the metal end was projected towards Sid Platter's head like a bullet.

As luck would have it, the noise of the buckle parting from the other end of the belt and the sudden lurch of the tractor had made Sid instinctively look round. By looking round, he had leaned to one side and the buckle missed his head by millimetres. For a few minutes, he was unaware of what had happened and looked quite unperturbed when people started to ask if he was all right? It wasn't until he looked round and saw the webbing belt with the heavy buckle lying over the port side of the tractor that he realised what had happened. He turned a very pale shade of white.

The aircraft had continued on its unfettered way across the peri-track until someone had shouted for the brakes to be applied. By this time the tail wheels were on the grass verge and were sinking into the soft Irish bog.

The captain was going ballistic by this time. He was running around shouting about incompetence and how could this have been allowed to happen. His last action was to rush up to the rear of the aircraft and tried to stop it sinking further into the mire by pushing up on the rear perspex cupola. His arse was on the line – and he knew it.

'Don't just stand there, give me a fuckin' hand to stop this thing sinking any further,' he wailed.

Several aircrew rushed over and tried to help but to no avail – the wheels were determined to plant themselves in the loam. However, the wheels stopped sinking when the axle had been reached. The starboard rudder fin was dangerously close to the concrete track and the other was nearly at grass level on the other side.

'How the fuck are we going to get that out of there?' the captain shouted. 'Somebody's responsible for this and will pay for it.' He was hysterical.

'You're the one that's responsible,' I thought as I hobbled out of the way, not wishing to be in the firing line.

The Irish fireman just rubbed his chin with his right hand, closed his eyes and shook his head in disbelief. Was this the pride of the Royal Air Force that he was watching?

He came over to where I was standing. 'Jeeze boy, yon is one big fuck-up. Whit are youse goin' tae dae aboot dat?' Sid Platter arrived.

'It's a real problem because the wheels have sunk so close to the concrete track that we will not be able to lift them directly back onto the track without some sophisticated equipment. We will probably have to dig down behind the wheels to lay a steel track out further into the grass and pull them onto this before we can lay another track back onto the concrete. Have you got any of that expanded metal track anywhere?'

'Jeeze boy, you're a hard one tae please. First it's a bloody towrope and now it's bloody expanded metal track. Do ye tink dis is a bloody ironmonger's shop?' he retorted good-humouredly. 'I'll be back in a tick.'

'And bring some spades,' I shouted after him. He waved in understanding as he roared off in the Land Rover.

I hobbled across to where the aircrew had assembled around the captain.

'Sir, can I see you for a minute?' The captain turned round towards me and his eyes were bloodshot with either crying or rage or both.

'Well, what is it? We're in a terrible mess with this and I can't see a way out without bringing in some equipment from Ballykelly. Somebody will pay for this.'

I thought that I was perhaps the somebody that he was referring to. I shrugged my shoulders as if to call his bluff. 'I think that we can get us out of here by digging a trench behind the wheels, laying a metal track in the trench, pull the wheel onto this track which will then allow us to install a ramp back up to the concrete level and tow the wheels up this ramp. I've already asked the firemen to fetch some track and spades. What do you think?'

'Do you think it will work? I suppose we will have to try as we can't spend all day here doing nothing. I'll go back to the operations room and phone Ballykelly – see what they think.' He strode off with a purpose but I was sure that he just didn't want to be around if the plan did not come off. Someone else could be responsible for any fuck-up.

The fire truck came hurtling back at an alarming rate of knots. They obviously had a mission as well.

'Got di spades and di track!' the fireman shouted.

The track was heavy-duty and exactly what was needed. The first bit of luck today. I had already briefed the aircrew about the plan to extricate their beloved aircraft. Because it involved work for them, they were not very enthusiastic about it and there were a few dissenting voices.

'Look, we either try this or have to endure the embarrassment of waiting for help to come down from Ballykelly. What do you want?'

The engineer and one other asked what had to be done, picked up the spades from the Land Rover and started to dig a channel behind the wheels. The soil gave way remarkably easily and the channel took shape in no time at all. The wheels did try to sink more into the soil but they stabilised fairly quickly. The track was laid out in the channel slightly lower than the wheels so they could be rolled onto it.

How to get the wheels to roll onto the track? The brakes were released and everyone excluding myself started to rock the fuselage back and forth to overcome the inertia of the wheels stuck in the soft soil. The rocking only succeeded in making the wheels sink more into the soil. We would need more horsepower to pull the thing round.

Sid was dispatched to drive the tractor onto the grass and it was connected to the rear undercarriage with the buckled webbing once again.

The tractor took up the strain and started to slip and slide on the grass which was longer away from the verge. Fortunately, however, the tractor had not become entrenched by the spinning wheels. Unfortunately, the aircraft had not moved an inch.

'Right, everyone back pushing the fuselage as the tractor pulls.'

The tractor took up the strain once more and everyone else put their shoulders to any part of the plane that they could get to. The thing was rocked back and forth and finally it moved in the right direction onto the metal track. It moved fairly easily for the six or so feet that were necessary.

The earth that had been removed for the channel was piled up between the wheels and the concrete perimeter-track and a metal track was laid on top of this.

126

The tractor was brought round onto the peri-track and connected to the webbing once again at an appropriate angle to pull the tail out of the mire. The tractor took the strain and everyone pushed as before in the opposite direction. The tail started to move and was just beginning the ascent of the ramp when THWANG – the bloody webbing buckle gave way once again and nearly took Sid's head off for the second time.

'Strewth! I thought you said that this webbing was good for a hundred thousand pounds pull,' I said to the fireman.

'Ah, certainly it is that for sure but I never said nuttin' about di buckle – did I?' he retorted as if I was stupid.

'I don't think we should use the buckle any more, it's too dangerous. Can we try tying the webbing instead?' I said as I hobbled over to the scene once more.

The webbing was tied but as soon as the tractor took up the strain, the knot just came undone. Several ex boy scouts among the aircrew came forward to tie different knots in the webbing but they all pulled out because of the slippery webbing material.

'OK, we'll have to go back to using the buckle and perhaps we can tie it into a loop to stop it taking all the strain? What do you think?' I addressed the assembled mass.

The webbing was duly passed through the buckle and then this was tied in a rather ungainly loop – but if it worked we could be on our way home.

One of the aircrew had a bright idea. He thought that Sid should have some personal protection during the towing operation. He had gone into the aircraft and had come back with a 'bone-dome' helmet for Sid to wear. Sid tried this on but it would not go over his rather large head. Back into the aircraft and the largest 'bone-dome' was produced. Even this was much too small for Sid but he did manage to stretch it over the upper part of his cranium. As the bone-dome was perched there, it gave him a surrealistic look like some space alien similar to the Mekon of Dan Dare fame. On seeing this apparition, I laughed so much that I fell off my crutches. Everyone else was in hysterics but Sid was so taken with the idea of wearing the bloody thing that he ignored us.

So the Mekon went on the tractor once again – one pull, no webbing break and the tail wheels moved but got stuck as they tried to get up the ramp. The angle of the tractor was wrong and we could not move it further round because we would be fouling the undercarriage door – Bastard!

'What in hell's name are we going to do now?' I asked Sid.

He looked at me with a blank stare – well, he was an armourer after all!

One of the aircrew came running up. 'I've just had a thought. If we started the starboard engine up the aircraft could be slewed round onto the track.'

Eureka! Why had we not thought of this before?

The co-pilot and the engineer went on board and started up the number three engine which would give a bit of lift to the tail plane and help to lighten the load on the tail wheels so they could be slewed up the ramp. The brakes were released, the engine was revved up and the tail of the aircraft came neatly up the ramp and onto the concrete. The engine was shut down once again.

'Thank Christ for that.' I said to nobody in particular. 'OK, now we have a bit of momentum going for us we should try to tow her out now. We must keep the rear wheels straight so we need one guy either side to kick them back in line if they start to wander off course. Shout to stop the tow if you can't kick them back in time – OK?'

The aircraft was lined up by manpower and the wheels were kicked into position. The tractor took up the strain. Two men were stationed at the wheels, everyone else pushed at the front wheels undercarriage and the motley procession started off down the peri-track. I hobbled along on my crutches shouting words of encouragement.

Every now and again one of the men at the rear wheels would get down on his back and crab his way along the track to maintain position with the moving load all the while kicking out at the moving wheels to bring them back in line. It looked like a Cossack dance routine performed by a crab. Sometimes the wheels could not be easily kicked back so the procession was brought to a halt to allow more strenuous force to be applied – two men kicking.

By this method, the aircraft made very slow but steady progress towards our goal. God only knows what the crowd of passengers that thronged the terminal building made of all this. They were lined along the terminal-viewing platform and at every vantage point possible and cheering loudly at the antics. All very embarrassing.

It took about thirty minutes to cover the hundred yards back to the intersection where we could finally get the plane on course to move in a forward direction. The wheels were kicked round to steer it to the right direction and it was all over to the accompaniment of a loud cheer from everyone.

As if timed to perfection, the captain arrived in a small bus. However, I personally was not one to hold such suspicions.

'Great job, chaps!' he enthused. 'Good news as well. I have just been talking to the guys up in Ballykelly and they have told me that the Customs Officer who was there to meet us has had to go off duty so there will be no one there'.

Bloody typical, I thought. Here we had been stuck up an alley without much chance of easily getting out and all this prick was interested in was bloody duty-free whisky and cigarettes – pillock!

'C'mon chaps, we can get back to the duty-free shop before we take off.' Everyone except Sid and me leapt onto the bus.

'Aren't you chaps coming?'

'No, I got my duty-free in Gib and I don't have the money to get any more. How about you guys?' addressing the other groundcrew.

There was shuffling of feet and pissed-off looks and mutterings of 'Naw, can't afford any either.'

The bus roared off down the road.

'Those bastards get paid more than is good for them,' said Sid giving them the V sign as the bus disappeared into the distance.

'Dat's right but der's no pockets in a shroud so dae can't take it wid dem,' said the fireman stoically.

Everyone looked at him sceptically as if he was mad. He went off whistling to his Land Rover and drove it round to the front of the aircraft again to await the final start-up.

The aircrew came back in about half an hour loaded up with duty-free goods. They must have had about six bottles of spirits and a thousand fags each. Lucky bastards!

I said my thanks and goodbyes to the fireman and was then manhandled onto the aircraft and made my way up to the engineer's panel along with the engineer. Everyone else except Sid and one other got onto the plane. The pilots got themselves into their seats. We were all anxious to see what would happen when the number two engine was started.

Number three engine was started after a bit of a struggle. The batteries were becoming a bit drained. However, it kicked over and gave a false start – running for a few seconds and then dying. The starter motor was kicked in again and it seemed very reluctant to turn the engine over. Eventually the bloody thing fired and roared into life – thank God for that!

The number four engine was started and then it was the turn of number two. Once it had kicked into life and settled down, the oil pressure gauge was rock steady. The number one engine was started and the oil pressure gauge was as erratic as it had been on the number two before.

The captain looked round and gave the thumbs up with a smile on his face. 'Must have been the pressure transmitter after all,' he shouted, more in disbelief than pleasure.

'Bastard, we could have been home hours ago if you had not been so pig headed,' I thought – wishing I could say it to him.

The other guys got on the plane and we taxied down to the runway and roared off into the blue with frantic waving from the crowds around the terminal building.

It took just over an hour to reach Ballykelly and we landed in the evening dusk. The aircraft was taxied round to the large aircraft servicing hangar and the engines were shut down. The door was opened and I was helped down the steps. As I reached the ground I caught sight of a sinister figure lurking in the shadows. It was the Customs Officer. He had probably been tipped off about the excess purchases by the Customs at Shannon. Perhaps they didn't take a liking to the aircrew buying extra duty-frees?

My wife and kids were at the hangar to meet me and it only took a few minutes for me to clear Customs. We did not hang around to see what happened to the hapless aircrew.

My foot healed remarkably quickly. I did have to suffer getting the stitches out again and this was not pleasant but I didn't have to be held down and I only cried a little.

There are two morals to this story. Never try to over-manage a crisis, and never trust the Customs!

15

The Storemen

The RAF relied heavily on the supply chains that serviced each and every need of the operations. From aircraft to underpants, everything had to be supplied through what was known as 'The Stores'.

There was a major problem with the stores system in the guise of the people who worked there – they didn't really 'work' there, they mainly skulked and hid away behind the racks of all sorts of everything that they had amassed over the years. It must have been part of the selection criteria for storemen that they should be very shy and when they were finally tracked down and asked to do something, they become very aggressive. They were a bit like upland gorillas in as much as they were very placid as long as they were allowed to piss about without any outside interference.

It was a fact that, when visiting the main stores at Ballykelly, there was a button on the counter with a notice alongside that proclaimed 'Ring Here for Attention'. There had never been a bell attached to this button, which had been worn down to the base by many years of frantic people trying to gain attention for their specific requirements. It was a source of wonder that there were not skeletons lying on the floor around this counter. Perhaps there had been, and the storemen with their squirrel-type natures had hidden them away in among the shelves behind the counter where no other living soul had ever been.

It was obvious that all the articles in the store were the personal property of the quartermaster warrant officer in charge. He had clearly put the fear of God into his subordinates that any article that did leave the store would be paid for in blood – theirs.

This system had for many years stood in the way of progress and had played a significant part in reducing the British standing in the world. The populace was told that it was the crippling war debt built up by Britain during the Second World War that had toppled her from being a major world power. This was clearly erroneous, as everyone in the forces knew the real answer – quartermasters! They only slept easy at night if nothing had left their clutches so they did not have to do any work to get anything replaced.

To overcome the daily fracas, and sometimes multiple fracases, that would take place in trying to extract some spare or other from the store to keep the pride of Coastal Command flying, it was deemed necessary to set up a local store depot within the H&R section. This was done so the section storeman could be the go-between and the gofer to mediate with his own species in the main store and make the aircraft fixers' lives much easier in their daily grind.

The setting up of this store was not considered by everyone to be a good move, especially the night-shift workers. This was because the section store had been unmanned at night and it had made the ideal place to go to get some shut-eye in the early hours of the morning. Early hours for the fairies meant about two minutes after arriving back from their supper.

After the stores became permanently manned, it was no longer possible to get in there, as the door was locked and any spares had to be booked out by the chief on night shift, under pain of death if anything went missing or was not signed for. At least that is the way it worked for the first week of operation. After that it was the usual free-for-all and the poor old storeman would get a kick in the bollocks from his boss when a stock check was made.

Other sleeping arrangements had to be found though, and for this reason the night shift dispersed into every nook and cranny. This made it very hard to find some of the people, especially the fairies, when starter crews were called for early in the morning.

The only good thing about the local stores was the fact that the storemen became part of the front-line organisation and in the main they were very helpful in filling out the necessary paperwork required to extract useful items from the main store. However, one storeman in particular – LAC Dan McLiver – was not the sharpest tool in the box. Dan, whether through guile or stupidity, had this infuriating habit of never understanding what was required. If the required item was not on show at the back of the service counter where it could be pointed out to him, there was the guarantee that it would be a long time before the job was restarted with the correct spare part in hand. It was not unusual to see grown men close to tears as Dan returned to the counter with ever more bizarre objects in his hands that bore no resemblance to the required spare. The bit needed would be explained once more and even the part number given sometime with comments like 'They're on the third row, second shelf right-hand side.'

Off Dan would go and bring back something totally irrelevant.

'I thought I told you where they are kept? They're on the second shelf right-hand side. Where the fuck did you get this from?'

'Well, there are five shelves on each rack so I didn't know if you meant the second shelf from the bottom or the top.'

'Fuck me, I'm not a million miles away. You could have asked before bringing this lump of shit out here. They're on the second shelf from the bottom – OK?'

Dan trotted returns with something again that is completely the wrong item.

'What's that? I told you, they are on the second shelf from the bottom.'

'Yeah but you didn't say what row it was on that time.'

'Fuck this! I'll get it myself,' invariably followed by a leap over the counter then pushing Dan aside to get to the goodies therein.

'Hey – you can't do that! I'll have to tell my chiefy about this.'

'Tell him all you like – my chiefy's bigger than yours.'

All this was put down to Dan having a very short memory span. Rumour had it that he had been hit on the head with the butt of a rifle during training with the SAS before he was transferred into the air force. This would seem to be true, as it looked like all storemen had been hit on the head with a rifle butt in order to qualify for the job.

This short memory span became evident when a new Autolycus unit was required. The Autolycus was a device fitted into the Shackleton that allowed it to 'smell' the exhaust fumes from surface vessels. Hopefully these surface vessels would be submarines recharging their batteries – predominately during the night. The stealthy Shackleton would then track down this invisible trail of exhaust fumes to pounce on the quarry and bomb the shit out of it. The irony was that the Autolycus was updated and perfected in the 1960s just about the same time as nuclear subs came into fashion, and they did not give off any exhaust fumes. More often than not the Shackleton crew would find that they had been stalking the *Queen Mary* or some other such trans-atlantic liner as they obviously gave off more exhaust fumes than a little submarine. If Shackletons had been around in 1912, they probably would have got the blame for sinking the *Titanic*.

Dan had been asked for a new Autolycus unit but there was none in the H&R store. This had been verified by the usual leap over the desk and rummage among the shelves. Dan was dispatched on his bike to the main stores, about a five-minute ride away, to get one of the units. After about thirty minutes the phone rang in the chiefy's office.

'Did someone send Dan across to the main stores to get something?'

'Yeah – it's an Autolycus unit.'

'That would explain it. It's the chiefy from the stores on the line – he says that Dan went to him and said that he had forgotten what he had come for, but he asked the chief to "say some big words".'

Another regular figure around the H&R crewrooms was the Irishman, Tommy Craigden, the petrol (POL) storeman.

Tommy was as thin as a rake, a blanched rake that had been left out in the sun for too long. He had very gaunt facial features with blond hair that made him look like he had just come off the set of a Hammer horror movie.

Tommy had never been seen to eat anything solid in his life – he had an aversion to even the thought of food. His main diet was drink, any drink and as much drink as he or anyone else could buy for him. He was to be found only where there was drink. He would come into the crewroom for a cup of coffee – but only occasionally as he did not want to ever sober up – he could not stand the pain of it. Tommy was the mother of all anorexics and the father of all drunks!

He mostly ensconced himself in the pigs' bar in the NAAFI because it was here that he could best serve his requirements of buying the occasional drink for himself, cadging or being offered drinks from others and 'mine sweeping' when the odd drink was left on the table. With him emptying all the glasses like some carrion crow and Molly the Mask wiping the tables, the bar was kept scrupulously clean.

And so it was on one winter's night that Tommy and a civilian fuel tanker driver were sitting in the bar when a crowd of about eight of us from H&R night shift went in for an after-supper pint. Tommy was as pissed as a fart and the tanker driver was even worse.

'What yi drinkin', Tommy?' someone enquired.

'Don't know – yi hivna fuckin' bought it yet!' came Tommy's standard reply. 'We'll hiv a couple o' Guinness for your askin'.'

'Are you finished work for the night, Tommy?'

'Na, we hiv still tae empty the tanker down at the fuel dump afore we're finished!'

'Do you not think you've maybe had enough to drink if you've still got work to do?'

'Fuck off, yi moralisin' bastard. Just get us the fuckin' drink, will yi!'

The drink was bought and presented to Tommy and his companion and it disappeared. Within five minutes. Tommy was up at the bar buying more drink.

We were in the bar for about forty minutes and Tommy and partner must have drunk another five pints of Guinness in this time. They finally decided that they had had enough and staggered out of the bar. The tanker driver obviously had difficulty seeing straight, as he had one eye closed and had to focus very hard with the other in order to make headway. Headway was two steps forward, one back, two to the side and then another lurch forward at a half run. He eventually exited the door.

We got up and left the bar shortly after and all eight of us piled into my Zodiac. This was not unusual as it was the normal mode of transport for the night shift and sometimes up to ten lads would pile in.

We travelled down Dukes Lane, the main artery road on the base. We had come to the bottom of the hill when I spotted something in my headlamps.

'What the hell is that down there?' I asked and everyone started to peer very hard out the front windscreen.

By this time, we had come to the right-angle corner at the bottom of the road, I had turned to the right and as the headlights traversed the night they had picked up the full sight of the twelve wheels of the 20,000-gallon tanker rolled over onto its side. This looked like utter devastation as there were huge gouge marks in the grass, and the tanker engine appeared to be still running or in the last throws of life.

There was one hell of a smell of petrol in the car.

As I turned the corner, we were confronted by the driver staggering all over the grass. At least he was unhurt. Someone rolled down the window and shouted to him to get away from the tanker but he just stared back uncomprehendingly, apparently in considerable shock – or drunken stupor.

When we fully rounded the corner we were further confronted with the sight of Tommy Craigden in the middle of the road. He was almost bent double and waving his hands in the air to get me to stop the car. I drove the few yards up to him and stopped and he flopped onto the bonnet of the car and rolled off. I thought he must have died. I stopped the engine as the smell of petrol was now overwhelming and I was scared that a spark could set the whole scene ablaze or worse. I left the headlights on, got out of the car and went round to the front where I was joined by a couple of others. A couple of the other guys went to see to the driver.

135

Tommy was on the ground and was obviously distressed. He was covered in petrol-soaked dirt and this did nothing to improve his normal appearance. His hair was hanging in rat's tails around his face and his uniform was torn in several places and looked like it had been used as an oil rag on a thousand Griffon engines. He of course would have taken the worst of the crash, as he would have been on the inside track as the tanker went over – unless he had been driving of course. He was moaning to himself and his shoulders were shaking, worse than usual.

'Are you all right, Tommy? Are you hurting anywhere? Can you remember what happened? Are you all right?' I asked, as I tried to see if he was in any immediate need of first aid.

After a couple of seconds he rolled over onto his back and looked up at me with very wide and startled eyes. He grabbed me by both lapels on my jacket and pulled me down close to him. The stink of his breath mixed in with the petrol made me retch as he said into my ear, quite matter of factly, 'Jeeze, boyo we've hid a wee accident, cud youse help us tae get it back on its wheels?'

'I don't think we should attempt that just right now, Tommy. Best if we get you and the driver some help quickly and get you away from here.'

We lifted him away from the scene and laid him out on the grass next to the driver who was completely comatose. We pushed the car down the road away from the petrol that was still soaking into the grass and onto the road. Luckily, the wind was from the east and blowing the worst of the fumes away from the direction we were going.

Someone stayed with Tommy and the driver as it was thought this was best. In reality I didn't want them in my car as the bloody thing might have blown up with their petrol-soaked clothes inside. I started the car with a degree of apprehension but it was safe enough. We got round to the H&R offices and called for the fire section, ambulance and RAF police to attend the scene and telling them to be careful of the spilt fuel. Only the police asked why they should be careful. We did not elaborate.

We didn't see Tommy for some time after this incident. I think he must have been taken to one of the forces 'compassionate' rehabilitation centres for 'lovers of fine wines'.

Wherever he went, he returned looking fit and healthy. He never spoke about where he had been and after a week back on the base he probably couldn't remember – as the 'black nectar' had called to him once again.

PART II

Sharjah

16

Sharjah Bound

During October 1969, Ballykelly was given the great honour of supplying the detachment of Shackletons to Sharjah for the protection of what were then known as the Trucial States (in 1971 they were renamed the United Arab Emirates). Any keen observer of social history and geography might have noticed that the Trucial States were desert nations and therefore the Shackleton, being a submarine and marine reconnaissance aircraft, was an odd choice for the job of patrolling the borders of these threatened nations. This is especially so as the main enemy, whoever they were, had no submarines and very little in the way of a surface navy at all. So why the detachment was set up was a bit of a mystery all round.

All that could be said in the defence of detaching the Shackletons to this part of the world was the fact the Shackleton would fly very slowly, mainly because it could not fly fast, and they were fitted with twin twenty-millimetre Hispano cannons up front. These weapons were ideal for killing camels in the desert should the main threat come from that direction. This had to be the real reason that these detachments existed, as there was little threat at all from the seaward side.

The Shackletons were operating in conjunction with 8 Squadron flying Hunters and the Trucial Oman Scouts, these last being special forces who continually patrolled the desert areas. These special forces could call on the Shackletons to bring down their full fire power on any insurgents that they might come upon in the wilderness. For this reason, in every detachment at least one Shackleton had to be kept on readiness alert at all times to go and shoot at some nomadic unsuspecting camel caravan in the desert. The trouble was that 'scrambling' a Shackleton took the best part of an hour so even the slowest-moving caravan could be long out of sight or back across the border long before the wrath of the British Empire could be brought to bear on their hapless heads.

However, there was always the comforting thought that the sight and sound of a relic from the Second World War might scare them shitless or drive them mad, as they thought they were experiencing a desert mirage of gigantic proportions.

And so this was the reason that almost a full squadron complement of the worthiest personnel from dear old Ballykelly found themselves on the way to the sunshine for two months' rest and recreation – not!

I was not part of the first detachment, managing to stay at home for Christmas, but as soon as the festive season was over the desert beckoned. As with all detachments, prior to the final selection of the people who would go, a notice was posted on the H&R noticeboard. Normally for detachments to, say, Key West in Florida or round the world 'west about' or even Majunga there was always a great deal of interest from all over the base. People who had never even seen a Shackleton close up, like those who worked in the relative luxury of the engine bay or electrical and instrument workshops, would sneak across the divide to surreptitiously append their names to the list for these high-class sorties. For the detachment to Sharjah there was neither hide nor hair of them and therefore the whole of the detachments were made up of the first-line H&R personnel. This was a mistake, as to stack all the reprobates together without the calming influence of some outside forces was a recipe for social disaster.

The names of the unfortunates who would make up the happy band of brothers had to be pulled out of a hat as nobody would volunteer to go to the desert for two months, away from the relative civilisation and Guinness that was available in Northern Ireland. However, as certain names were forthcoming and no lame excuses were accepted, and it appeared that two months' exile was inevitable, other mates of those condemned souls would begin to volunteer – just for the hell of it.

As I was one of *les miserables* I was mightily glad to have the usual gang along for company: Jimmy Curry, Terry Waffal, Steve Bentit etc. There were about twenty souls in all on this detachment to keep three Shackletons in tip-top condition.

We flew out of Ballykelly to RAF Brize Norton where we were to stay overnight before getting a flight from there to Sharjah via Bahrain the next day. At Brize Norton we had supper, then inevitably the bar in the NAAFI beckoned and we just had to go to drown our sorrows, for the sure and certain fact was that this would be our last night of civilised freedom for some time to come.

Once a few pints had been pitched over the throats, the singing started, as it always did, and while it was appreciated by some in the bar initially, the longer the singing went on the more people became a little annoyed by it.

This was especially so of a group of four army 'pongoes' that were bound for some cesspit part of the world, probably even worse than Sharjah. They started heckling us singers and trying to drown out our mellifluous tones by shouting over them. This got us pretty angry and we of course had a song that denigrated the army and their professional standing. This made them even more pissed off and they were ready to do battle and we were ready to reciprocate. After all we outnumbered them by five to one and were certain that we could take them on – even if they were SAS-trained killers!

The sabre rattling had started and this would have escalated further if the NAAFI manageress had not phoned the police, who appeared from nowhere. They must have been on their way down to the NAAFI for supper in any case to have arrived that quickly.

So the situation was defused and we were unceremoniously dispatched from the NAAFI and escorted back to our accommodation to make sure that was where we ended up. This was just as well as we were to be flying out early the next morning and should not really have had as much to drink as we did, but it was our last night after all.

The next morning saw a weary and very hung-over bunch of guys, with the stench of last night's beer rancid on their breath, making their way to the terminal to be transferred to the departure point. We were glad that the previous evening's events had ended when they did and that everyone was at least in one piece in body if not in mind. Still, nine or ten hours on a Britannia aircraft out to Bahrain would be sufficient time to sober up. But what a way to sober up! The Britannia was known as the Whispering Giant when it first came into service as it was the first turbo-prop passenger airliner. However, the idiot that had named it thus was standing on the ground some twenty thousand feet below this flying object when he heard it whisper – he had obviously never flown in one! They were nowhere near as noisy as flying in a Shackleton but they certainly did not whisper, it was more of a shout. An unsynchronised roar that is always present with a multi-turbo-prop aircraft.

Even this roar could not keep us awake for very long and we probably woke up reasonably sober somewhere over the Mediterranean with still some five hours flying time left. One could get drunk again in that length of time if there had been any beer on board. But this was not

BOAC. Still, there were always the air hostesses to look at as this would be our last glance of the female form for the duration of our sojourn in Sharjah. That was a very sobering thought in itself.

Bahrain was reached and we were thrown out into the heat and flies. I had taken off my shoes on the flight and now could not get my feet back into the bloody things so I had to disembark in my stockinged feet.

We were unceremoniously processed through military immigration and sent to stay for the night in grotty billets that were packed full of three-tiered beds. We dumped our gear and went out to explore the base.

The mess was duly found for some fodder and then the NAAFI for a few beers before retiring. Drinking those beers was fatal because by the time we returned to the billet a load of pongos had been drafted in and they had moved all of our kit from the bottom bunks to the upper bunks. Still we got our revenge as we kept them awake by climbing into and out of the beds as each got up in succession to piss the beer away. This disturbance caused a fair bit of animosity, as climbing down from the top bunk in a three-tier arrangement in pitch darkness is not easy. Getting back in is just as interesting as the whole bloody thing sways around in a very precarious way. Served the bastards right.

It wasn't until the next morning that we realised that our bedfellows were the same lot of pongoes that we had had the altercation with at Brize Norton two nights previously. This time, although there was some cat calling and sarcastic comments thrown about, it was done in a reasonably good-natured way as we were here to fight a common enemy – enforced solitude. We breakfasted and then boarded a flight down to Sharjah, arriving there in mid-afternoon.

There had already been one detachment in Sharjah so all the stores and organisation had been established. At least we did not have to get stuck into that side of the business, which was always a pain in the arse. We went down to the squadron site and had a look around at the facilities – nothing to write home about.

However, the boys on the homegoing detachment did warn us to keep away from our next door neighbours, who happened to be 8 Squadron who were operating that other fine senior citizen of the RAF, the Hawker Hunter. This aircraft was classified as a fighter but in essence they were nothing more than an ejection seat mounted on a blowlamp. The fact that there was nothing remotely resembling a propeller on the Hunter made the Shackleton groundcrew very sceptical about its ability to fly. Worse still from their point of view, it had no facilities for making coffee or sandwiches.

In general, relations between the two sides had been reasonably good. There would be some social events between the factions such as darts matches and dominoes in the bar followed by a contest to see who could sing longest, loudest and rudest. This last could usually be declared 'a sing-over' as the 'Boys from Ballykelly' had much more experience in this sport.

This state of affairs began to be affected by some occurrences which, while unconnected, had a cumulative effect that led to an almost complete severance of diplomatic ties between the two groups. Long-term strategic theorists at the MoD had been messing about with RAF command structures so that the two commands previously known as 'Fighter' and 'Bomber' had been combined to form the new 'Strike Command'. Needless to say, this did not go down too well with the proud members of either. On the other hand the diehards of the Shackleton squadrons were still operating autonomously as 'Coastal Command', which was as it should be of course and only fair because they single-handedly protected the realm from maritime intruders.

Pride is a terrible thing however, and the chaps from the former Fighter Command felt hard done by. The feelings of both can be imagined therefore when some daft sod at MoD decided that Coastal Command should also become part of Strike Command and this heinous act was to take place on 27 November 1969. This fall from grace was greeted by a massive amount of piss-taking from our erstwhile colleagues of 8 Squadron which cooled relations by several degrees.

The coastal people did their best to ignore this lack of respect and on the day of the merger carried out a simple ceremony using a symbolic coffin inscribed 'Coastal Command RIP' and the date of its demise. Coastal Command was interred in a little corner of sandy ground in Sharjah near the Ballykelly detachment crewroom. A day of mourning was declared and the troops retired to the bar to get rat-arsed.

One of the Shackletons on this detachment had developed an engine problem which caused it to be grounded for a relatively long period. This was not the fault of anyone on the detachment but attributable to the usual logistical errors, wrong part sent from the UK, right part sent to the wrong place by our friends the 'suppliers' née 'stores'. This lack of blame locally in no way reduced the hysterical glee demonstrated by the former colleagues from 8 Squadron and their urine extraction was redoubled. Comments like 'When are ya gonna dust the bloody thing', 'It's been there for so long you should open it as a café' and 'Why don't you plant another one to keep it company?' were just some of the printable ones. Relations between the two sides went from cool to arctic.

During the detachment winding-down evening in the Khunja Club bar the jokes and comments reached boiling point and one of the Ballykelly boys decided enough was enough and commenced on a course of action that was to have a reaction far beyond his wildest hopes. No punches or glasses were ever thrown, no violent act undertaken but, from the commanding officer down, the hurt and humiliation felt by their 8 Squadron tormentors was to be satisfyingly deep.

When the beer stocks of the Khunja Club were exhausted a few of the stalwarts with hollow legs made their way to the Gliding Club to continue the festivities and enjoy three or four of the celebrated fried egg rolls they made there. Of course the singing continued and in the middle of a particularly noisy song, when all attention was elsewhere, a small leprechaun-like figure in the shape of Norman left the club and headed out, safe in the knowledge that his absence would go unnoticed for long enough to complete his task. He walked back to his billet, changed into KD and, picking up a couple of items he thought might be needed for the job, he left the accommodation and headed for the airfield.

To reach the aircraft dispersal area from the domestic site meant him dodging from hut to hut, then crossing a road and passing through a wide gate at the entrance to the dispersal. Unfortunately some security freak had chosen this very spot to situate a guardroom and a guardroom was very likely to contain RAF policemen, who might even be awake. As our man arrived at this point, a member of this elite force appeared out of the darkness, the two practically bumping into each other. It would be hard to say which of the two was more surprised. The policeman's training soon asserted itself and the questioning began.

'Oh shit, ah, hi there.'

'Allo, allo, allo, working late then, are we?'

'No mate, working early, gotta get off the ground before the heat gets up.'

'On yer own then, are you?'

'No, just getting a few things ready for the other lads arriving.'

'Still, I suppose you'll get some time off later?'

'Oh yeah, our motto is, sleep all day while the aircraft's away.'

'OK mate, have a good night.'

'Cheers, you too.'

'Oh, by the way, if you see my boss on your travels,' said the cop, 'Tell the skiving git to get back soonest or there will be no bloody Bonio for him tonight.' Christ, was the dog really on the loose?

This piece of social intercourse completed (in Sharjah there was no other kind of intercourse) the pair separated, one for a cuppa, the other on 'the mission'.

The area where the aircraft were parked was illuminated by floodlights mounted on pylons about sixty feet high, and drooping lifelessly from high up on one of the pylons was the 8 Squadron flag, deployed with all the arrogance often displayed by the insecure or overconfident.

Our man moved to the base of this pylon and began to climb. However, not being used to more exertion than lifting a pint of beer to his mouth, after a short climb he stopped for a break and released half a gallon of Tennant's best tinned lager and three egg rolls into the atmosphere, whereupon, feeling a bit lighter, he continued the climb. At the top he stopped for another short breather, this time the remaining contents of his stomach stayed put. Just shows how quickly you can get fit when needs must.

The flag was well secured to a vertical post by ropes that could have held a battleship in place, tied in very professional knots which caused our man to speculate that 8 Squadron might have some Royal Navy moles infiltrated into the ranks. This would be no bad thing in a place like Sharjah where the human female was an endangered species and the old sailor refrain 'any port in a storm' could take on a whole new meaning. Removing the multi-tasking penknife from his pocket he carefully cut through the ropes so as not to damage the flag – working behind enemy lines doesn't mean you have to be a vandal.

The flag was neatly folded into a manageable size and slipped inside his shirt which, being RAF KD issue, could double as a tent. He then made his way back down the pylon, carefully avoiding the bits of second hand-fried egg roll sticking to the ladder handrail. He got back to his billet uneventfully and placed the liberated flag under his mattress and inside the mattress cover.

The fury of the 8 Squadron personnel was awful to behold but their cries of pain fell on deaf ears and, try as they might, they never found the hiding place of their beloved flag. After some days their bile was demonstrated by an unspeakable act of desecration on the recently constructed tomb of Coastal Command. They covered the grave, headstone and all, in toilet rolls. There was no better way of ensuring their squadron standard remained a hostage.

The flag was eventually spirited back to Ballykelly where it hung on display in the Handling & Rectification Flight crewroom coffee bar. It dangled above the urn of boiling water where it was kept clean by regular steaming. In the meantime much shit had collided with the fan, high-level signals between units etc. had begun to cause a lot of embarrassment. As the object of interest was now 'in the public domain' it could no longer be denied that it had been purloined and so in the fullness of time it was duly returned to its owners.

The irony in all of this is the fact that 8 Squadron was to become the eventual and final operators of the Shackletons in their role of airborne early warning radar aircraft flying out of Lossiemouth in north-east Scotland. This seemed to be a very harsh snub to all the proud Coastal Command squadrons that had nurtured these aircraft over near forty years of active service – bureaucrats at work again in a modern world. And 8 Squadron never did say thank you.

17

The Swimming Pool

There was one day of handover before the departing crew left us to the sand and the flies. The good old boys had set up a party for us in the evening as much to celebrate their imminent departure as it was to welcome us to the desert.

The party, or more realistically the booze-up, was held in the Gliding Club on Sharjah camp and was a very raucous affair with lots of beer swilling and singing as only a Ballykelly contingent 'choir' could manage. It was very hot and sticky for us new boys on this first night as the club was quite small and it was jam-packed full of bodies each of which had consumed about three thousand calories of booze and were giving off this energy at a tremendous rate. When we were finally thrown out of the club in the early hours of the morning we were soaked with sweat and initially failed to notice how cold it had become outside.

It had not escaped our attention on our way into the club that the swimming pool was nearby. It could hardly be missed as it was an above-surface pool and the structure stood some twenty feet above ground level. In our drunken state this edifice seemed to call to a few of us – me, Norman Lindsay and Jimmy Curry in particular. We tried the gate at the pool entrance and wonder of wonders, it was unlocked. We climbed the stairs and there shimmering in the moonlight was the quiet and inviting surface of the water. We searched for lights but could not find the switches anywhere.

I stripped off and dived in first. I can still remember the sensation of the very cold water causing almost instant near sobriety. I did a length of the pool and climbed out at the far end. I didn't think we should push our luck too far by outstaying our welcome. We were not doing any harm but there was always some rule or other that would state that we should not be there.

I looked about the pool and I saw that Norman had stripped off and was swimming around in the shallow end. Of Jimmy there was no sight. I shouted to Norman, 'Have you seen what happened to Jimmy?'

'Well, he dived in fully clothed before me,' came the reply through chattering teeth.

I looked around the surface of the pool and especially in the areas that were more in shadow than others while shouting 'Jimmy, Jimmy, where the fuck are you?' There was no reply. I kept casting my sight over the pool as I thought that he was probably playing some sort of game of hide and seek with us. By this time Norman had extricated himself from the pool and was standing next to me shivering violently, teeth chattering from the effects of the cold water on his wee body in the cold night air.

'I'll have to jump in to find him and see what the fuck is the matter with him,' I said as I prepared to hit the cold water once again. I was not as pissed now and it did not seem to be such a good idea any more. Just as I was getting set the surface of the water erupted as if had been breached by a large aquatic mammal. In the middle of this maelstrom was Jimmy spewing up the contents of his stomach once again – all over the pool. It was not just a straight sick, as he was struggling to keep his head above water while he was discharging so his head moved to and fro and this dispersed the vile bile over a very large area of the water. I was even more reluctant to dive into the pool now, not because of the sick but because I thought that he could easily drag us both under if he panicked. I hunted around for a pole or something that he could get a hold of. I found a pole with a large boathook on the end of it. This was just what was required to harpoon the whale in the water.

Jimmy had gone under about three times. Each time he surfaced his head was covered in the solid bits that adhered to his thick hair and bits of egg roll were glistening in the moonlight. Luckily he was pointing towards the shallow end and each time he erupted out of the water he was propelling himself closer to this relative safety. On his fourth discharging eruption he was indeed able to stand on the bottom with his head out of the water. He stood there retching and coughing but at least he was alive and breathing. I passed him the pole and he had regained enough composure to grab it. We helped him to the side of the pool. It was no wonder that he struggled in the water because he still had all his clothes on, including his boots.

We got him round to the steps and helped him out of the pool. He stood bent over, retching the remaining pool water out of his stomach and eventually he started to feel a bit better but then the cold hit him and he started to shiver and chatter.

'Should we strip him here and try to dry him with our clothes or should we just get back to the billet?' I think we decided that, in case we were seen, discretion was the better part of valour as it would not look good for two drunks to be seen trying to strip the clothes off another.

We therefore picked up our clothes, got Jimmy supported between us and quickly departed the scene. We were apprehensive of being seen as we marched along at a brisk pace. We could have been mistaken for two naked homosexual bodysnatchers that had been successful on this night by abducting a junior NCO – this was probably a hanging offence. Christ, it was bloody cold and Jimmy was now in some sort of torpor and was not helping us too much.

We eventually reached the room that Jimmy and I were sharing for the night and noisily bundled into it, much to the annoyance of the other couple of occupants, fine sober young men that they were. We dumped Jimmy on the floor and towelled ourselves down in an effort to rub some warmth into our bodies. We stripped Jimmy while being looked upon with further disdain by the others. We towelled him down and tried to massage heat into him. We dressed him in some of his clothes and bundled him into his bed and covered him with his bed-sheet and counterpane. I threw my counterpane over him as well as I had started to feel quite warm from all the recent exertions.

After a while it was obvious that Jimmy was not improving as his shivering was becoming more violent. I had been out to the showers to see if there was any hot water so we could dump him in there but it was only lukewarm. It seemed ironic that in a country that had temperatures of over thirty degrees that we should be lumbered with somebody suffering from hypothermia. The only thing to do was for both Norman and I to get into bed with him and warm him up a bit. We discussed this, and thought what the hell! I told Norman to keep the sheet between him and Jimmy as we didn't want any accusations of impropriety – he was a randy little bugger. We lifted the counterpanes and jumped into the bed. Christ, he was cold! We lay there and sung songs to each other for about half an hour and there was a perceptible improvement in Jimmy as he had woken up and joined in the singing without even asking what two other blokes were doing in his bed.

Norman departed to get himself ready for the trip home later on that morning. Jimmy slept, while keeping the rest of us awake by snoring all night. Ungrateful bastard!

149

We never heard anything about the swimming pool being polluted with the contents of Jimmy's stomach. Presumably they had to drain it off and refill it. Hopefully some fitness fanatic did not dive in for an early morning swim because he could have had a secondhand breakfast at the same time.

18

The Graduate

On the morrow, we took possession of the rooms that the outgoing crew had vacated and made ourselves at home. Christ, it was hot and there was no air-conditioning anywhere. By the time we had transferred our kit, there was a mass queue for the cold showers.

In that era of the distant past, the effects of the sun on the skins of the northern hemisphere personae was not recognised, nor was the use of sun block. Even if sun block had been available, it would have been regarded as 'poofy' and therefore nobody would have used it in any case. Of course the first thing that those who had not been exposed to the sunshine for any more than two hours at a time (this constituting a summer in the UK) wanted to do was to get their kit off and get into the sun. The sun beat down relentlessly and enjoyed being soaked up by the unwary. This caused a lot of problems in the first few days as guys were out working on the aircraft for several hours at a time without protection.

The effects of this was to have lads walking around like robots trying not to bend or crease their reddened skins, which were stretched like papyrus over their skeletons, especially their arms and legs. Blisters appeared on faces especially above and below the eyes, ears and lips, giving them a very strange appearance. There were cries of 'Don't touch me for fuck sake!' if anyone came within six feet.

After a few agonising days, the blisters had scabbed over and their skins began to peel off so there was an army of lizards walking around as they shed the skin in expectation of a new sun-friendly layer underneath and one that they would hopefully fit into. After about two weeks, all had healed and everyone looked very healthy in their new sun-kissed brown livery.

The work was really quite strenuous as there was a significant flying programme and with only three aircraft it took a lot of effort to keep at least one of them serviceable at all times. There was also the minimum of each trade to keep them airworthy.

There were four engine fitters made up of one sergeant – Bob Vicary who had delusions of grandeur and never went outside. One corporal – Scouse Dickbury who was from Liverpool and was the most affable drunk and laziest bastard that ever came out of that city. I, as junior technician and Senior Aircraftsman Taff Jenkins completed the party.

Because of the work-related allergies of the other two, Taff and I were assigned all the work that could be piled on to us. This meant that very often we would be working ten and eleven hours a day, for day after day with propeller and engine changes and all the other routine stuff that needed to be done. I confronted Dickbury and told him he was as 'much good as a chocolate fireguard' and was certainly not pulling his weight. This prompted the little bastard to go and 'sprain his ankle' so he was put on light duties by the MO and hobbled around the place on a pair of crutches doing sweet FA. I threatened to shove his crutches where the sun never shines but he just giggled and hobbled off. Taff and I were getting more tired and rattier by the day.

Back in those days, pornography was not available for general distribution and if it had been it would not have been easily attainable in the middle of the desert. The place was also completely devoid of women except for the Arab women in Sharjah town who were completely covered from head to foot. So after a few weeks of complete isolation away from the female form, guys could become extremely frustrated as memories of their past sexual encounters or fantasies receded into the distance, and relief by the five-fingered widow became harder as the memories waned.

This fact was epitomised by one of our number who could only masturbate himself to ejaculation by listening to a woman's voice, so he would perform the act whilst listening to 'Mrs Dale's Diary' on the radio as this was the nearest contact to a woman that there was to be had in this part of the world at that time. In those days most of the radio announcers were male and unless one was of the 'limp-wristed' persuasion one had to seize every opportunity that was available to keep the imagination going to avoid being driven mad by sexual frustration. I bet Jessie Mathews, the pre-war film star and latterly the voice of Mrs Dale who was always 'worried about Jim', never suspected that she would become the object of sexual fantasies in her dotage – even through the ether by radio in the middle of the desert.

The films of that time did not give any mental stimulus, as they were sexually sterile after the British Board of Film Censors had cut out every scene of a remotely sexual nature, to preserve the eternal souls of the great British audiences and to ensure that they were not driven mad by tantalising images on the silver screen. Even the sight of a female cleavage was enough to categorise the film as X-rated and to see a glimpse of stocking-top was enough to make it XX.

This was to change when one particular film was to be shown at the station's Astra cinema. Imagine the ecstasy and expectation of going to see a movie that featured nearly naked tits used in a very provocative manner for several minutes on the screen, and a scene of a woman removing her stockings. Tales of these voluptuous tits circulated around the camp and those who had seen the film were the envy of all those who had yet to see it as they were one up in the 'choke the chicken' stakes.

The film was *The Graduate*. Anne Bancroft took off her stockings and a 'stripper' waggled her tits around with tassels attached to her nipples – don't talk about nipples. I had been working overtime every night that this film was featured at the Astra which was an open air cinema, so I was determined that I would not miss it on its last screening otherwise I would be well behind the others in porno material and may myself have to resort to listening to 'Mrs Dale's Diary'. Perish the thought!

I had ensured that all the work was completed down at the squadron so that I would have an uninterrupted viewing of this piece of soft pornographic cinematic artistry. I was showered and powdered as if I was going on a date and had a real sense of anticipation as I waited at the head of the queue to get into the Astra.

Once we were seated on very hard wooden seats inside the canvas walls of the cinema, the night air wrapped its cooling fingers around the person and this required that a jersey was put on to stop the heat of the day escaping from the body. In reality, the temperature had probably only dropped by about five degrees but compared with the daytime temperatures under constant sun, this felt bloody cold. I am sure there were those that used the excuse of the coldness to wear loose-fitting coats or anoraks so they could play with themselves as the film rolled on – nothing proven, just a suspicion.

When the programme started there was always the round of 'Pathe News' that was usually about three weeks old and normally featured the Queen and Duke of Edinburgh visiting some God-forsaken hole in the Commonwealth or the Brits beating the shit out of some other God-forsaken hole somewhere in the world. After this there was every forces favourite – *Tom and Jerry.* The director of the Tom and Jerry films was one Fred Quimby and he was a real hero to all the forces personnel. As the credits rolled at the start of the film Fred's name was always greeted with a resounding 'Good old Fred!' by all those present in any forces cinema anywhere in the world.

These films, although commonplace today on children's television, were revered in those days as a cult and were therefore always welcome at every showing – even if you had seen them ten times before.

After Tom and Jerry the credits for the main feature began to roll and then there was Dustin Hoffman floating in the pool with his new wetsuit that he had been given for his birthday. The tannoy blasted out 'JT Blair please report to the front door of the cinema.'

'Bloody hell!' I thought. 'Why in the name of hell would I be wanted at this time of night?' I decided to ignore the message as if I had not heard it.

Five minutes passed and Anne Bancroft was becoming very fruity with young Dustin – things were hotting up towards the bedroom scene.

'JT Blair please report to the front door of the cinema.' Bastards, how could they do this to me? I decided to sit still. The bedroom scene has just started and they are about to get down to business. The screen went blank and the lights in the cinema were turned full on to the accompaniment of a hundred voices bellowing 'What the fuck?'

'Blair – get your arse out of there now!' It was that stupid bastard Vicary who was doing the shouting.

Now I had been spotted there was nothing left but to get out of my seat and go to see what the stupid bugger wanted. I stood up and was immediately pelted with all manner of debris by the rest of the audience. I was being told in no uncertain manner where to go. I protected myself as best as I could and gave them the two-fingered salute as I made my way along the aisle to the exit.

'What the fuck's the matter now?' I asked irritated as I picked bits of crisps and Mars Bar wrappers from my person.

'The son of the Sheikh of Sharjah is flying with the CO tomorrow and he wants to ensure that the aircraft is one hundred percent serviceable for the morning. You need to come and check over and run the engines so that there will be no hitches when they are started with the VIP onboard.'

'Are you fucking crazy? I could come and run the engines all night and there still would be no guarantee that once stopped they would be serviceable again.' I was thinking fast on my feet as the film had started again and things were happening in there in my absence. 'Why don't I come down early in the morning and run the engines so at least there will be a better chance of them being serviceable soon afterwards – or the CO could take over the aircraft with the engines still running.' My hopes were raised with this suggestion.

'No, I have been given orders that it has to be done tonight so you will need to come now,' he said sniffily. He did sniff a lot in any case.

'Well, why can't you get hold of that lazy bastard Dickbury and get him to do it? He's only skiving with his pretend sprained ankle and he could easily run the engines and if there is anything wrong I will come down and fix it – how's that?' I asked, hopeful that I had suggested an acceptable compromise.

'I don't know if he is skiving or not but he has an excused duty chit and I cannot put him to work. If anything happened I'd be for the high jump.'

'Well, send the lazy little bastard home! I've asked for this before and nothing's happened. This is the first night I thought I was to have off and we've been here for five weeks now. I'm tired and pissed off. At least let me go and watch the end of the film and then I'll come down.' Another fair compromise I thought.

'Look, that would be OK with me but I should have told you that the CO is waiting to see you before he knocks off. You need to come now.'

'What is the silly bastard doing out at this time of night? He should be on the outside of several gins and tonics by this time. He must be pissing himself about this sortie.'

'He is,' was the glum reply.

I went quietly having decided that I had been well and truly corralled.

Down at the squadron offices we were confronted by the CO prowling around like a bear with a sore head. As soon as we arrived he came across to the Land Rover and was anxious to put his tuppence worth to us as we walked back to the office.

'Ah Blair, sorry to drag you down here so late in the evening but I have been put in a bit of a spot. Just been informed that the Sheikh's son is to fly with us tomorrow and as it is a bit sensitive from the security point of view I need to be sure that the aircraft will be serviceable for take-off as soon as possible. Can you give me some confidence in this respect?'

'Aye, Sergeant Vicary told me of this requirement. I did a lot of work on Kilo during the day including three sets of plug changes and this was deemed satisfactory on the final engine run and magneto checks. I could run the engines again now but as you know there is no guarantee that everything is going to be OK in the morning.'

'No, you are quite right but is there anything that can be done to assure reasonable confidence? We really only need the engines to be serviceable for this sortie. Is there anything you can suggest?'

'With respect sir, I have already suggested to the sergeant that it would be better if we come down early in the morning and did everything, including running the engines to ensure that they are all serviceable. If we give ourselves about two hours then there will be plenty of time to do a plug change or whatever small job needs doing. Also it would be good if the flight engineer was here to accept the aircraft once it is verified serviceable. He could also keep the engines running until the rest of the crew got on board.'

I looked across at Vicary and I could see that he was not best pleased with me putting this alternative solution to the CO. It was obvious then that it had been his idea to try to do the job that evening.

'Splendid, that's the ticket! That should ensure success. I'll get the flight engineer down here for what time? Take off is at nine.'

'If he is here by seven or seven thirty that should be OK. Do you want to use Kilo?'

'I am told that Kilo has the least Red Line Entries so I suppose that is the one that we should use for the VIP – OK?' and he turned on his heels and disappeared at a rate of knots.

I looked at Vicary and shrugged my shoulders as if to say 'That was easy, why couldn't you have done that?' However, I said nothing.

My thoughts immediately returned to *The Graduate*. Would I be in time to see the stripper?

'Would you give me a lift back up to the cinema, Bob?' I almost pleaded with Vicary.

'Aye, suppose so, but I've got a couple of things to sort out here yet,' he said sullenly.

I thought, you rotten bastard – but I said, 'Well, couldn't you give me a lift first and then come back again?'

He did not have a chance to reply before the CO put his head round the door and enquired. 'Anyone need a lift to the accommodation?' My heart soared as I leapt off the table where I had been sitting and gave a resounding 'Me sir – thanks!'

I jumped into the Land Rover and we were off.

'Thanks for that tonight, Blair, I really appreciated your input. Too often we cannot see the wood for the trees and it needs some practical thinking to come to a solution – thanks.'

'*Per Ardua ad Astra* sir, *Per Ardua ad Astra*!' I replied. He laughed. 'Can you just drop me off here, sir? I was in the movies before I went down to the squadron so I want to catch the end of the film if I can.' I still lived in anticipation.

He stopped the Land Rover and I got out and ran like hell towards the cinema only to be met by the entire audience coming out of the place. I must have been away for much longer than I thought and had missed the whole bloody thing.

I met up with some of the boys and went to the bar to be regaled about the sex scenes and the size of the stripper's tits. All exaggerated for my benefit of course. Bastards! Best to do was to get a few pints down the throat and forget all about sex for now.

I told young Taff Jenkins about the night's events surrounding the aircraft for the morning and he said that he would like to come along and give a hand if required. So it was set then – I would not need the help of the hapless Vicary with his miserable face and I was sure that he would be happy at being relieved of any responsibility in the affair as any backlash might ruin his illustrious career.

Taff woke me up at five-thirty and we trudged off through the cold morning air for the twenty-minute walk to the squadron offices. It never fails to surprise me how cold it can get in the desert regions at night. With all the heat that is blasted into the sand, concrete, tarmac and buildings during the day, one would think that this would be given back into the atmosphere at a slow rate during the night and therefore keep the place warm, but this is not the case and it gets bloody cold very quickly after the sun goes down. On this day there was a frost on the ground.

We got to the squadron and had a bit of an altercation with the RAF police dog handler who was on patrol over this area. I had forgotten about this security and he gave us quite a shock when he leapt out from behind one of the offices and demanded that we remained very still and to identify ourselves. Luckily the dog was calmer than he was and gave no sign of aggression, however I was certain that it could be encouraged to take a dislike to us very quickly if required. We stood very still and produced our ID cards, laid them on the ground at the dog handler's instructions and retreated a few paces while he picked them up and verified that we were indeed RAF personnel. I wouldn't have been surprised if he had given the IDs to the dog to verify them for him.

After some explanations as to what we were doing there at this early hour of the morning and a radio call to the guardroom we were free to go about our business. We even gave the dog a pat before we went.

Next problem was trying to get into the offices – they were locked. I had not thought about this before but it was obvious now that this would be the case. I shouted to the dog handler who had continued on his lonely vigil. 'Hey mate, have you got any keys to get into this place?' I think he said something like 'Fuck off!' and continued on his way.

'Bollocks, Taff, we don't really need to get into the office right now; we can do all we need to and if we need any tools later we can get them.' He nodded and shrugged his shoulders in agreement.

We trudged out to Kilo and pulled a Houchin power plant up to the aircraft, plugged it in, started the engine and engaged power. Immediately the inside of the aircraft lit up.

I went round to the back door and placed the steps at the side in order to get at the door handle. This was always a precarious operation as the metal sides of the steps were hook-shaped at the top to locate over the door threshold when the door was open. The points of these hooks could not be placed against the skin at the side of the door in case they pierced the skin when a body weight was on the steps. Instead, to facilitate the operation the steps were placed backwards on the skin, but this then put the angled feet of the steps on their points so there was never much contact with the ground. Additionally, the angled treads were now the wrong way round and had to be treated with caution when stepping on them as they were quite sharp. The steps had to be positioned at just the right angle against the aircraft so as they would not skid away when weight was applied. I have seen several incidents caused by unsuspecting men unskilled in this operation, when they had 'come a cropper' as the steps slid from underneath them and they ended up on the ground wearing the steps! What price Health and Safety in those days?

I unlatched the door, positioned the steps properly over the threshold and went into the body of the aircraft. The usual odour pervaded but it didn't smell too bad at this time in the morning, at least not as bad as it did during the heat of the day. I wondered what the Prince would make of the 'aroma de shack'.

Taff and I checked all the fluid levels on all four engines just in case there had been any leakages. There had been none and all levels were correct so the next job was to test the engines. I went back into the aircraft and selected fuel tanks and fuel booster pumps to check for leaks from any of the engine's fuel priming solenoid valves. This was always a favourite snag of flight engineers and I was determined that it would not feature on this sortie. None of the solenoid valves was leaking.

Normally it took a minimum of three men to start the engines. One on the throttles, one on the engineer's panel to press and tweak the starting buttons and switches while the third manned the fire extinguishers outside and was in charge of safety around the immediate vicinity. However, over the years, mainly out of necessity caused by not being able to always find a willing volunteer for the extinguishers, engine fitters were skilled at starting the engines on their own. This was achieved by operating the buttons and switches on the engineer's panel, which took two hands, while operating the left-hand seat throttles with the feet when required and sometimes the throttles had to be worked hard to get the engine to 'catch'. This was the modus operandi on this day. It was pretty difficult to start all four engines in this fashion as the other throttles got in the way when starting the selected engine. I got over this problem by removing the bondu boot from my left foot which gave my toes a better grip on the throttle.

Eventually after much persuasion, cursing and swearing, all four engines were running and Taff came in to watch the engineer's panel gauges for the run-ups. Once the engines were warmed up, I put them through their paces one by one, hopefully wakening everyone else on the base in the process.

The sun was just broaching the horizon by this time and the rays poured in through the windscreen raising the spirits considerably. I thought how much like cold-blooded animals we are, if not in the physiological sense then certainly in the psychological sense, as we all take sustenance and pleasure from the sun – very deep thoughts for an engine fitter.

Someone was waving at me from outside the aircraft. It was the flight engineer and I closed the engine throttles to idle and waved to him to come inside. Taff went down to the rear door and positioned the steps for him to climb aboard. He came up to the front and asked how everything was going. I told him what we had done and that everything was OK and the engines had checked out. I asked him if he wanted to verify the engine runs but he declined with a shake of his head. The engines were left running for a few moments to stabilise then Taff shut them down – the silence was deafening! It always took several minutes to recover hearing and other faculties after an extended engine run and especially after running all four. Hearing protection was not regarded as best practice in those days.

'Bloody hell, you two must have been at it early this morning. I couldn't believe my ears when I heard the engines blasting away at that ungodly hour – I thought World War Three had started! The whole bloody place must have been woken,' the flight engineer proclaimed.

I was internally pleased at this and wondered if it had woken Vicary and Dickbury – I hoped so.

'Well, with all the pressure that the CO placed on this sortie we didn't have much choice. If we needed to fix anything we would only be starting now, on bloody hot engines, so we needed plenty of time to fix and then carry out more runs to verify.'

'Aye, I suppose you're right but what am I going to do for the next two hours?'

'You please yourself but as you are satisfied with the checks that have been done, as soon as we have signed for the pre-flight servicing we are going off to breakfast.'

By this time the flight sergeant had arrived and opened up the office. 'Vicary told me about your meeting with the CO last night and he wasn't best pleased with you persuading him to put off the checks until this morning, he thought you should have done them last night.'

'Fuck him and the horse he rode in on. It's just that he is so mealy mouthed that he is scared to speak up for himself and in any case it was the CO's ultimate decision. If Vicary had a brain he would be dangerous,' I retorted.

'Aye, you're right and by the way, confidentially, I agree with you. Everything OK with the kite?'

'Aye, luckily, for once in its life. By the way it only has minimum fuel load – is that all right?'

'I'll find out from Ops and get back to you.'

'Perhaps you can get Corporal Dickbury to do any refuelling,' I said sarcastically and gave him a wink. He cast his eyes heavenwards in response.

The upshot was that after all this protracted and frenetic exercise the kite took off for the sortie on time and was back on the ground about an hour and a half later as the Prince had had enough of the privation and hospitality afforded on a Shackleton. He looked decidedly queasy and not a little disorientated when he disembarked and was whisked away in his air-conditioned limousine. No one could blame him for that as an hour and a half was more than enough time to endure this flying dinosaur of ours. Still, we loved them even if he didn't. I bet he didn't think much of the British government for sending these ancient flying gunboats to protect his Sheikhdom. He probably convinced his father to stop paying for them.

I never did catch up with *The Graduate* during the rest of my time in the RAF and certainly no more films of a pornographic nature passed through the Sharjah cinema, not that I had any time to go to them. Still, there was always Mrs Dale to fall back on when the sap started to rise.

19

Going Home

The next weeks went on and on, seemingly interminable, and this feeling got worse the closer the time of departure came. In reality I was quite enjoying myself as I really felt great in the sun after becoming acclimatised to it once again. However, there was a different feel to the sun in this part of the world to that of the Far East, in that it did not feel as humid or sultry even although the humidity was very high. It was probably the lack of trees and a fresher wind blowing across the land. It might have been that we were being fed 'happy pills' by the establishment. We did have to take salt tablets daily so it might have been that these were doctored to include some sort of stimulant. Whatever the cause, I felt very well and even the twin evils of Vicary and Dickbury could not get me down.

Finally, as always happens, the day dawned when we were to go home. The new detachment had arrived and had been shown all the ropes so there was nothing left for us to do but to pack our bags and go.

The bags were duly packed with all the dirty washing that could not have been washed by the billet boys over the past few days, along with a few presents for wives and kids that had been selected from the meagre assortment of goods in the NAAFI store on camp. The main thing was to get out of there as quickly as possible and get home just as quickly.

The journey home was a retrace of the journey we had down to Sharjah. First leg was to Bahrain where we stayed overnight and then on to Brize Norton by VC10 the next day. The whole journey went off without a hitch.

On arrival at Brize Norton we were subjected to the same procedures that could be expected at a civilian airport. First through passport control, collect luggage and then stand in a long line to be subjected to custom clearance. As was customary at that time, everyone had to present themselves to a customs officer and he would decide whether you were worthy of further investigation or not. More often than not, after you had declared that you had nothing to declare you would be dismissed by being given a chalk mark on your luggage and the flick of the officer's finger pointing to the exit door.

God forbid that the customs officer took a dislike to you or that he had some suspicions that you were smuggling some illegal goods. In this case, very much the same as today, the luggage of the hapless soul was torn apart without ceremony, sometimes to the delight and amusement of the 'innocents' that were waiting in line watching the proceedings. Not so nice for the victim whose dirty washing was strung all over the bench, especially his underpants covered in piss stains and skidmarks!

This was very different and more formal compared with the way that crews were treated by the customs at Ballykelly. At home base the customs officers were more restrained in their treatment of the returning conquering heroes who had endured a harsh three weeks playing golf in the Caribbean. Perhaps this was because they had learned over time that the aircrew personnel were scared to blight their careers by being caught smuggling and the groundcrew personnel would not have any contraband on them as it was all hidden in the aircraft to be collected later.

This is not to say the customs did not know that there might be contraband on the aircraft, and they used to go around new arrivals from overseas banging on panels and fuselage, having access panels opened up and cowlings removed. Occasionally they had the aircraft towed into a hangar and did a deeper search of the voids by having more panels removed and used stronger lights and longer mirrors. I am sure that in the far and distant past they did find some goods hidden in these obvious places but as tradition demands, the smuggler must always stay one step ahead and the level of ingenuity increased to avoid detection! This was an ever-improving evolutionary process.

Also the selection of contraband had to change to avoid detection. Everyone would have wanted to avoid duty on a thousand cigarettes or a dozen bottles of booze but in practical terms these items were difficult to hide because of their bulk. However, it was not impossible to the ingenious to hide several thousand smokes and several bottles of drink in places that the customs never knew existed. For example, the Autolycus unit that 'sniffed' exhaust fumes had a large drum over which was printed 'Danger Radioactivity'. This drum could hold well in excess of a thousand fags, and the customs would not go near it in case their balls fell off. The radioactive source was a very weak affair and would not have had the power to penetrate the cellophane on the fag packets never mind the fact that they were double wrapped in cartons.

The ability of the groundcrew to plant this contraband was due to their accessibility to the aircraft at the foreign departure point and their ability to recover it because of their access to the aircraft at the home base. This accessibility at home base could be at their leisure because the aircraft could safely fly again before the smuggler had a suitable opportunity to recover his goods.

However, the most sought-after contraband at that time was duty-free watches and jewellery and these could be easily hidden in undetectable places that were easily accessed at both ends of the journey. The biggest problem of all was having the cash to pay for them out of the pittance that the RAF paid. Only the aircrew had the wherewithal to purchase the real goods. This resulted in a bit of a Mexican stand-off, where the aircrew had the money to buy the goods but were too proud or too scared to approach the groundcrew to hide it for them, and the groundcrew had the ability to hide goods but no money to buy them. In the end the customs won.

This was perhaps a reason for disbanding the squadron's groundcrew and corralling them into collectives of H&R – so nobody would have real trust in anyone else any more. The collectives never worked for Stalin so why should they be any more successful in the RAF?

On this day, standing in line to be browbeaten by customs officials at Brize Norton, I was behind my dear old pal Dickbury. He had not improved his performance over the last few weeks of the detachment and somehow made himself into some sort of office 'gofer' ingratiating himself to all the officers and senior NCOs. I never saw him close to an aircraft and I was convinced that he had an allergy to them.

The same was true of Vicary and after the episode with the Sheikh's son he hardly spoke to me at all, which was not exactly heartbreaking. He was not going to do anything for my career as I was to leave the RAF in just something over a year's time. He could go and hide anywhere he wanted to keep himself away from the necessity to make decisions as long as he kept out of my face.

So here I was behind Dickbury and he did not look very comfortable at all. His eyes were popping out of his head, he had a very sallow, pale skin and he was sweating profusely. He looked like he had flu, so I kept several feet away from him even though I knew his most desperate disease was malingering! He kept wiping his forehead and his mouth with a sodden hankie and I thought he was going to collapse at any moment. He kept looking around as if trying to find an escape route away from this place. I felt moderately sorry for him and asked if he was feeling all right. I got a grunt as a reply!

The queue shuffled forward towards the customs officer. 'Have you read the list of your entitlements – and have you got anything to declare?' Each was asked in turn. This was normally answered by a monosyllabic 'Yes' accompanied by a shake of the head and a shrug of the shoulders as if to show a certain disinterest in the whole process and a presumption of total innocence. All of this was in hopes that there would be the chalk mark on the kit bag and the dismissive wave of the hand from the customs man.

Dickbury finally reached the front and presented his baggage on the counter. 'Are you feeling all right, sir?' asked the customs officer. Dickbury reply with a nod of his head and swallowed hard. 'Well then – have you read the list of your entitlements – and have you got anything to declare?' asked the man behind the desk staring into Dickbury's evasive eyes. This was answered by a high-pitched squeaky 'No.'

'Let's have a look then, shall we. Can you please open up this small bag?' Dickbury's knees physically gave way and his hands were trembling as he opened the zip on this bag. The customs man thrust his hand into the bag and stared to feel around the contents inside. He then tipped the contents of the bag onto the counter and started to separate the various items that were unfolded to his eyes. While doing this he kept looking up at our hapless hero.

'Are you sure you don't have anything to declare sir?' Again this was greeted by a high-pitched squeaky 'No' followed by a very hard movement of his adam's apple as he tried to swallow his dry spit.

The customs officer had separated a pack of cigarettes and a bottle of Johnnie Walker Black Label whisky from the rest of the contents of the bag which he was now replacing whence it came. 'All right, let's have this kit bag open, sir.' Again there was the jerk of Dickbury's knees and his trembling hands tugging at the zip in an effort to force it open against the bulk of the dirty washing that was inevitably lurking inside.

As Dickbury struggled the customs officer asked once again, 'Are you sure you don't have anything to declare?' At this Dickbury burst out crying, stood back from the desk and sobbed 'Only these!' as he simultaneously unbuckled the belt on his trousers, unzipped the fly and let the trousers fall to the floor. The customs officer looked on in amazement at this sight and those of us who were close by started laughing. This laughter got louder and louder as more and more guys caught sight of this apparition standing there in his shirt tail with his trousers around his ankles.

It was obvious that it was not immediately apparent to the customs officer what Dickbury was declaring, as he leaned forward on his arms looking over the open case lying on the counter. He looked around and gave an uncomprehending shrug of his shoulders. He could not help himself and started to laugh along with the fifty others in the hall who were now falling about with tears flowing down their cheeks. Even Dickbury, like a naughty child who had been brought to an unwilling, sobbing confession about a misdemeanour, now realised that he was the centre of attention and even he started to smile at the ridiculous situation he was now in.

'Sir, what do you have to declare?' The customs man shouted over the din of the still resounding laughter. The laughter somewhat diminished at this, as we also wanted to see what he had to declare.

Dickbury looked at the customs man with a frown as if he was mad not to see what was being presented to him but the customs man was looking up and down uncomprehendingly. At this Dickbury looked down and perceived why the man could not avail himself of his secret – his shirt tails, which came down almost to his knees, were in the way.

Dickbury gripped the front shirt tails one in either hand and parted them like the image of the traditional flasher. This revealed an awesome sight that had not been apparent when he had dropped his trousers. He was wearing nylon stockings supported by a rather fetching suspender belt, all capped by rather stained Y-fronts. This was only 1970 after all, and these things were not done – or more likely not displayed.

This display set the whole hall into another and even more raucous round of laughter and people were jumping up on to anything that would give them a sight of this apparition! Some moralistic bastard shouted, 'That's fucking disgustin'. He should be put away for that!'

The customs officer could not believe his eyes and put his hand up to his forehead and shook his head as he tried in vain to stop laughing. Eventually he regained some of his composure, and with his hand outstretched he said dismissively, 'Is that *all* you have to declare?'

Dickbury looked down at his legs and then back up again as if he had only just realised what the officer meant – was he was consciously outing himself as a transvestite?

'No! Not the stockings – these!' As he said this he was struggling with the clasp on the suspender belt that held the stocking up. He succeeded in releasing front and back in short time so he was obviously well used to the operation. He rolled the stocking down to reveal at least half a dozen watches strapped to his inner thigh. He repeated the operation on the other leg and revealed another half dozen or so watches secreted in the same way.

'I think you had better pull up your trousers and come with me sir. Please hold the line where you are, sir,' he said to me with an outstretched hand.

I barely heard him because of the continuing hilarity that was still ringing round the hall. There were comments shouted like 'He had better watch his step!', 'I'll bet he's been a bit strapped for time!', 'Have you got the time if I've got the money; Ducky Dixy!', 'Hope he gets a suspendered sentence!', 'We never saw his knickers!'

Dickbury pulled up his trousers and the customs officer picked up his bags and indicated with his head that he should be followed down the customs hall. The pair joined up at the bottom of the long counter and disappeared together through a door marked 'Customs Official Only'. Would they conduct a full internal search of the little bugger – one could only hope, as it would be just rewards for his constant malingering!

After a few minutes another customs officer replaced the first and I was called forward to place my luggage on the desk. 'Have you read the list of your entitlements – have you got anything to declare?'

I was still unable to stop laughing completely and could only answer by closing my eyes, biting my lip and shaking my head – I badly needed a piss!

Chalk mark on the bags and I was out of there as quickly as the weight of them would allow me to move – looking for the toilets. I just managed to get to a piss stall in time and the relief was all embracing and allowed me to giggle some more at what had just happened. It had seemed like an eternity but I bet the whole thing had happened in no more than three or four minutes – obviously a long time in comedy!

There was a bus outside the terminal waiting to transport the Ballykelly contingent to a waiting Andover turbo-prop passenger plane out on the dispersal. This seemed like extraordinary service and organisation for RAF transport but then Brize Norton probably did not want us hanging around for too long after our altercations of some eight weeks previously. Get them back to the bogs of Ireland as quickly as possible!

We embarked with our kit and dumped this to be covered with a cargo net at the rear of the kite. We took our seats and were ready for the off. An air steward came up the aisle counting the heads. He repeated the exercise on the way back up to the front. 'There seems to be one missing?' he enquired to no one in particular.

'Yeah, one of the guys was picked up in customs for smuggling and is probably in the nick by now – we better just leave without him,' said no one in particular.

'I'll have to check this out,' he said as he disappeared into the flight deck. He appeared after a few minutes. 'Captain says that we should wait a few minutes to see what happens. He is in touch with Operations who are trying to find something out.'

'Aw, fucking hell, leave the little turd behind. We want to get home, not sit here waiting for him to finish his fucking jail sentence.' None of the senior NCOs that were on the plane made any comment on this.

'OK – just a few minutes then.' He disappeared once again into the flight deck, no doubt to tell the captain that his passengers were turning ugly. He came back into the cabin and indicated by rotating his hand and index finger that the plane was to be started. At this there was a wry cheer from the dissenters. He went to the door and signalled to the groundcrew that they should remove the access ladder. This done, the door was closed and the engines started their long wind up to self-sustaining speed. Great, we were on the last leg and I could feel the stirrings in between mine at the thought of the arrival!

The aircraft started to move and then came to a sudden stop and the steward, who had been on the intercom by headphones got up and opened the door. Those on the port side of the plane relayed the fact that the access stairway was being brought into position. This was greeted with shouts of 'I'll bet the little bastard has been set free.'

Sure enough, a few seconds later Dickbury came bounding up the steps and blustered into the cabin with a big smile on his face! He deposited his bags with the steward who placed them with the rest while Dickbury bundled himself into a seat. There wasn't a man jack of us that was pleased to see him there, however there was no way that he could be ignored as he boasted how he was smart enough to declare his contraband as this made his treatment by the customs more lenient.

This statement has always puzzled me, because if he had been man enough to stand his ground and not revealed his underpinnings he would have probably got away with it. At least he could have waited until the customs had finally knobbled him before revealing himself. He ultimately revealed what a prick he really was!

The customs confiscated all his watches, his cigarettes and whisky. However, they did allow him to keep his stockings and suspender belt as they could not prove that they were not part of his clothing. Dickbury said that he had bought these items as a present for his wife; could he possibly have bought these in Dubai? I was never sure but it did give me an idea of what he was doing with his time while I was doing all his work. Listening to Mrs Dale while dressed in sussies perhaps?

168

The homecoming was as great as ever. It never failed to amaze me how the kids had changed over the space of a few weeks.

Several years later the British MoD tried to modify the successor to the Shackleton, the Nimrod, into an airborne early warning (AEW) aircraft to safeguard our shores from the threat from the Eastern Bloc. The Nimrod was a derivation of the first jet airliner, the Comet, which goes to show that the British can never throw anything away! After many hundreds of millions of pounds had been spent on this project the British public were told that the radar systems installed in the Nimrod, being quite revolutionary in design because they looked forward and backwards at the same time, were in fact too sensitive for the job, so the project was scrapped.

The MoD therefore ended up purchasing the originally recommended Boeing AEW. They had been successfully deployed for years in the USA as their radar was located on top of the fuselage and conventionally, and simply went round and round. As usual with British/USA procurement exercises there would be some delay in delivery of these, and because of this total fiasco a stop-gap had to be found. The Shackleton had been progressively replaced operationally by Nimrod, the mighty hunter, which although not blessed with pistons and propellers carried on the great Shackleton tradition of delivering letters to the navy and occasionally scaring the shit out of our submariner friends.

On the demise of the Shackleton operational squadrons, some Mark 2 Shackletons still survived and the MoD decided they could be converted for AEW operations until the new Boeings were in service. This was done and the Shackletons and their crews carried out their new duties with the same efficiency, skill and aplomb as of old.

Who was to be given the honour of maintaining these thousands of rivets in loose formation in this new role? Ironically, it was none other than those confirmed Shackleton haters, the famous Hawker Hunter fighter operators and flag misplacers of Sharjah, 8 Squadron! I have no doubt they came to be as sentimental, protective and blasphemous about their new charges as we had been.

PART III

Majunga

20

Unilateral Declarations

Mr Ian Smith, last colonial leader of the country once known as Rhodesia, will be best remembered in the history books as the man who in 1965 invented UDI or the Unilateral Declaration of Independence. UDI was meant to redirect the 'wind of change' that was blowing across Africa at this time and was not well received by those who were concurrently inventing 'political correctness' and the split-up of the British Empire. Ian Smith and his boys treated the 'wind of change' as a very smelly and lingering fart.

The then prime minister, Harold Wilson, was very pissed off at Smith's UDI and he tried to thrash out a political compromise at a meeting onboard HMS *Tiger* somewhere in the Indian Ocean. Wilson was not to be put off and told Smith that if he did not rescind his action of UDI, international sanctions would be brought to bear on Rhodesia. Smith was made of sterner stuff though and told Wilson to 'fuck off'. This was a brave action in the face of the combined capabilities of the British Armed Forces and Harold Wilson's pipe, which apparently nearly snapped in two as Wilson's jaw clenched at Smith's response.

However, courageous as he was, even Smith might have reconsidered on his chosen path if he had foreseen that among the forces to be pitted against him would be included the elite of the Royal Air Force, namely the air and ground crews of Coastal Command with their Shackletons. This bastion of defence for the preservation of peace around the world was not so much derring-do as derring-couldn't!

The very cunning plan set up by Whitehall mandarins was to have a couple of Shackletons with appropriate numbers of personnel detached to the island of Madagascar at the holiday resort of Majunga. This location was chosen because it had the only runway on the western side of the island. The mere fact that it was the next best thing to paradise was of no consequence to the boys behind the Whitehall desks. However, it did have some dire effects on the poor souls who had to endure this onerous term of duty to save the face of our once great nation, now wrinkled and withering away at the edges.

As Rhodesia was a landlocked country, all supplies and especially oil supplies had to be shipped into Beira, the capital of Mozambique. The president of Mozambique was obviously being well looked after by Ian Smith and did not subscribe to the same scrupulous ethics as the British government so the trade went on unabated.

The Shackletons were to perform their world-renowned role of reconnaissance up and down the Mozambique Channel, between Madagascar and the African mainland, and identify and photograph those ships that were bound for Beira with their cargoes for Rhodesia. The Shackleton's crew would then pass on this information to a flotilla of Royal Navy frigates that were there for the sole purpose of apprehending these 'pirates' and trying to show them the error of their ways.

On successful interception an exchange something like this would take place:

Royal Navy: 'I say you chaps, would you mind stopping a mo?'

Tanker: 'No, of course ve no stopping, vot do you vont?'

'What is your cargo?'

'Ve are a tanker, vot do you zink is de cargo?'

'I believe you are carrying oil!'

'Verry good, you no blind after all.'

'Which company owns the tanker?'

'Blitish Petloleum!'

'Oh I say! What is your port of destination?'

'Beira.'

'You cannot take a British oil tanker to Beira.'

'Why no?'

'It's not allowed.'

'Sez who?'

'Harold Wilson.'

'Who Halold Wilson?'

'The prime minister of Great Britain.'

'Plis to send message to Mr Halold viz our compliments.'

'What is your message?'

'Tell Mista Wilson fuck off, ve going Beira.'

'No need to be rude old boy, do you mind if we send a boarding party of our Royal Marine chaps? You are a British ship after all.'

'Piss off, no bootnecks on my boaty, matey.'

'We have your photograph taken by our surveillance aircraft this morning and your company is in breach of international sanctions against Rhodesia.'

'Go wipe your arses with your bloody phlotoglaph!'

'Oh, very well old boy, bon voyage then.'

The whole exercise was as futile as trying to change the laws of gravity but it went on unstintingly for several years at the expense of the good old British taxpayers. All because of a fit of pique by Mr Wilson and his Labourites! In the future they would add the word 'New' to the party name, but nothing much changed really.

Sometime in 1968 the Majunga detachment became the sole preserve of the brave boys from Ballykelly who shouldered the burden without complaint until the demise of the base in 1971. However, others had been there before to pave the way. One could say that they were the 'pathfinders' or more likely the 'brothel creepers'.

21

Something Lost, Something Gained

Norman was a young, innocent and unsullied soul making his way in the world of Coastal Command if such a world existed. He was now twenty-two and had never experienced the pleasures of the flesh. This was nothing to do with his religion, he had not taken a vow of chastity, nor was it something that he was proud of and he was determined to do something about it very soon. As luck would have it he was stuck in the desert regions of the world where even camels became desirable after a time.

It was 1966, at the initial stages of the Rhodesian oil embargo, code name Operation Mizar, and 37 Squadron based in Aden were charged with carrying out this onerous duty. Norman happened to be, by Royal Command, in the said locality of the Aden Protectorate as it was then known. At least, that's what the diplomats called it. To those who had to live and work there Aden was the arsehole of the world and the 37 Squadron Shackleton base at RAF Khormaksar was situated some twenty miles up it. It was therefore something of a blessing that the squadron had established a temporary detached base in Majunga on the tropical island of Madagascar from where they could exercise the wrath of Harold Wilson on the world's crude oil marine transportation business.

Life at Khormaksar was pretty sterile, as can be imagined, so when Norman was invited to go to Majunga to help change an engine on a marooned Shackleton it was an offer not to be refused, for two very good reasons. Firstly, it meant escaping from the sand flies for a few days, but more importantly, the person who invited him was large and persuasive as well as being a senior NCO. In addition, although somewhat unimportant, some comrades on the squadron had recounted to him in great detail their sexual exploits in Majunga where the local girls were 'user friendly'. This fact in no way influenced his decision to accept the invitation even though he was in pristine and virginal condition for a twenty-two-year-old male in the 1960s, when sex, drugs and rock and roll were being discovered all over the world – except in Aden. They say that 'if you can remember the 1960s – you didn't live the 1960s'; well, he must have been dead because he remembers every last day spent in this shit hole.

The little engine-change team of three along with a replacement engine set off southwards courtesy of Transport Command in an Argosy aircraft. This machine emitted a high-pitched whine from its turbo-prop engines and this, along with the nipple-shaped radar dome on the nose, led to it being nicknamed the 'Whistling Tit'.

The trip down to Madagascar was uneventful and Norman managed to sleep for most of the way in order to be rested and refreshed for the rigours that lay ahead. On arrival at Majunga the team were met by the guys who were there already on detachment and bombarded with the usual questions about home and loved ones. Sometimes they asked about wives, not always their own. Then would come the sports quiz:

'Ashes?'

'In Australia.'

'Five Nations?'

'In France'.

'Americas Cup?'

'Dunno!'

'World Cup?'

'Still going strong.'

After this exchange the veterans departed but not before inviting them out for few beers later on. The team collected their bits and pieces of luggage, boarded a minibus and were driven to the luxury of the Hotel de France in downtown Majunga. Unpacking took ten seconds and off they set back to the airfield to make a start on the job in hand. They worked until about seven o'clock and called it a day, then back to the hotel, a quick shower, change of drawers cellular and off to check out the bright lights in the town.

The veterans ensured that they saw all that there was to see in the town, which took about ten minutes, and then they repaired to Madame Chegal's for drink and anything else that came to hand. By about ten that night everybody was pissed and this hostelry was awash with hooting, roaring and the beginnings of a Coastal Command choral session which brought on some fits of laughing. The laughing being contagious, the locals were spontaneously convulsed without even realising the joke.

As the evening progressed and the drinks flowed, Norman could see that one of the girls, who he noticed had disappeared several times during the course of the evening, was showing a definite interest in him and the more he discreetly studied her the more enchanted he became with her enigmatic beauty. By about midnight he realised that this was truly a vision of loveliness the likes of which he had never before seen and it seemed, by her shy smile and coy looks in his direction, that she harboured similar feelings towards him. Could it be that this statuesque creature was one of those rare finds, exotically beautiful and also intelligent enough to observe in him something irresistible that others of her gender had missed up to now?

So captivated was he by the girl he failed to notice that the place was now almost empty, so before any of his drunken comrades still present could pre-empt him, he decided to take the bull by the horns. Plucking up the courage that only large quantities of drink can bring, he stood up to his full five feet two inches and stumbled his way to the table where she sat splendidly alone and aloof. With a mixture of schoolboy French and sign language he asked if he could join her. Just as well it was sign language as by this time he could hardly speak. She answered with a friendly smile and a flippant gesture indicating that he should sit in the chair nearest her.

'*Je m'appelle* Norman,' he said through thickening lips and tongue, brought on by the anaesthetic affects of alcohol.

'*Je m'appelle* Monique,' she said huskily as she held his gaze with the brown limpid pools that were her eyes. He wondered if he should be bold enough to kiss this vision of loveliness but she pre-empted him by kissing him on both cheeks. He was now doubly in love.

A waitress came and they ordered another beer for him and a glass of red wine for her. As he sipped the beer, he frantically tried to think of some other suitable subject for conversation that would suit his little bit of French and her non-existent English. While he was contemplating this dilemma she nonchalantly reached under the table and caressed his left thigh. By coincidence this is the side he 'dressed' and it therefore removed the need for conversation, which was just as well because he was wearing shorts and as her featherlight touch moved higher under his shorts the power of speech deserted him altogether and he could feel his eyes glazing over. Under other circumstances, in the Camel Club bar at Khormaksar for example, he would have felt great embarrassment at these proceedings. But tonight she was his and his alone. He was suspended in some sort of spell and couldn't have cared less what anyone else in the bar was thinking, which was in fact 'not a lot'.

While she carried on a conversation with a couple of her friends at the next table, she knew just how far to go with caressing his 'one-eyed bed snake' to avoid having it spit venom at her right there in public, so before he went into pre-ignition she removed her hand and indicated that they should leave the bar. Before standing up, however, he did check that nothing unseemly was peeking from the leg of his shorts. They were, after all, very short shorts.

As she supported him out of the place he was grateful to notice a full moon lighting up the night because streetlights were not a feature of this neighbourhood. It wasn't fear of mugging or an attack of some kind that made him glad of the light, because none of the veterans had ever felt any sort of threat from the locals although the 'Blancs Françaises' gave cause for concern. The veterans had let it be known that these abominable people were known to drop flowerpots on them when returning to the hotel late at night as they sung a spoof version of the French national anthem, the lyrics of which told the story of a Frenchman and some missing toilet paper. At least it was thought that they were flower pots but the contents were a bit dubious so they could have been something that resided under their beds. No, his gratitude was more to do with being able to see where his paramour was taking him because he had a feeling he would need to retrace these steps later to find a taxi to take him 'home'. However, in his befuddled state it was very unlikely that he would be able to find to his way to anywhere.

Arriving at her pad she lit a candle and from what he could see he thought it to be pretty basic but very clean and well kept. All the essentials were present although not exactly with all mod cons. Once his eyes became adjusted to the gloom of the low-powered lighting he could see that she was talking to someone and shaking him or her awake in the only bed that was in evidence. Once this person was awake and was hurriedly preparing to depart, he could see that it was an old man with grey hair and he was muttering to himself, no doubt pissed off that his sleep had been disturbed – probably for not the first time that night.

However, business was business and this was family business. Once the old man had departed the scene Norman could see that the bed was large enough for a rare romp, even to his inexperienced eye, and it was warmed by the departing occupant. It also did not escape his notice that she had acquired one or two little luxuries around the place that were not of local origin but appeared to be more of a Ministry of Defence, airmen for the use of, kind of import. This may indeed have been one of the first examples of a Foreign Aid Programme initiated by the UK government, albeit unwittingly. Whatever it was, he was happy to play his part in pioneering this entente cordiale and adding to the local economy by the business in hand.

For him, that night was like Christmas and he, like a child, spent all of it playing with his new toy, a toy which he has declared to be his favourite ever since and shall surely never be displaced. The time positively flew by and before you could say 'premature ejaculation' several times, the sun was streaming in through the gaps in the corrugated iron from which the cabin was built. He woke up drowsily at first but then his senses started to work and he heard a strange hissing sound coming from somewhere inside the hut. He sat up and looked around in the direction of the noise and there in the corner was his partner squatting over a bucket evacuating her bladder in a cloud of steam. She noticed him looking and merely smiled at him, at least he hoped that she was smiling and not grimacing at evacuating her bowel at the same time. He was bursting for a piss and when she had finished he took his place at 'La Toilette', thankfully there was no smell of excrement. Could this be one of the 'flower pots' he had heard about?

He leaped back into bed. The sunlight and morning sobriety had somewhat altered the appearance of his partner and her pad but he was too much of a gentleman to show it. Suffice to say he now observed a couple of points that had escaped his notice the night before, the least of which were her missing teeth, loss of the luxuriously long hair that was now hanging from the bed post, the squint eye, and the moustache. He thought her old man had sneaked back into the bed during the night! There were cockroaches running everywhere around the place, geckos looked at him suspiciously from the walls and ceilings and a trail of rather large and evil looking ants marched just above his head. It was a veritable zoo. Fuck it, he may as well get some more of his money's worth before departing so he closed his eyes, gritted his teeth and dived into the abyss once again.

Then something happened that he never thought would happen, he had to admit that he had had enough shagging for now. With all the window shutters tightly closed the sun soon made the room like an oven and he would have died for air conditioning and a shower. These, however, were luxuries that were not available so he made do with an all-over wash from a basin on a stand in the corner. By the time he was dressed she had somehow found a taxi for him, he did the necessary business transaction and they said their goodbyes. He didn't see her again before leaving Majunga but he has fond memories of that night and hopes she occasionally thinks of the youth who, many times, made up for his lack of expertise with the tremendous enthusiasm of the novice. Somehow there are doubts if she can remember any of her customers, enthusiastic or not.

The day saw the team at work bright and early and the engine change was completed by late afternoon. Everything was checked and double checked in readiness for departure to return this Shackleton to Aden and them with it. As soon as the aircrew were happy with the engine tests the plane took off into the evening sunset. When they could leave their take-off positions Norman found a place to settle down for the long flight. His choice was the port beam seat in the tail section, about halfway between the food preparation area, 'the galley', and waste disposal area, 'the crapper'. This made it easy for either end of the alimentary canal to be satisfied with the least effort – something that was very important to a fairy! He still had a smile on his face and a little stirring in his underpants as he remembered the previous night's activities.

Soon after reaching the top of the climb and going into the cruising altitude, dinner was served courtesy of one of the signallers taking his turn as in-flight caterer. When this culinary masterpiece had been seen off, the excesses of the previous couple of days began to take effect and Norman fell into a dreamless sleep, expecting to know nothing more before a wake-up shake as they approached Khormaksar.

He did get the wake-up shake from Harry the signaller but unfortunately they were still a long way from Aden. Instead the signaller looked a bit serious as he shook his shoulder and shouted something he had difficulty hearing due to the engine noise. When he eventually got the message he forgot all thoughts of sleep. The signaller was shouting and indicating that he should put on his Mae West lifejacket and go to his ditching position by the navigator's station. In this situation there is no point asking a silly question like 'Why?' so he headed forward towards the crew working area. To get there he had to pass through the galley where he found both of his team mates on their knees on the bottom rest bunk. They were not praying but looking intently out of the window so he squeezed between them and had a look. He immediately regretted it because the view was not encouraging; it was dark but the whole of this side of the aircraft was bathed in artificial light – the number two engine was on fire and bloody great flames were arching over the wing and trailing away behind them.

It's odd the kind of things that pass through the mind at times like this. Obviously the first was 'Oh fuck.' Second was 'It's actually true what we were told about airflow in the theory of flight lectures. The venturi effect that makes flying possible is being presented in living colour by the flames curving over the wing but never in contact with it.' But the most pressing question that kept rattling round his skull was 'Why the fuck don't they put it out?'

He remembered, at last, that he had a 'Biggles' headset and put it on to listen to the intercom conversation in the hope of getting some information about their problem and possible solutions. Nobody had to tell him it was serious, he'd worked that out all by himself, because sometime previously, at the end of 1964, a Mark 3 Shackleton from Kinloss had crash landed on Culloden Moor because of an uncontrollable engine fire, like this one was turning into.

Thankfully the fire was eventually extinguished and everyone started to feel a bit better but a problem still remained: the propeller would not feather. Pilots frequently practised flying and landing Shackletons on three engines as part of an ongoing mandatory training programme. In this exercise the propeller on a chosen engine would be feathered and the engine would be stopped, then the aircraft dumped on the deck – hence lots of experience doing it on 'three'.

Feathering meant turning the propellers edge-on to the airflow thereby reducing the amount of drag, or braking effect, produced by the propeller to the forward motion of the aircraft. Under normal operating conditions the pitch of the counter-rotating propellers was controlled by a constant speed unit which was a centrifugally controlled valve, mounted on the engine, that passed pressurised engine oil through an oil pipe installed through the counter-rotating propeller shafts to the propeller dome which activated the forwards and backwards motion of this dome against an internal sealed piston. The dome was connected to the three front propeller blades by a rack and pinion and therefore, as the dome moved, the pitch of the propeller was adjusted accordingly. The racks of the front propeller extended through the rear of the propeller housing and were connected to an ingenious device called a translation unit. The racks of the rear propeller blades were also connected to the rear of the TU. The TU was a bearing unit that housed its own oil reservoir as it was not part of the engine system. Its job was to translate the forward and backwards movement of the front blade racks to the rear blade racks that were being driven in the opposite direction.

Because the propeller feathering relied on engine oil pressure for operation, it is obvious that when the engine is stopped, by default, the propeller could not be feathered. This was taken care of by having a separate feathering pump located in the main oil tank that would supply oil pressure to feather the propeller when required. However, as is often the case, there was a certain flaw to this philosophy in as much that if all the engine oil was lost, in an engine fire for example, or the transfer oil pipe had been punctured, the propeller could not be feathered.

Unfortunately, whatever the reason, this was the case in this incident; the fire had been put out, the engine was stopped but the bloody propeller refused to feather so it continued to windmill in the airflow.

This was a double whammy as the increased drag reduced the air speed and made even more work for the other three engines. Gravity dictates that an aeroplane needs to maintain a given speed to remain airborne but they had reached a condition whereby they were still flying but gradually losing altitude. Decisions had to be taken to alleviate the predicament.

The most obvious solution was to reduce weight and suggestions were solicited. The favourite one was that the signallers, now that all the food had been cooked, were of little further use and should depart the aircraft, they probably had eaten more than anyone else so were the heaviest. However, this did not get the required majority vote so heads were bowed again in thought. There was nothing inside the aircraft heavy enough to make much of a difference and although there was some stuff hanging in the bomb bay, there was no way of releasing it to fall on some unsuspecting tribal village below. Ideas were submitted and discarded in turn, and for a while the favourite option appeared to be to ditch into the ocean, until the navigator pointed out that they were four hundred miles from the nearest water. Mae West has never been so surplus to requirements. Options were disappearing by the minute, the only answer was to find an alternative airfield and in the part of the world beneath them, and at this time of night, they were as rare as rocking-horse shit!

An invitation came from an airfield in Ethiopia with a hard sand runway but no landing aids. They offered to light some fires either side of the strip to help them down but after due consideration the captain declined with thanks and the search went on. After hanging on for what seemed another couple of centuries, Nairobi was roused and became a possibility, then a probability and finally the definite emergency landing destination. Not the common old RAF airfield at Eastleigh but Nairobi international civil airport, Embakasi. Now that a landing had been secured

183

the fuel could be jettisoned to help keep the kite flying. Without much further incident they landed at Embakasi at one am local time.

Civil airport meant bar, bar meant drink which in turn meant that the post-landing examination of the offending engine was necessarily cursory, not that the mess needed much looking at even in the dark! However, the wing was still intact so there was some hope of being able to fly the plane out of there sometime in the future.

In the bar the captain bought the first round which was thought by all to be a very gentlemanly gesture, since it was he who had faced the brunt of the emergency and got them there safely. Understandably, he might have expected to be supplied all night by the rest of them. They left the airport bar at five am, feeling no pain, in search of accommodation and ended up at a place on the outskirts of the city called the Spread Eagle Hotel, was this name an omen? It was not the most luxurious establishment but it was better than Aden and beat the hell out of a liferaft floating around the Indian Ocean.

Later that day they felt obliged to pay a visit to the Shackleton in the intensive care unit, only to arrive at the airport to find it had been stolen! Or at least, that's how it seemed because it wasn't where they'd left it. Their investigation into the mystery started at the offices of the RAF Transport Command detachment that operated Britannia aircraft from this airfield as part of the same campaign to keep peace in the area and oil out of Rhodesia. Their engineering officer soon confessed under interrogation that they had moved the Shackleton to a remote site during the night because it was 'an embarrassment' due to its fire-ravished appearance and the widening oil stain beneath it. The said babyfaced engineering officer was left in no doubt as to *their* opinion of *his* opinion and thereafter he did all he could to help. They were taken to the sick friend and ripped off a few panels to reveal the extent of the injuries. It was immediately obvious that nothing could be done in the short term to heal the wounds so they tidied up and returned again to the Spread Eagle for more poolside sustenance. For the historical record, the engine that was changed in Majunga was not the one that had externally combusted en route. A further four days passed hazily by before somebody remembered about them and they were transported back to Aden on an East African Airways flight.

During these four days Norman enjoyed another unexpected bit of 'luck'. One night in the hotel whilst wending his drunken way from the bar to his room at the end of a pleasant evening, he met a large local gent who had a young lady in tow. As their paths crossed in the corridor the large local gent grinned, pushed his lady friend in Norm's direction and made a gesture that he might want to accept his kind offer. She didn't appear to object to the arrangement so he accepted and took her to his room where nature took its course again, many times. How lucky could he be? He had waited twenty-two years to lose his virginity and here he was having his second shag in a week and he didn't even need to go chasing it. What a place! What a continent! He considered himself in heaven and admitted to making a real pig of himself that night as this girl was much younger and much more enthusiastic than the one in Majunga and she made better use of his weapon. Considering what came later, perhaps she was a 'Woman of Biological Destruction'?

During those days of idleness the happy band listened to the BBC World Service coverage of the 1966 football World Cup final, along with an Israeli El Al airline crew who were also in residence at the hotel. This crew booed and hissed loudly every time the German team got hold of the ball although they didn't seem to be actively supporting the other finalists, who were ultimately victorious, but whose nationality cannot be remembered and whose success has never been mentioned since.

On returning to Aden Norman's boss must have decided our man was good detachment fodder because in no time flat he was heading off to Sharjah, then a small staging post in the Trucial States situated on the Arabian Gulf which was up round the corner on the other side of the Saudi peninsula. The unhappy thing about Sharjah was the unavailability of female company, which made the invasion of small 'non-marine crustaceans' around his genital regions that occurred soon after he got there all the more surprising. Unless he had been recently interfered with one night unknowingly, whilst being 'tired, emotional and pissed', it must be concluded that the visitors were a strain from either Madagascar or Kenya – or both! However, this fact did him no good at all when he turned up on sick parade and told the medical orderly of his predicament. The orderly did not ask how long he had been in Sharjah and he gave him a very knowing look with pursed lips in the way that only practising homosexuals can do. If the orderly was on a recruiting drive he was out of luck. Our man had recently lost his virginity in one way but he sure as hell did not fancy losing it in the other!

22

Majunga Bound

I was to be part of a detachment to Majunga in 1970 and the normal way to travel was by RAF transport from RAF Lyneham in Wiltshire. Most of the rest of the detachment had travelled by this route some days before, however it was decided that I should be part of the groundcrew that would accompany a Shackleton down to Majunga. As there were no second-line servicing facilities near to the detached base, the Shackletons had to be changed out at regular intervals to ensure that they were kept in tip-top condition for the strenuous tasks they were involved in.

Because the trip to Majunga would take several days with stop-overs at Gibraltar, Malta, Khartoum, Nairobi before reaching Majunga, a full complement of groundcrew tradesmen would be required. This complement consisted of myself – engine fitter, Terry Waffal – electrician, 'The Reverend' Jimmy Curry – instruments, Steve Bentit – radar, John 'Bumbly' Barfly – armourer and Jimmy Asore – airframes.

This fine body of men would overcome all adversities that might present themselves en route and see the intrepid flying machine to its destination. The main adversity being the bars that were to be visited at each port of call.

We said our goodbyes to our loved ones and set off on the first leg of the journey down to Gibraltar early one morning. This was an uneventful trip and there were only minor snags to be cleared when we arrived, so the aircraft was left in the tender care of the resident 224 Squadron groundcrew, to prepare for the next morning's flight to Malta.

Early next morning we were on our way and again the journey to Malta was uneventful and I didn't even have a hangover to nurse, which was unusual on these trips. We arrived in Malta and again there were a few minor snags that had to be cleared. The aircraft was prepared for the onward journey.

186

We were to stay two nights in Malta so this gave us ample opportunity to make up for the one night of sobriety in Gib and we made good use of it. The NAAFI here at Luqa sold the cheapest drinks in the world and drink could be bought outside for peanuts. A veritable drinker's paradise!

After supper, we made our way to the NAAFI watering hole. Jimmy Curry was first up to the bar.

'What will you have?' says he.

'I'll have a pint of bitter.' says I.

The barman arrived. 'My friend here will have a pint of your best bitter and I'll have a half of Drambuie.'

'Very conservative drinking on behalf of my friend,' I thought.

The barman came back with the drinks. A pint of bitter and a sherry glass filled with the amber nectar. Jim's attention was elsewhere when the barman had asked for the payment. Jim turned round and looked at the drinks with disdain.

'What's that?' he said, pointing to the glass of Drambuie.

'That's your half of Drambuie, sir,' came the reply.

'I meant a half pint,' Jim retorted.

The barman's face grimaced and he went away to empty the best part of a bottle of Drambuie into a half pint mug. Jim paid the few shillings that were required and proceeded to sup his drink like it was beer.

We're in for trouble here, I thought.

I had another pint of beer while Jim finished his sweet sickly brew and then we caught a bus down to the area known to thousands of multinational servicemen as 'The Gut'.

The Gut was a street in Valetta town that ran down to the harbour and was the centre of debauchery on the island. There were bars filled with ladies of easy virtue and shops filled with duty-free goods but in essence it was all a bit of a sham. This was the place of renown where supposedly young maidens gave blowjobs to rampant servicemen under the bar-room tables for the price of a packet of duty-free fags. This was the stuff of legend where all the sailors sailed their ships in the bars and fucked all the women while sailing on the seas! This was the place that could rob you blind in seconds if you did not have your wits about you, and many young men woke up in the morning with raging hangovers and nothing else. It was, on the surface, titillating and tantalising but underneath it was sordid and seedy. This was 'Sin City' with not so much 'Sin' but more 'Take You In' and it was a major industry for the island.

The only sort that got a good deal out of The Gut were the rampant navy homosexuals and that was only because they were picking each other up in the bars which had nothing to do with the industry of The Gut. They only needed the use of a quiet corner for a few minutes to satisfy their lust!

One such bar on the street was the Silver Horse, affectionately known as the Galvanised Donkey. This bar was run by 'Precious', the biggest poofter of them all and he was a close friend of Sugar who ran Sugar's Bar in Gibraltar.

Jimmy and I had done the rounds of the other bars on the street and as was usual we were drawn inexorably towards the good old Galvanised Donkey. Jimmy by this time was well pissed and was bouncing off the walls as I tried to persuade him to just come back to the base. He would have none of this and, bent over, he was making his way up the hill as if being pulled by a magnet.

We had been in the bar for a few minutes when a crowd of people came in. It was obvious from the way they were dressed that they were Italians, and arty Italians at that. They were flamboyant, talked rapidly and very loudly and occasionally someone would burst into song for a few seconds.

I started to talk to one of the ladies who spoke good English. She was pretty in a buxom, dark-eyed, Mediterranean sort of way and was wearing a shawl around her shoulders. After we had been talking for some time she removed this shawl and revealed what was underneath. She was wearing an extremely low-cut dress that exposed a fair proportion of two orbs the size of watermelons. They were obviously very firm and not pushed together by any tight-fitting bra thereby revealing a very ample cleavage that did a lot of heaving up and down. I was very taken by this view and I could tell that she quite fancied me by the way that she kept brushing against me and touching my face at frequent intervals. I thought that it might be a lucky night in The Gut after all.

It turned out that she and her companions were an Italian opera company on a tour of the Mediterranean area. I told her that I liked Italian opera and we discussed the merits of *Tosca* and *La Bohème* among others. We also discussed whether Caruso or Pavarotti was the best tenor of all time. However, while I was very interested in the opera I was more interested in her heaving chest which she was displaying with great effect.

During this conversation, I had been keeping an eye on Jimmy. He had had another couple of drinks and was now slumped over the table in the corner of the bar. His head was turned to the side on the table and he had a contented grin on his face. He looked very satisfied with himself. My female companion made several references to Jimmy and she was concerned about the state of his health. I assured her that he might as well be in heaven as he was in his favourite state of inebriation. She found it incredible that one so young could get in that state, so I told her it took years of practice. She liked that.

One of her companions came across and jabbered to her in Italian. She turned to me and said. 'Someone has asked that we should sing. You pleeze excuse me for I go to sing here with my friends? You will listen?' I smiled and nodded my head. I went and sat near to where Jimmy was still relaxing on the table.

They started to sing, and opera sung at such close proximity was one of the most wonderful things that I have ever heard. The music was so touching that I had tears running down my cheeks. Now I was in heaven! The buxom lady was something of a diva as she sang solo parts unaccompanied by the rest. She kept singing directly to me and was making her message very plain for all to see. I was really chuffed at this attention and her probable intention.

They sang several songs on requests from the people in the bar and the more they sang the more people came in from the street and the applause was beginning to become deafening. The singing and the applause were having an effect on Jimmy who was stirring out of his stupor and was now sitting up staring around the room with one glazed eye, trying to focus on something or anything. When the singing was going on he would smile benignly while trying to keep his head still. In this he failed miserably and his body rocked back and forth completely unsynchronised with his head. When the applause started he tried to clap but he could not get his hands to make contact with each other and he would hold them out in front of him and look at them as if they were alien to him. He did laugh good-humouredly though and seemed quite content with life.

The company had sung their last song and were waving away requests to continue. The buxom lady came back over to the table. She was very flushed with her exertions and was dabbing her face with a wet handkerchief to cool herself down. I stood up and the tears were still running down my cheeks. She trotted into my open arms and she kissed me tenderly on both cheeks. I thought I had fallen in love, and the stirring in my trousers was evidence of this!

Just at this point, Jimmy stood up and the table with all its contents went tumbling to the floor with a terrible crash. This did not faze Jimmy at all as he had other things on his mind. I had turned round to see what had happened, and my arm was around buxom lady's waist. He somehow staggered out of the clutter on the floor and managed the couple of steps to where we were standing. Buxom lady was obviously shaken by this sudden movement but she need not have worried, as Jimmy did not mean any harm. I gave her a reassuring squeeze and she stood her ground.

Jimmy put his hands on buxom lady's shoulders, stared into the ample bosom and said, 'You're fuckin' beautiful, your singin' wiz fucking beautiful an you've got beautiful tits.' At that he promptly threw up the contents of his stomach right into her cleavage, which quickly filled up and overflowed down the front of her very expensive designer dress.

For a nanosecond she did not comprehend where this warm sensation had come from but when she realised what the drunken bugger had done she went ballistic! She pushed Jimmy away from her and he ended up in a heap on the floor among the spilled drinks and broken glass caused by his table-turning exercise. She pushed me away and stood there mortified and stunned with her arms outstretched, eyes nearly popping out of her head and her mouth open. She was silent for a moment and then she let out a blood-curdling scream that probably could be heard down the other end of The Gut.

I grabbed some napkins from a table and made to wipe the sick from her bosom, which was now covered in diced carrots and other unidentifiable solids. The whole sorry mess was steaming and the smell was acrid and horrendous. She would have none of it. She pushed my hands away and started to give me a tirade of very hot Italian combined with hand gestures that obviously showed what she thought of me and my mate. She rounded off the tirade by spitting at me. Luckily with all her shouting, she didn't have very much saliva left, but I got the gist of her intentions and I didn't think she was being very fair, as I personally had done nothing to offend her.

She turned away from me and some of her female companions came running over with towels and napkins to clean her up. A couple of the male variety came over and started to give me dog's abuse once again. There were a lot of hand movements again involving the particular upward thrust fist with the fingers touching and then the placing of the thumb nail behind the front teeth and clicking it forward. This I believe was a real threatening movement. I had had enough by this time and made as if to punch them and they ran off following the ensemble out the door. They were still looking back, still giving me dog's abuse and still gesturing as they went.

It was obvious that any treat that was in store for me that night was no longer available and I was now very pissed off. I shouted after them, 'I suppose a shag is out of the question then?' The door slammed shut.

I never saw buxom lady again and I realised that I didn't even know her name and, what was even better, she didn't know mine. I remember lightly kicking Jimmy before picking him up off the floor and getting him out of the bar.

However, things were not all bad because as I supported Jimmy along the street to the bus stop I found a ten-pound note lying on the pavement. I am still looking for the guy who lost this money. If he can give me details of when and how he lost it and the serial number of the note, I will willingly return it to him. I must be the only person ever to make a profit out of a night out in The Gut.

We didn't dare go off the base the next night and repaired to the NAAFI for a few bevvies, paid for by the money I had found. We got pissed on about ten bob.

The morning after, we were off to Khartoum.

23

Khartoum

The flight down to Khartoum was uneventful and boring. Not quite so boring as flying over the sea as there were things to look at while flying over the desert at an altitude of a few thousand feet. There were the myriad camel tracks, there was the sand and then there was the occasional clump of green foliage. Then eventually there was the mighty Nile that we followed south until we reached our destination: Khartoum, the capital city of the Sudan and witness to some of the very best traditions of the glorious British Empire.

Khartoum, where General Gordon had withstood the siege of the Mad Mahdi in the late nineteenth century and lost his life there when the Dervishes sacked his palace. Khartoum, where the glorious British expeditionary relief column under the command of Lord Kitchener eventually sailed up the Nile to defeat the Mad Mahdi and his Dervish army at the battle of Omdurman just across the Nile from Khartoum. They were only two days late from being able to save poor old Gordon!

Khartoum had been governed by the British for the past eighty or ninety years and had become very prosperous as a result. It was the stuff of legend and derring-do, now in the hands of a Communist junta who were kicking all the colonials out and, as a result, leaving the land to revert to desert.

We landed in the late afternoon and as soon as the aircraft hit the runway the temperature inside soared and everyone scrambled to open every available door and window just to get a bit of air circulation. In the case of the Shackleton, air conditioning had not been invented yet but the four big fans on the front of the aircraft could shift air throughout the cabin.

The aircraft was taxied to a remote part of the airfield and the engines were stopped. Immediately the temperature seemed to soar another twenty degrees. The steps were positioned and the cabin was evacuated by all in a very short space of time, with shouts of 'Ya bastard, feel that heat!'

We were met by the British chief engineer of the airfield who was there to enquire what we needed in the way of services before we took off the next day. We told him of our fuel and oil requirements and the need of an electrical generator if he had one with the same socket connector. Fuel he had but the heavy grade of oil that we required he didn't. He said there wasn't much need for it as he had never seen a maritime reconnaissance aeroplane in the middle of the desert. I scratched my head and wondered who the hell organised these stopovers and the stores requirements?

I checked the oil tanks and luckily they were more than half full, having used only about five or six gallons on the journey down from Malta. I hoped that they would not use more than this on the next leg down to Nairobi as I would hate to ditch in the wilderness and be eaten by lions or baboons, or even worse, cannibals.

We were also met by a chap from the British Consular Office and he fussed around organising the transportation and handing out the immigration forms that had to be filled in. Christ, it would take us all night to answer all the questions and we were only there for a few hours.

We completed the servicing on the aircraft and were transported to the immigration office where in addition to answering all their questions we had to produce all the money that we had individually and this was counted and handed back to us. Mine did not take long to count! The money was to be counted on the way out of the country and any expenditure had to be accounted for. It didn't seem likely that there would be any great expenditure here in any case.

By the time that we had finished with immigration and customs it was getting dark. The BCO chap was hovering around very excitedly to get us into the transport to the hotel. I don't think he had seen any strangers here for ages and wanted to make the most of the company.

We were transported to the Port Sudan hotel which is situated at the confluence of the Blue and White Niles. Very old English colonial place and a bit tattered at the edges but it did have air conditioning in some rooms and it was nice to get out of the heat that had become quite oppressive but was now beginning to cool off with the onset of evening.

We went up to our allocated rooms, showered, changed and were back down stairs in a trice. The bar was beckoning and a couple of cool pints on expenses before dinner would go down a treat.

After dinner we went back into the bar which was full to bursting and it seemed that every expatriate in Khartoum wanted to speak to the strangers from the 'old country'. The main theme was how harshly the government was treating them. Some of them were fourth or fifth generation Sudanese and ran successful businesses around the country. Some had estates growing tobacco and foodstuffs. And then there were others who thought they would be in for a few free drinks from the strangers. Little did they know that we were penniless ambassadors of Coastal Command and it was us that bummed the drinks – and we managed to get a fair few that night.

The government was throwing these people out of Sudan and all they were allowed to take with them was four thousand pounds! They were desperate and wanted to give us all sorts of money and goods to take out of the country, not specifically for themselves but just to stop the government getting their hands on their treasures. I think that when they heard that a British military aircraft had landed they thought the British government had reverted to 'gunboat diplomacy' and that we were sent to be their saviours. I was very tempted with some of the offers but the intensity of the authoritarian procedures to let us into the country foretold of the procedures to let us out again and as I didn't want to end up in some black hole prison in Khartoum, I declined. This engendered some very long faces as it seemed that we were probably their last hope. Poor buggers!

Next morning we were up bright and early to get into the plane and into the air before the sun had a chance to burn the arse off us. Our chap from the BCO was there with the transport to take us to the airport and clear us through immigration once again. He handed us papers that had to be filled in for our escape. These were the replicas of the ones that we had filled in the night before. Bureaucracy gone mad!

We cleared the procedures and this allowed us out to the aircraft and as we approached something did not look quite right. The port main wheel tyre was as flat as a pancake. How the hell had this happened? Somebody blamed the BCO chap as he wanted to keep us there for the company.

Jim Asore, the airframe fitter whose responsibilities included toilets and tyres, thought that it was probably a leaking valve, so he would change this and blow the tyre up again. I went off to find the airfield engineer to ask him for an air compressor. We hitched a compressor up to his Land Rover and towed it out to the plane. Jim had just finished letting the remaining air out of the tyre and had changed the valve. We offered the air connector on the compressor airline to the valve and the bloody thing would not fit. It was too small! What to do now?

194

The airfield engineer thought that he might be able to modify the hose to make it fit onto the valve. He disappeared with the compressor to see what he could do.

The aircrew arrived at the aircraft and were told the 'good' news. They hurriedly re-embarked onto the bus and disappeared to some air-conditioned grotto somewhere.

We hung around the plane for about an hour and the engineer came back with the compressor onto which he had managed to fit a larger connector that miraculously fitted the tyre valve. My heart soared at the thought of getting away from here.

The compressor was started and passed air into the tyre. We all stood around expectantly to watch the tyre being inflated. Nothing happened! There was definitely air going into the tyre but just as much must have been passing out. Bastard!

By this time it was becoming very hot indeed and the sun was so strong that it felt very uncomfortable being in direct light. A bit like Dracula waking up early in the morning with a hangover and the sun pouring in through his window, and beginning to turn to dust.

Jim thought that it was because the weight of the aircraft was pressing down on the flat tyre and was perhaps partially pushing it off the wheel rim that the tyre would not inflate.

We asked the engineer if he had a jack that we could use to slightly lift the aircraft to take the weight off the tyre. We took some measurements of different positions that would accommodate a jack and he disappeared once again in his Land Rover.

He came back in a few minutes towing a large under-wing jack. Jim stripped off the wing jacking point panels and we tried the jack. Miraculously once again it was perfect and it was indeed a Shackleton jack that had been used here when the aircraft had been on hot temperature trials in the fifties. They could not have chosen anywhere hotter. We started to pump the jack handle and the piston extended up to the jacking point but once it encountered the weight of the aircraft, it refused to extend any further. The bloody thing had not been used in years and the hydraulic pump seals were probably dried out and knackered. It was getting even hotter and sweatier now after all this exertion.

The engineer thought that there might be some suitable seals and O rings in the store if we wanted to strip down the pump and fix it. We had no other option so we removed the jack, hitched it up to the Land Rover and headed for the workshop. We were glad to get there as there was a cool water dispenser which was put to good use for drinking and dousing.

With the help of a very competent local employed mechanic called Ahmed we stripped the pump down and replaced the seals with some that were of dubious origin but seemed to fit quite nicely. The pump was reassembled, primed and bled and we were on our way back to the aircraft once again. It was about eleven o'clock by this time and it was very hot and oppressive.

The jack was repositioned under the wing and the handle was pumped again. This time the piston extended and continued to do so once it had contacted the jacking point. Eureka!

It was very hard work pumping the handle. To lift a forty-ton aircraft full of fuel off the deck takes a lot of energy and taking it in turns in this heat soon sapped the strength out of us. But millimetre by millimetre the bloody thing was moving and the weight was coming off the tyre.

We had been at it for about an hour and it seemed that there was sufficient gap between the wheel rim and the ground to allow another go with the compressor.

The compressor was started and air passed into the tyre once again. After about half an hour the bloody tyre still had not begun to inflate. Was there something wrong with the compressor? The only way we could test it was by connecting it to the other tyre valve and see if it would pump this tyre up. This was done and the tyre pressure started to rise progressively. Nothing wrong with the compressor.

We went back to raising the jack once again and got it up to a height where the undercarriage oleo leg was fully extended but the tyre was still marginally touching the ground. The jack was fully extended at this point so it had to work.

The airline was reconnected and the compressor started to pump air into the tyre. We decided to let it run for much longer this time to ensure that we were not being fooled by the amount of air that was required for the inflation exercise. We waited and waited but nothing happened. We felt all round the tyre but we could not tell where the leak was. We got some water and laced it with washing up liquid and poured this all over the wheel and tyre to see where the leak was, but there was no indication at all. Bastard!

We were all very dejected that we were facing the possibility of failure to get away from this place. What else could be done?

By this time it was very, very hot and every one of us was filthy and sweating. It then occurred to us that the bloody aircrew had not even had the decency to come out to see how we were doing, nor had they brought us any sustenance and we were starving and somewhat demoralised that our efforts had produced nothing. The buggers had not even left any flight rations when they scuttled away from the scene some hours before.

We got a lift into the flight operations building to try to find something to eat and drink and to gather our thoughts once again, out of the heat. There was a shower adjacent to the room where we were ensconced and we took it in turns to dive into this to cool down and get rid of the worst of the carbon and rubber dust from the filthy tyre. I personally was beginning to hate that bloody tyre.

After the shower we felt much better and someone had produced some food and drinks from somewhere and we felt even better still.

The captain came in for an update. It was good of him to bother. He seemed almost agitated that we were inside and not fixing the problem.

'What's next then?' he enquired.

Jim summed it up thus. 'I can't remove the wheel as we can't get enough height on the jack and even if I did remove the wheel and managed to inflate the tyre we couldn't get it back on because of this height problem. We can't see where the leak is, so unless there is a puncture at the bottom of the tyre that we cannot see, I am wondering if it could be a crack in the wheel hub? In that case there is no point in taking the wheel off before we have another to replace it. Apart from continuing to pump air into the bloody thing I don't see what else can be done. We just don't have the equipment to do the job, sir. I think we have to issue an Aircraft on Ground report.'

'Well, think about it a bit more before we go that far. There is no hurry to issue an AOG at this stage.' He departed.

It should have taken a nanosecond to think about it. There was no way that we could do anything else.

We sat around for another few minutes and we did try to consider other actions. The only thing we were not sure about was the possibility of the puncture being on the bottom of the tyre. We decided to try to lever the wheel round so we could get a look at this area. We went to see Ahmed and he gave us a couple of long crowbars to lever the wheel round.

We tried every way possible to move that bloody wheel but to no avail as the tyre was too thick to allow the flattened section to reform and revolve. It was as if it was stuck to the ground like some great slug.

We quickly gave up as we realised that even if we found a puncture, we could not do anything about it – we were AOG. We let the jack down and removed it. The plane looked very forlorn leaning over quite significantly as if it had broken its leg.

We went back to the flight operations building and Jim went to report the latest to the captain. The only thing on our minds at this time was how long we would be marooned in this God-forsaken hole. We took another shower.

We had to clear immigration once again and this meant filling in yet another bloody form which was a dead ringer for the one that we had filled in when we arrived and when we had cleared this morning. The chap from the BCO was still there and I am sure he was smiling. He had organised the transport once again to take us back to the Port Sudan hotel. On the way to the hotel he explained that the consulate had arranged temporary membership for us at the Sudan Club and that he was taking us there first so we could sign in and get membership cards to use as we wanted.

We were taken to this place of social sanctuary in a country that was becoming extremely hostile to such decadence, greeted by the club manager and given a tour of the facilities which included the only swimming pool available to us south of Cairo. We were shown the bar and the only question that was asked in the whole tour was 'How much is the beer?' It was about half the price that we had paid in the hotel the night before so for the first time that day there were smiles on faces. We duly signed in as temporary members and were given cards with our names on them. Bills were to be settled before our departure. Heaven!

We went back to the hotel, showered once again, changed into civvies, got our swimming trunks and headed downstairs to the waiting car that had been placed at our disposal. 'Sudan Club please' to the driver, and we were off. This is the game!

The Sudan Club was the epitome of all things colonial. It had obviously been allowed to become a little dilapidated around the edges. The furnishings were fifty years out of date, faded, frayed and well used. The attitude of most of the members was more like a hundred years out of date and just as colonial as the surroundings. Waiters were summoned by either shouting for them at the top of one's voice and then shouting at them once they appeared to make them understand the order, or by loud clapping and then shouting at them if they did not respond quickly enough. This method of treatment had obviously evolved since the establishment of the club many years ago but it had significantly failed to make the waiters move any faster for their grand masters.

We lowly airmen who had not had the benefit of an English public school education, where corporal punishment was a major hobby and boys took A-level exams on the subject, were a little more reserved in our treatment of these beleaguered black workhorses. Catching their eye with a wave of the hand or a nod of the head gained a far quicker response, but still the shouting went on.

We went out to the pool, primarily to have a swim but also to eye up any totty that might be hanging around. Visions of air hostesses or BCO secretaries in skimpy bikinis were soon dashed. The only totty were mainly married matrons with upper-class screeching accents, horsy faces, varicose veins on their large thighs and cellulite on their fat arses. They would spend the day running after spoiled brats who were not yet old enough to withstand the rigours of public school three thousand miles away.

However, the water in the pool was heavenly in the early evening air and washed away the traumas of the day. The beer was even better!

We went back to the hotel and the captain informed us that in communication with HQ they had said it would take at least seven days to get a new wheel out to us. Seven fucking days – in this place! It defied contemplation.

We went into dinner and bemoaned our sorry lot. The chap from the BCO came and joined us in the bar after dinner and asked if we would like to have a tour of the city the next morning. We agreed and thanked him.

24

The Battle of Omdurman

The next morning we were up bright and breezy. It was a beautiful day – again! We had breakfast and sat around the hotel waiting for our tour guide to arrive. The main conversation between us was of the burst tyre and was there anything else that could be done to get us out of here, but it was generally agreed that we were snookered.

The chap finally arrived at about ten-thirty and we filed outside to find that he had brought two open-backed Land Rovers for our sight-seeing trip around the town. We got ourselves loaded into the vehicles and off we went. It was hot as we passed along the tree-lined roads next to the Nile.

We stopped next to one of General Gordon's steam-driven gunboats that was still moored up to a little jetty. It looked very isolated and was definitely of a past era. It reminded me of the little boat in the film *The African Queen* and I could envisage Humphrey Bogart stoking the boiler on this vessel and having to kick the relief valve to stop the bloody thing blowing up. All very romantic but this boat had probably seen some terrible carnage during the episode of the siege of Khartoum, some eighty years before. How the boat had survived at all was a mystery. Probably some eccentric colonial chappie had purloined it as a picnic boat and had kept it river-worthy.

We went on down the avenue and then crossed the Nile by bridge into Omdurman, then through the town and out into the desert where the main battle had been fought with the Mahdi. While we were going through this ramshackle town, we were plagued by gangs of children chasing after the trucks and asking for *baksheesh*. Poor little buggers, they obviously had never seen a bar of soap or a pair of shoes in their short lives. Although they were very black, the dirt and sand gave them a whitish sheen and every one of them had snot running out of their noses, also sand encrusted and covered in flies. We had nothing to give them.

There was not very much to see at the so-called battle site as the shifting sands had probably shifted significantly over the intervening period. There were no dead bodies lying around or any old rifles, so any battle scene had to be conjured up in the mind's eye. I could only think of good old Corporal Jones in 'Dad's Army' shouting 'They don't like it up 'em, you know!'

Winston Churchill took part in the cavalry charge at this battle and he declared that this was the last great battle of this type. Little did he know, nor did we, that he was to be proved wrong.

We saw the Mahdi's tomb. He wasn't at home at that time as he had died in the relief of Khartoum shortly after General Gordon was killed. Lord Kitchener who was late for the party had the Mahdi's body cremated and the ashes thrown in the Nile.

We made our way back through the town and now we were going against the light breeze, such as it was, the temperature was unbearable. The faster the Land Rover went, the hotter it got, and we were being desiccated sitting high up in the back.

The driver was asked to slow down but sedate driving was not part of his philosophical make-up. Any part of the body that was exposed to the sun was being burnt, even through clothes. Clothes stuck to our bodies with salt as the liquid sweat had rapidly evaporated. It was painful peeling the material away from the skin, and this had to be done continuously. Christ, it was hot and there was no shade in the back of this bloody truck.

To make matters worse, when we were on the outskirts of the town, near the camel market, the same bloody children that had greeted us so warmly on our way into the place were waiting and started to throw bricks at us. At least, at first we thought they were bricks but it turned out to be lumps of camel or goat shit or possibly even human. It did not smell very much as most of it had been dried out, as we were ourselves, and it was rock hard. However, some of it was quite fresh and soft. There were so many of them that the drivers had to virtually stop the trucks so we were subjected to this barrage of shit and we had no protection from it. The only thing we could do was to throw their shit back at them and a real battle ensued for several minutes. The longer we were there, the more of the buggers arrived and we were in real danger of being the first British military in history to be shitted to death, although by no means the first to be up to our necks in it.

We urged the driver to get going through this throng and he started to ease forward, revving the engine hard as he went. With this and blowing the horn, the crowd dispersed somewhat. It might have been that they were beginning to run out of ammunition as most of it was in the trucks by this time. We kept urging the driver on and finally he got the message and started to drive fast once again to get away from these abominable brats. This made the evaporation process worse again and we had to get him to slow down once we were safely out of throwing range. The tailgate of the Land Rover was let down while we were moving and the worst of the shit was kicked out, but the soft stuff was splattered around and some was on skin and clothes. Ugh! We were not amused and were happy to get back across the river into 'civilisation'.

We were driven round the town a bit and went to the Austrian Embassy building where General Gordon 'copped his whack'. The Khartoum garrison had been under siege for months and had withstood privations and skirmishes during this time. After today's incidents in Omdurman, I knew how it felt.

25

The Zoo

Apart from going up to the Sudan Club for a swim, there was little to do during the day. There was even a restriction on taking pictures around the place in case they revealed establishments of military significance, like bridges. The British had been around for a hundred years or more so one would think that all the military establishments were known to them. After all they built the bloody military establishments! However, no one wanted to end up in jail so very few pictures were taken by our happy band.

Just behind the Port Sudan hotel there was a zoological garden. It was never advertised anywhere as being a place to visit but we knew it was there – we could hear the animals at night and what's more we could smell them during the day.

Terry Waffal and I elected to go for a walk one afternoon, having been cooped up in the hotel all day. We strolled down the avenue outside the hotel to the actual place where the two mighty Nile rivers meet. It was quite fascinating to see the waters from the different directions coming together. The White Nile from the south is so-called because of all the silt, sand and shit that it brings down from the plains of Africa. The Blue Nile is so-called because of all the black silt that it brings down from Ethiopia. At the confluence, it is quite fascinating to see that the two rivers do not merge. The White Nile flows predominantly on the Omdurman bank side and the Blue Nile stays on the Khartoum side. It takes hundreds of miles before they fully merge.

Once we had contemplated this fact, we walked on round the corner on the banks of the Blue Nile. We had not gone very far when we saw the gates to the zoo. Having nothing better to do we decided to go in. Terry had his camera with him as he was becoming more emboldened the longer we stayed in the place.

We paid the few pennies entrance fee to get into the zoo, which seemed very dilapidated and not very clean. However, it had probably been like this for years.

In the middle of a pedestrian square there were elephant tusks piled twelve feet high. Every tusk was numbered in white paint. There were some tusks eight feet long and some were only about a foot long. There were hundreds of them. These tusks had been confiscated from poachers and were to be burned to stop them getting into the ivory trade. I felt very sad at the thought of all the elephants that had been killed in support of this evil trade and this would only be one pile out of many around the continent.

There were not many animals in the zoo and those that were there looked pretty mangy and sad. Not a very uplifting experience to see them like that.

There was a flock of ostrich running around a corral that was surrounded by a low-slung fence. They seemed to be fairly friendly beasts and were curious as all ostrich are and they searched around the bodies of anyone that got close enough obviously smelling for food in pockets or bags. We had nothing to give them.

Terry wanted to have a photo taken with these birds. We didn't think that they were of military significance so it would be OK. Terry got himself up against the fence and immediately the birds started to crowd together and their heads were going everywhere around his torso. He looked like he was being attacked by a mythical multi-headed Hydra.

After I took the picture with him standing in the middle of all this activity one of the birds had obviously become a bit disappointed at not finding anything edible. It turned round and shat all over Terry! I don't know if the bird was suffering from some sort of bowel upset or whether this was a normal defecation; all I do know is – thank the Lord that the buggers don't fly!

Terry's back was covered in this greenish shit very similar to a cow pat and it smelled just as bad. He just stood there as the full impact of what had happened dawned on him and he gave a physical shudder as the hot liquid permeated his shirt and shorts. The shirt was quickly removed.

We hurried back to the hotel where the staff greeted us enthusiastically but soon backed off when they got a whiff of Terry. We tried to explain that it was an ostrich that had done it and flapped our arms about and used our arms as an imitation of the ostrich neck and head, but I bet none of them had ever been to the zoo and didn't know what an ostrich was. With our gesticulations, they probably thought that we were trying to imitate a flying elephant and they looked nervously skywards.

They looked at him very suspiciously as he made his way through the foyer with the rear of his shorts covered in shit. I looked back and they were hysterical with laughter although good grace would not allow them to laugh aloud.

It seemed that we were destined to be shat upon in this town.

26

The Consular Party

After having been been in town for a few days, we were invited to a garden party at the Consul General's pad. At first, none of the groundcrew wanted to go to the party as we thought it would be a lot of standing around with a sherry and then the bum's rush out the door. However, as we could not answer the question 'Well, what else will you be doing?' we decided that it might be a bit of a wheeze and there might just be a bit of totty to latch onto. So our acceptance was duly given to the chap from the BCO and he passed it on.

On the night of the party we were well scrubbed and dressed in our best attire, slacks, shirt and tie. The chap from the BCO sent cars down to the hotel to pick us up and we slid off into the evening. When the car arrived at the gates of the house, the security guard glanced inside and waved the driver on. We were then treated to the spectacular sight of the residence and the gardens.

The house itself was like a small colonial palace with turrets and minarets and the garden was vast and filled with all manner of trees and plants. We could see all of this because the whole place was lit by what must have been a thousand lights strung from the house, every tree and shrub. In the middle of all this was a gazebo and paved area that was also bedecked with lights but more importantly with tables loaded with all sorts of food, and more importantly still – drink! Our eyes must have been like snooker balls as we took in this wondrous sight.

We were deposited in the middle of all this where we were greeted by the Consul General accompanied by his beautiful and charming wife. They were probably in their forties and they both looked very healthy and happy. They shook hands with us, asked us to make best use of the food and drink and said that they would mingle later.

They had no need to worry about the amount of food that she had obviously been up all night preparing. We were becoming tired of the same old menu in the hotel and needed some good old buffet sustenance.

As at all of these occasions, everyone is a little reticent to make a move for the food and drink. However this was taken care of by a veritable army of robed and turbaned waiters to cater for every whim. There were food waiters carrying great trays of delicious spiced foods and trays of sausage rolls and chicken wings and sandwiches and a multitude of other offerings. The drinks waiters were everywhere. The first to approach asked what we wished to drink. When told 'beer' he replied, 'Yes sir, but what kind of beer would you like?'

'Well, what kind do you have?'

'There are cans of Tennants, McEwans, there's Stella, Allsops, Star, Guinness in bottles and Bass on draught.'

We must have died and gone to heaven!

Some time later the CG came over and started to chat. It transpired that I had gone to school with one of his wife's nephews. Small world! Mrs CG came across a little later after he departed. He must have told her about the coincidence and we exchanged tales and tried to find out if we had other mutual acquaintances, as she was originally from Perthshire. As she was a bit older than me we could not expand on this but we had a good natter anyway about the town of Crieff and surrounding district. She was really charming. I could see that I was getting jealous looks from some of the others as it appeared that I was monopolising the lady and she occasionally put her hand on my arm as we cracked a joke between us. She finally left.

The guys started to filter back around once again asking what we had been talking about. I told them we had a mutual interest in astral physics.

Jimmy Curry reappeared on the horizon and seemed to be fairly pissed, which was nothing new but we had only been there for about an hour and a half – far too little time for Jimmy to get drunk on beer. However, he was holding a pint mug half full of what looked like beer.

'See this place, this place is fuckin' great, see this drink? This drink is fuckin great!' He said as he thrust the mug under my nose. It was neat whisky.

'Where the hell did you get that?' I asked.

'Ah just asked the waiter fir a whisky and he asked me how I would like it so I just asked for it in a pint mug with a couple of ice cubes an' this is what I got,' said he as he staggered about the lawn.

I remembered The Gut in Malta and had no wish to see a repeat performance, even if it was only on the immaculately manicured lawn. I resolved to keep an eye on the boy.

I ordered another beer and sat with Jimmy on a remote bench in an effort to keep him away from the main body of the party as he was becoming a bit loud. By the time he had finished the drink he was well out of it and was beginning to stagger even while sitting down and one eye was at the closing stage. Time to go, I thought. It was a pity because this was the first time that we had really sat outdoors in the evening and it was really pleasant. Perhaps I was becoming acclimatised once again.

I was asking the head waiter if he could call for a car to take us to the hotel when I was approached by a tall man who spoke with a foreign accent.

'Excuse me, I overheard you asking for a car. Your friend looks like he is in a bit of a state. Can I offer you a lift home? I am just about to leave myself and my car is just over there.' He pointed to a rather large, sleek, black Mercedes.

With the state that Jimmy was in and with the quality of the car, I hesitated, but my new friend assured me that if anything happened, it would be all right. So I kicked Jimmy to wake him up a bit and told him that we were leaving and that he should not make a fuss. Some hope!

The whisky had mainlined to the brain by this time and 'When the drink's in – the wit's out.' Jimmy stood up, downed the rest of the whisky in the mug and immediately demanded more whisky at the top of his voice.

'Ah need mair drink, you're not takin' me awa frae the drink, ya rottin' bastard.'

I signalled to the other guys that we should get hold of him and restrain him. This was done and Jimmy was grabbed by his legs and arms and unceremoniously carried across the lawn face down, all the while shouting for more drink He was poured into the back of the Mercedes, which had a back seat and two dickie seats that pulled up from the floor. We all bundled in after him and continued to constrain him as he was determined that he was going back for more drink. He was shouting at the top of his voice.

The car took off and purred its way down the drive. In the headlights, there was the silhouette of the Consul General accompanying a robed black gentleman who was the Sudanese Minister of Defence – we had been advised earlier that he was to be there. These two gentlemen were surrounded by a group of large security men, a couple of whom stepped out of the shadows and indicated that the car should stop. They signalled that the driver should wind his window down.

This was a signal for Jimmy to try to escape once again and once again he was restrained but we could not get him to shut up. He was still shouting at the top of his voice, 'You can't keep me in here, you black bastards! I want mair drink.'

This was a common phrase used by our Jimmy and not directed at the people outside the car as he would have been oblivious to the fact that there were any black people within earshot. However, the reaction of the security man on the driver's side was to thrust his Uzi machine gun through the window and order everyone out of the car. We obeyed in very quick time, bundling Jimmy out the door causing him to trip and run headlong into a rhododendron-type bush.

'Agh, you black bastard!' he cried as he tried to untangle himself from the dense undergrowth. The rest of us stood there with our hands in the air, not daring to say a word.

'Who is dis man?' asked the security man pointing his gun at Jimmy.

'Eh, please excuse him, he's very drunk and doesn't realise what he is saying. I apologise for him. We're leaving before he makes a complete arse of himself,' I replied.

'Looks like he make fool of himself already,' the security man was giggling at Jimmy's antics trying to extricate himself from the bush, most of which he was wearing by this time.

The CG had left the Minister of Defence and was approaching the car.

'What's the matter, sergeant? Why have you stopped my guests from leaving?'

The sergeant was almost helpless with laughing and tears were running down his cheeks. He took a couple of deep breaths before he could answer.

'Dis man here was shoutin' abuse in di car an' ah thought he might be dangerous for di minister. He don look so dangerous now though!' He returned to his laughing.

'Please pick up your friend and leave before you start an international incident,' said the CG with a smile on his face. He too had caught sight of Jimmy in the bush.

We picked Jimmy up and brushed him down as much as possible. As we were doing this he caught sight of the sergeant.

'Oh, who's a big boy then with playing with a little pop gun?'

I shrugged my shoulders at the sergeant and we bundled Jimmy back into the car, quickly followed by ourselves. We shouted our thanks and goodnights to the CG, gave a cursory salute to the sergeant and sped out of the gates.

'Hey man, that was a close shave. Ah was shittin' myself,' declared our driver. 'You don't piss around with these guys, they can be very trigger happy. Your friend is lucky he didn't get that Uzi stuck up his arse and his brains blown out. He's one lucky bastard ah can tell you.' He shook his head in disbelief.

After a little while Jimmy fell asleep. The driver said, 'My name is Ad Overdulve, I'm Dutch and I own a tobacco farm from which I am to be deported within the next couple of days. Can you believe that? I have lived here all my life and my father before me and the bastards are throwin' us off our land. Where do you want to go now?'

'You may as well just take us to the Port Sudan hotel and come in for a drink with us.'

'Christ no, we don't want to pay those prices for a drink, we should go to the Sudan Club if you want to drink some more.'

My initial thoughts were about taking Jimmy into the club in the state he was in, but I relented anyway. 'OK, let's go there then.'

We arrived at the gates of the club and were waved through. Obviously the car and driver were well known around these parts.

When we had got ourselves settled in the bar and Jimmy was ensconced in an armchair fast asleep, Ad said to the barman, 'All the drinks for these gentlemen are to be put on my tab all night, OK?' The barman nodded.

'That's very generous of you,' I said as I contemplated how much this could cost him.

'Well, if I must leave with only a few pounds in my pocket ah might as well spend some of it now.' I could see the reasoning behind this and was grateful for it.

There were only a handful of people in the whole club, and apart from ourselves there was no one else in the bar. It was all very staid and proper.

Ad recounted some tales of life in Khartoum and the Sudan and we had a few drinks. We had some more drink and then the singing started, quite quiet at first but each successive song got louder. After about the third song which was probably the 'Irish Rover' the bar started to fill up. Lord knows where the people were coming from, but in they came and started to applaud and call for more singing, as if we needed any encouragement for that. We had probably repeated our repertoire twice over, and by this time we were probably so drunk as to not remember how many times we had sung each song.

Some aircrew came in and looked on with a certain degree of jealousy as we were plied with unpaid for drinks and they were nursing a half pint of beer. The bar was in an uproar with everyone joining in the choruses. We had just finished a song when a little old lady came up to me. She was one of three old ladies who had come in to the bar and had sat at a table by the window. They looked like they had been around when Gordon was there. They were all dressed in chintzy dresses and buckled shoes and had grey hair tied back in a bun. This lady had a great big smile on her face and her eyes were sparkling and I thought they were wet with tears.

She said, 'Oh we haven't had a night in here like this since peace was declared in 1945, it has been wonderful. Thank you all very much. To finish off the night, do you think there would be a fourth for bridge?'

'Have you been waiting for a fourth for bridge since 1945 as well?' I enquired jokingly.

'No, not really but our oldest sister Emily passed away some ten years ago and we have struggled to get a fourth since then. We don't go out much you see.'

'I'll come and play a couple of rubbers if you like but I'm a bit drunk so don't chastise me if I make a mistake – and no flirting with me, I'm a married man.'

She giggled and blushed. I told her my name and we set off to meet the other two sisters. There was Mildred, Joan and Agnes. While the conversation was pleasant, it was somewhat stilted due to the utter concentration on the game and of course there was the normal in-depth analysis after every hand. I felt like I was Omar Sharif sitting in on a professional bridge competition, a very pissed Omar Sharif! I think I fell asleep during one of my dummy hands and so to the chagrin of the sisters, I called it a night.

'We're here most afternoons if you would like to join us again,' said Mildred.

However, I never saw them again, and on enquiry I was told that they had been part of a contingent that had been repatriated at little notice. God bless them!

Ad acted as our guide around the town for the next few days and nights. As no expense was spared, we visited all the high spots and low spots. There were more lows than highs but we did go to a local nightclub where there was belly dancing and hookahs – that's the things you smoke, not the things you shag.

27

The Birthday Party

It was Saturday. Christ, had we been here for only a week? It felt like forever. Would we ever get away from here? The only people getting away were those who didn't want to go. We had said our goodbyes to Ad the previous night as he was to depart within the next couple of days. He had been a good friend and companion for the few days that we had known him.

We had been up to the Sudan Club for a swim and a couple of beers but now we were returning to the hotel. As we entered the lobby, the head man came across smiling and bowing to greet us. All this was to ensure that we took note of a message that was written in chalk on a blackboard in the lobby.

Tonite Saturday

There will be a splendid evening of dancing

On the Roof Garden

To the Accompaniment of a Gazz Band

As the only dancing we had seen was the belly dancing, we resolved to see what a Gazz Band was like and to compare the Roof Garden to the Agricultural (Aggie) Hall dances back in Limavady.

But first it was Steve Bentit's birthday. We were to celebrate this with a slap-up meal in the hotel dining room and it was then quite appropriate that a dance should follow. We had not eaten much at the hotel restaurant as it was a fairly limited menu and expensive, as most hotels are. We had preferred to eat up at the Sudan Club as the menu was more acceptable to our Western taste – beefburger and chips, pie and chips, bacon, eggs and chips. So tonight was to be something of an occasion.

We duly dressed for dinner and assembled in the bar for a couple of beers before going into the dining room. The menus were brought through to the bar and the choices were given to the head waiter who would call us when the meal was ready.

After about twenty minutes we were called through to the dining room and we ceremoniously made our way there and seated ourselves at a table that had been decorated with flowers and balloons. Someone had tipped off the staff that this was to be a birthday celebration and they had risen to the occasion.

The first course was presented and consumed and the last of our beer was drunk before it became too warm and flat. This left us without anything to drink with the main course.

Steve Bentit magnanimously declared that he would like to buy a bottle of wine to accompany the main course. He waved at the wine waiter and shouted in his inimitable sonorous West Country accent, 'I say my good man, could I have the wine list please?'

The wine waiter was a man of giant proportions. He was about six feet eight inches tall and this was made higher by the turban he was wearing. His jet-black face shone like polished mahogany and was covered in tribal scars cut at every conceivable angle and place. He wore the usual long white robe with a red cummerbund around his waist, and thrust into this was a rather large curved dagger in a sheath. This gave him a very impressive appearance but his appearance paled into insignificance when one was confronted by his strongest attribute – his smell.

His personal odour could have brought the elephants in the zoo round the corner to their knees and it pervaded every corner of the dining room, especially when he first entered. He did not smell too bad when he was stationary but the wafting of his robes when he was in motion caused fits of gagging and choking among those of us who were not used to this phenomenon. However, the white locals seemed to be so accustomed to this that they were immune and showed no reaction to this walking compost heap. God knows when he last had a bath or had his clothes washed, but it seemed like it couldn't have been this side of the Second World War. There was a lot of curiosity about what could be producing this prodigious smell under the robes.

He shuffled across the floor on sandals of which the soles were so thin that they could have been used for shaving. His great toes protruding out of the sandals looked like large chipolatas that had been fried to a gnarled crisp. The toenails were like scallop shells and no doubt hid some indescribable material underneath.

He handed over the wine list to Steve and shuffled off to take his place standing motionless once again beside the waiter's sideboard. Unfortunately the smell did not diminish with his departure and the ceiling fans only served to spread it around the room so that every diner got his share. It was so bad that it could be tasted in the air and immediately replaced the taste of the first course – prawn cocktail.

Steve opened up the menu and gave out a startled cry. 'Bloody hell, you should see the price of this wine. I wouldn't pay this much to buy the bloody hotel!'

'It's OK Steve, we don't need wine anyway. Let's have some more beer.'

'No, I said we were going to have wine and wine we shall have, even if it costs a week's wages.'

He waved again at the wine waiter who now looked really pissed off at being disturbed for the second time in one evening. He shuffled back to the table bringing his fragrance with him once again to the accompaniment of more gagging from the assembled group.

'I'll have a bottle of Mateus Rosé, please,' Steve said, pointing to the name on the menu.

The waiter took the menu and shuffled off to a locked cabinet in the corner. He fumbled in his robes and extracted a huge bunch of keys and proceeded to unlock the cabinet. He took out a bottle of Mateus Rosé, locked the cabinet once again and shuffled back to the table with the precious liquid.

He held the fat squat bottle in the palm of one hand and it seemed very tiny in comparison with the size of the hand. He held it out for Steve to examine the label. Steve nodded his approval and the man fumbled in his robes once again and produced a corkscrew. He proceeded to thrust and twist the corkscrew into the cork through the foil top. He pulled up on the corkscrew and extracted about half the cork. He jettisoned this piece of cork on the floor and thrust the corkscrew back into the bottle but the remaining part of the cork just turned in the neck as he tried to get the corkscrew to bite into it. Try as he might he could not get that screw into the cork. He stopped the exercise and looked at Steve with some alarm, shrugged his shoulders, mumbled something incoherent and shuffled off into the kitchen with the bottle in his hand.

About two minutes later he reappeared with a smile on his face and the bottle now minus the cork. He came up to the table and once again presented the bottle for Steve to inspect. Steve nodded gloomily and a little wine was poured into his glass for him to sample. Steve nodded once again and the wine was duly dispensed around the other glasses.

We sat there expectantly waiting on our second course. This was served and it seemed an appropriate time to wish Steve a Happy Birthday and to drink his health.

'Here's wishing Steve a very Happy Birthday and we thank him for buying this wine to toast his health, gents, raise your glasses and wish Steve a Happy Birthday.'

There were echoes of 'Happy Birthday, Steve' followed by a slurp of wine. As soon as I had got a whiff of the wine under my nose, I knew that it was not 'right'. I took a little sip and it was warm and rancid, I immediately spat it into my side plate.

'Fuckin' hell, Steve! This wine is bad!'

'I know,' he said, 'but you go and tell the big bugger.'

We never drank the wine and we never told the wine waiter that his wine was off – mainly because his personal aroma had diminished a little over time and we did not want a close-up re-infusion before the end of the meal. We had a sweet course and coffee and then repaired to the bar once again to await the appointed hour and attend the dance on the roof garden.

At about ten o'clock we decided that the time was ripe to go upstairs. None of us had ever been to the roof garden but we were clever enough to realise that it was probably situated on the roof. We had no great expectations of what this dance would be like here in the middle of the desert, as nothing we had seen around Khartoum had inspired us to think that it was anything other than 'Hicksville' and a very poor Hicksville at that.

We eventually found the stairs that led to the roof. This was no mean feat as the stairway was well hidden and dark – at least the one that we found was. We were further guided by the sound of music that got louder as we stumbled up the stairs.

The way that we approached the roof terrace was from behind the bandstand and this area was in complete darkness. As we reached the end of the bandstand we caught our first glimpse of the terrace which was bedecked by fairy lights and was in stark contrast to the darkness we were standing in. Imagine our surprise when we were presented with the sight of about ten tables all occupied by women dressed in their finery. There were women in saris, women in evening dresses, women in cocktail dresses, women made up like film stars, or at least that is how they seemed to us rampant beasts chomping at the bit to get in amongst them. The best thing of all was that there were no men around to compete with. We had found the female oasis of Khartoum, the motherlode of womanhood, all there for the taking and none of them dancing. They were obviously waiting for us to show them a good time. Where had they been all week?

We did some preening of hair and clothes before making our entrance onto the terrace from the dark recesses of the bandstand. The music was a strange mixture of jazz with a distinct Arabic influence. It was very evocative and seemed just right for the occasion of ravishing the dusky maidens of this fair city, because that is what it had become in the past few minutes.

We emerged into the light, full of testosterone and hope. We could see that a general air of excitement was rippling through the female contingent as they caught sight of us. This spurred us on to get right in and 'go for it'. It looked like there might be three of them to every one of us. The mind boggled!

Our aspirations were short lived, however. As we cleared the side of the bandstand and had a full view of the dance floor we could see that it was packed with men all dancing individually and with each other. These were obviously the husbands of the sex-hungry females who so longingly ached for our British sex-charged bodies. Bloody hell, who invited them?

Dejectedly, we took seats at the nearest table and tried to look nonchalant and unfazed by this state of affairs. We ordered more beer and when it was delivered there was much glancing at our table by the assembled masses and nudging and nodding in a disapproving way. It was then that we realised that we were the only people there who were drinking alcohol.

We sat there drinking our beer and enjoying the music. It transpired that the women were not allowed to make a display of themselves in public so were not allowed to dance. The men enjoyed it though, but we preferred not to join in – just in case the tale of it ever got back to Ballykelly. It seemed a shame that we could not have become better acquainted with their wives and girlfriends while they were on the dance floor.

We drank up and left to go to the Sudan Club in case there were any stray nymphomaniacs waiting for us up there. No such luck.

Steve's birthday in Hicksville had gone off like a damp squib.

28

Departure

We had been in this place for nine days and we were becoming demoralised over the prospect that we might never get away from it. It seemed to be becoming more oppressive in heat and social attitude, and we were running out of beer money even although we were being supplied through the aircraft imprest fund, doled out by the captain. We needed something to do but we had already done it all, apart from the obvious. Even the chap from the consular office had run out of enthusiasm for us and had abandoned us to our lot.

On the ninth day, the captain received a communication from Coastal Command saying that a new wheel would be dispatched from Sharjah in the Trucial States either the next day or the day after. Hallelujah! We were not forgotten after all, left to wither in the shifting desert sands like some latter-day Beau Geste.

The next day we went down to the airport to meet the C130 Hercules aircraft that had arrived with the means of our salvation on board. A dozen cases of beer. We offloaded the wheel and the jacks and got to work changing the flat tyre.

The captain of the Herc had said that they had to take off within two hours, and they would go without the flat wheel and the jacks if they had to. We had the wheel changed and the equipment stowed in the Herc within an hour. We waved bye-bye to the Herc and thought about getting away ourselves on the morrow.

The Shackleton was given a pre-flight going over. I started the engines and put them through their paces to ensure that there would be no glitches when we were finally given the all-clear to depart. I was still slightly worried about the oil situation but reassured myself with the thought that the journey down to Nairobi was only some eight hours. However, it was over some of the most inhospitable terrain in the world.

We had a good piss-up that evening with the beer that the Herc had deposited on our doorstep and the singing was on the go as the captain had announced that we could depart first thing in the morning. Even Jimmy did not get too drunk that night for fear of being left behind, an indication of the general enthusiasm for departure.

The morning dawned. We packed everything into the BCO transport, said our farewells to the hotel staff who had looked after us so well, fortunately the wine waiter wasn't there, and departed.

We went through the form-filling exercise at the airport customs and went out to load up the aircraft. The engines were started, the starter crew got on board and we taxied forth. For Christ's sake get this tub off the deck – it's boiling in here.

The brakes were released and we surged down the runway – ROTATE – and we finally waved goodbye to Khartoum on the confluence of the Great Nile Rivers, which I now knew was also the confluence of socialist and capitalist societies. May Allah help them if the socialists won!

29

Nairobi

The aircraft droned on and on over the landscape of sometimes mountains, sometimes jungle, sometimes plain and sometimes scrubland. We were flying at a height of some eight thousand feet so most of what was below was reasonably visible. As we flew over rural settlements, the people were waving at the strange noise that they could hear in the sky. They probably thought that the Third World War had started – but with Second World War technology.

At this height the temperature inside the aircraft was very pleasant and I managed to get some sleep down on the tail observer's mattress. Time passes quickly when you are asleep, especially a restful sleep at a decent temperature.

We arrived at Nairobi airport in the late afternoon. As Nairobi is situated at an altitude of about six thousand feet, the temperature was very pleasant and a big difference from the oven of Khartoum, which now seemed a lifetime away. Just arriving at Nairobi you could sense the difference in social attitude, as people here were much more friendly and willing to help and there were no more of those bloody awful customs forms to fill in.

We had unloaded the luggage from the aircraft onto a waiting bus and gone into the airport operations centre to organise the fuel and oil requirements. As we were to be here for only one night the aircraft had to be prepared for flight early next morning.

As the civilian airport was being used by a RAF Transport Command Britannia detachment as part of the Beira patrol logistics network, there was an RAF contingent at the airport so they had all the necessary materials. The fuel and oil were delivered to the site and willing hands helped with getting the stuff into the right tanks. The engines took twenty gallons of oil each so there hadn't been a great deal of flying time left.

We completed the checks and top-ups in a couple of hours and were now on our way to the Safari Park Hotel on the outskirts of the town. It was about six o'clock. This hotel was set in acres of gardens and was very well appointed. This again contrasted favourably with where we had stayed in Khartoum. However we were not particularly interested in the flora of Kenya, we were more interested in the fauna that could be found in downtown Nairobi.

When we entered the hotel we asked the concierge what entertainment there was to be had downtown.

'Depends what you want. There is a cinema, a theatre, restaurants – there is a very nice restaurant here at the hotel or there are several nightclubs.'

'Nightclubs, that's what interests us. Are there any floorshows at any of them?'

He looked up some brochures.

'There's an African dance troupe at one, then there's Frank Ifield singing at another and then there's a stripper on at the Sombrero club. If you're going to the Sombrero, I recommend that you get there early as it will get packed. We don't get many white strippers here in Nairobi.'

A white stripper! Christ, all our prayers had been answered. There was a rush to get upstairs to grab the shower first – two to a room.

We were back downstairs within the hour well scrubbed and ready to hit the town. Two taxis were called and they deposited us in the centre of the town within ten minutes. We asked to be dropped off at one of the restaurants that the concierge had recommended as they served the best steak in the whole of Kenya. That was some boast but it turned out to be probably true. The steak was cooked to perfection and was very tasty along with the salad and chips and beer. We were bloated.

'Right, let's get to this Sombrero club before it gets too busy and we can't get in,' someone suggested. So off we set. The club was well within walking distance and we strolled along the main drag being pestered by taxis, rickshaw wallahs, prostitutes and pimps. We had to dive into a bar to get away from the throng that had gathered around us as they were becoming intrusive and a bit threatening.

After a beer in the bar, we made a dash out of the doorway and ran across the road, taking the waiting throng by surprise, and arrived safely at the door of the Sombrero, slightly out of breath but free of escorts. We paid the few shillings entrance fee to get into the club and entered a place that was dark and completely empty of customers. It was about nine-thirty by this time.

Once the eyes became accustomed to the darkness, one could see that the room was made up of a bar area and several tables arranged around a dance floor with a small bandstand.

Once the eyes had become a bit more accustomed to the dark, one could see that there were local girls festooned all over the place. Why were they there? Were they the waitresses? No, there were waiters there to take the drinks order once we had populated a table next to the dance floor. Why they were there was soon to become blatantly obvious.

We had no sooner got our drinks when the ladies swooped out of the darkness. They swarmed around the table and began harassing us in a very provocative way. It all started innocently enough, with them asking if we wanted them to do anything for us and when they got answers in the negative their advances became more overt and aggressive as time went by.

I was swung round in my chair and one of the dusky maidens pulled up her short mini skirt and straddled my legs. Even in the dark I could see that she was not wearing any knickers as she gyrated on my knee and tried to get me to buy her a bottle of champagne! I wished I had had the money for a bottle of champagne, I wouldn't have been in that dive if I had.

Some of the other guys were suffering the indignity of having their faces rubbed with hairy pussy, to which they objected profusely with cries of 'Christ, now I know where Brillo pads come from! Get off my face, that hurts!'

After a while they realised that we were really a bunch of skinflints with no money to satisfy their demands so they drifted off, but came back every now and then to try their luck once more.

The place started to fill up after a while so we were not the primary targets any longer. We did however observe scenes of sexual activity at various times and places during the evening. There were also some heavy-looking pimps hanging about to relieve the young maidens of their hard-won earnings.

It seemed to take forever for the floor show to start. We had several more rounds of beer and were beginning to become a bit more relaxed and noisy. Eventually the band came onto the floor, started to tune up and then went into some jazzy music. There was the inevitable troupe of local dancers that came on and did some sort of shaking and stomping dance that required drums to be played so loud, torturing the eardrums, that you didn't care if there were dancers there or not.

A local woman was singing some native song out of tune to the accompaniment of the dancers who were now out of breath and sweating so profusely that their smell permeated the room. It reminded me of the wine waiter in Khartoum. Still they were all smiling and seemed to be enjoying themselves so we gave them every encouragement by way of applause and whistling. Thankfully they only knew the one song so they departed the floor.

There then followed an intermission just to build up the atmosphere for the main event. We awaited this with baited breath as it had been a long time since we had seen a white woman without her clothes on. For some it would be a first.

Eventually the band returned and played a couple of tunes before the barman who had the microphone announced, 'Gentlemen, now is de time you have been a-waiting for. Please give her de clap – your stripper for de night – Daisy!'

The drums rolled and a spotlight was jerkily focused on the bit of curtain beside the band from behind which Daisy emerged. She must have been all of four foot six in her stockings but she was wearing very high heels at this time. She was dressed in a sparkly corset with fishnet tights and long gloves to above her elbows and she had some feathers in her hair. If she had been a foot taller she could have been in the Tiller Girls dance troupe at the London Palladium.

To the accompaniment of the band she proceeded to do some very sore-looking acrobatic contortions such as bending over backwards and lying on the floor on her front and bringing her legs up and over her head onto the floor in front of her. When she did the splits, Jimmy Curry shouted, 'Don't go bursting that thing before we see it, Daisy!' This brought forth great merriment from the assembled mass. Daisy gave him the V sign, this time with her fingers.

During the second set of music, Daisy started to divest herself of her clobber. It took about ten minutes for her to remove her gloves as she kept pulling them down and then pulling them on again as if it was cold. Eventually she dispensed with this sexy item of clothing. Next she did some sort of backwards contortion and undid the zip on her corset and she paraded around the floor holding this in front of her for another five minutes. Finally this was discarded with a flourish. Underneath she was wearing a bra and pants and of course the tights.

To get the tights off she had to remove her shoes and I have never seen such a palaver in getting out of a pair of shoes. Once these were discarded, she then had some difficulty in reaching the floor when sitting on the chair. She tried to look very seductive when toying with the tights and managed to extract one leg. The other leg was a bit of a problem as she bent over to roll the net down her leg with her toes on the floor, the chair gave way underneath her and she and the chair went careering across the floor, landing very undignified on her back with her legs akimbo. However, she was a good enough professional to pick herself up, playfully kick the chair and start on the tights removal once again. This was successful after she got a hold of the gusset and put her legs above her head while sitting on the chair and provocatively pulled the remaining foot out of the things.

Only bra and pants to go! She started into a very energetic dance routine that involved handstands and tumbling but there was no sign of the underwear coming off. This resulted in the usual crowd response of 'Get them off, show us your tits!'

Eventually the music became quieter and the lights were dimmed with only the jerky spotlight trying to follow Daisy around the floor. She was obviously in her element, she thought that she had every man in the place frantic with desire. More shouts of 'Get them off, show us your tits!' soon brought her back down to earth.

The bra was unclipped and yet again there was the interminable dance around the floor, this time approaching the men sitting nearest the dance floor and giving them a quick preview of the delights hidden inside. Eventually the bra was discarded with another flourish ending with her arms upright above her head. Someone shouted out, 'Fuck me, she's a boy, where've her tits gone?'

It was true, she hardly had anything that you could call tits and what seemed to be a decent pair were now lying on the floor inside her padded bra. Undaunted she carried on with her routine and started to flirt with those of us who had a ringside seat.

She came over to me and sat down on my knee and leaned back against me ruffling my hair provocatively. 'Christ, look at that bloody great spot in the middle of her chest! It's bigger than her other two tits put together. It looks like she's got three tits!' This from no other than Jimmy. Sure enough there was a bloody great spot that looked like a third nipple and was probably the result of a insect bite or something.

Daisy leapt off my lap with a cry of 'Fuck off!' She pirouetted into the middle of the floor, pulled off her pants to reveal a skimpy G-string underneath and with a roll of the drums she disappeared off the floor. We could only speculate whether she would have removed the G-string or not. Jimmy was not a popular person at that moment – again!

With nothing else to keep us in the Sombrero we departed and got a taxi back to the hotel. I felt almost cheated that our first encounter with a female for so many days had been marred by her having small tits and a boil on her chest — especially after we had waited so long to see her in the buff.

Next day dawned and we were off to Majunga. I would be glad to get there at last.

30

Majunga

We arrived at Majunga airport sometime in the afternoon and we were greeted by the guys who had been down there for the past three weeks. They were all suntanned but some of them looked decidedly knackered as a result of their night-time forays into the fleshpots, or more accurately, pots of flesh that abounded in this area. Others had been there much longer but could not depart until we had arrived and they were pissed off.

'Where the fuck have you been? We've been waiting for ages to get back home. We've been stuck here for eight weeks now! Thought you were never goin' to get here,' was our initial greeting from those who were all packed up and ready to take the returning Shack back home, somewhat delayed because of our paralysis in Khartoum.

'It's a long story and we'll tell you about it sometime. Hope you have a better trip than we did,' I thought as I remembered our Battle of Omdurman.

We were transported up to the accommodation, or what passed for accommodation in Camp Britanique. Camp Britanique was a collection of single-level aluminium huts serving as bedrooms, mess, ablutions block and a bar. There was no air conditioning apart from the lack of glass in the windows and there were four beds in each room. Each bed did however have the luxury of a rotating table fan. This was to be home for the next four weeks or so.

As normal, it took a couple of days to get settled in to the routine of the place but it was all easygoing with everyone mucking in to get the job done. There seemed to be more spares and supplies lying about the allocated area at the airport than there was in the whole of the rest of Coastal Command. I supposed Harold Wilson had personally requisitioned them to ensure his 'none shall pass' embargo.

There were three Shackletons in the detachment, two that were kept serviceable to fly and one to rob to keep the other two aloft. This last aircraft was the 'Christmas tree' as it donated all of its gifts to the other two.

My first job was to change out one of the engines on the Shack that had brought us here. The engineer had thought that 'something was wrong' on our way down from Khartoum and then across to Majunga but had not mentioned anything about it. It turned out the timing gear of the engine was shot and it had to be replaced. We could have stayed in Nairobi with Daisy for another few days. I for one was glad that he had not mentioned it. However, changing the engine manually here without the aid of an engine-driven crane in the heat was no joke. On top of this was the fact that the spare engine had to be robbed off the 'Christmas tree' in the first place, thereby making it a very protracted exercise. The loss of this engine left the Christmas tree aircraft in a very forlorn state as it sat there outside the civilian airport terminal building. It was reminiscent of a scrap yard with just one piece of junk in it.

The Shacks went out on sorties, and came back, and went out some more, and came back some more, but none was successful in its mission to divert supplies away from Beira. This was a good thing as the only people to suffer would have been the people of Rhodesia.

As well as trying to make the merchant marine see the error of their ways, another important and hazardous operation carried out by the Shacks was the delivery of mail from home to the brave crews of Her Majesty's Ships who executed the highly dangerous interceptions at sea so that the rest of us could sleep easy in our beds. I say 'our beds' but in fact this is academic as nobody cared too much which or whose bed they slept in. We were given to believe that these mail drops were passionately welcomed by the sailors, or at least by the ten percent of them who could read.

Unfortunately interservice relations can sometimes become strained by the most insignificant of incidents aggravated by the ill grace and total intransigence of one side – the navy – leading to the spitting out of the dummy in a general fit of pique. The mail was dropped in Lindholme containers which would float patiently on the sea surface until the 'fish heads' could get a small boat launched to recover them, or at least that was the plan.

I don't believe for a minute that the Shack crew intended the containers to splash down five miles from the frigate as their aim is usually quite good, but the bad-tempered buggers below on their holiday cruise didn't see it that way and what a fucking fuss they made. They accused the airforce 'crabfats' of deliberately sabotaging the drop, just because their latest consignment of *Beanos, Dandys, Playboys* and *Spick and Spans* took a little while to recover. The fact that the outboard motor on their little speedboat broke down and they had to row back to the ship probably justifies their attitude somewhat, but I have to say that airforce feelings were hurt and, sentimental old sods that we were, the supply of tissues was exhausted in minutes.

Apart from being sentimental, the crabfats are nothing if not forgiving so to try to make amends to our fish head friends and show there were no hard feelings on our part it was decided to lay on a little show for them. In this way it was hoped to alleviate some of the boredom of their long weeks at sea so far from home. In the subsequent mail drop to our mates some of the containers were filled with rocks, and the Shack was sent merrily on its way with a crew determined to do their best to cheer up the lads at sea and make up for the last little misunderstanding. Arriving overhead the frigate's location the aircraft did a couple of circles and a figure of eight around the ship and with a friendly waggle of the wings set off to come in on its 'bombing run'.

Back she came low and fast, well everything's relative, bomb bay doors gaping open ready to drop a load of happiness to the sailors below. As the Shack got closer the pilots could see the frigate's crew, from the captain down, lining the decks, their upturned apple cheeks and smiling faces gleaming in anticipation. From those lines of smiling faces came also friendly waves as hands were raised in greeting and not closed fists … it seemed the fish heads also wanted to be friends again. This time the Shack crew were determined that the containers would 'land' nice and close to the ship so the sailors would have a good view.

In she came flying parallel to the ship's course and from astern, navy speak for 'from behind', something to which sailors are (allegedly) partial. The bomb aimer stared unblinkingly through the bombsight until the crossed hairs were right alongside the bridge of the ship and about ten feet off the side and hit the button, calling 'Lindholmes gone.' As the signaller on the Shack watched through his camera viewfinder he could see the faces on the frigate change as the eyes followed the ever-accelerating plunge of the yellow Lindholme containers which was not in the least affected by the little stabilising parachutes on the arse end. The sailors' grins changed to fear, horror, blind rage and hate as their whole consignment of 'mail' hit the water and kept on going in a downward direction. Rumour has it that half the ship's divers were suited up and in the water before the package hit bottom, but this could be an exaggeration because no serving sailor had been known to move that fast since the rum ration was stopped. Had the worthy seafarers been more observant they might have noticed the extra Lindholmes containing the real mail sacks still securely attached in the bomb bay and which the aircraft then proceeded to drop in a textbook manner after making another circuit of the ship. Unfortunately this did nothing to repair the total sense of humour failure suffered by the mariners and the Shackleton crew departed the scene with cries of 'Bastards' ringing in their ears over the radio. 'Dear oh dear,' commented the pilot, more in sadness than in anger. 'They've gone and broken radio silence, now the whole world knows we're here.'

31

Majunga Nights

Facing these mind-bending dangers on a daily basis meant that some sort of rest and recreation was required outside duty hours, and this was provided enthusiastically by Madame Chegal in her drinking establishment located in the luxurious Majungan neighbourhood known as Tintown. Tintown was thus known because all the buildings were constructed from corrugated iron, not dissimilar to the houses in the west coast of Scotland and Ireland, so a lot of the airforce detachment felt quite at home and took up residence with the locals. Tintown should not be confused with Tinseltown in California which is a lot more luxurious but whose residents are morally bankrupt and sleep around a lot more.

Madame employed lots of girls who were, if anything, even more enthusiastic and much better looking than herself and provided our brave warriors with much needed solace and relaxation between the sheets. Such was the easygoing style of the place that many of the services provided, even the alcohol, were supplied '*bon pour*' – on credit. This was a great boon to our heroes who were only paid a pittance once a fortnight and were stony broke after the first week. And this was in a place where an all-nighter cost one thousand Madagascar francs, which was the equivalent of seven shillings in old money or thirty-five pence today. On paydays some of the lads were known to have a guinea's worth by having four in a bed for an all-night session. Unfortunately there was no discount for bulk purchase.

Of course there was always the risk of a greater price to pay and this was summed up by one senior officer who felt the need to record that 'I'm not sure what constitutes the greatest danger to my men, heatstroke, malaria or other diseases of a more dubious and sexual nature, acquired as a result of over friendly relations with the locals.'

Be that as it may, and certainly this officer was entitled to his opinion, but the men had been repeatedly told that they were ambassadors representing their country and as ambassadors, none of them was going to be so undiplomatically rude as to turn down a shag whilst supporting the local economy at the same time. After all this was the biggest source of revenue to the local economy.

The only other place that was worth a visit after a foray to Madame's establishment was the restaurant, Le Lampe Bleu. Here they served the best and cheapest steak dinners in town. This was an indisputable fact, as a million flies can't be wrong. The restaurant owners had never heard of insectocutors in those days nor had they ever used an insecticide. To be fair, it would not have done any good as the place had no walls to speak of. However, the place did have its charm, but the wise only ever bought one meal at a time, so as the others at the table could act as human fly swats or try to keep the flies at bay until the meal was finished and another could be ordered. If there was enough time everyone at the table could be served in the course of a couple of hours. This was the place to which those who stayed in Tintown brought their amours for a nice romantic evening.

Not surprisingly there were many heroes who were canny and before starting up a romantic relationship with a local girl would escort their chosen partner down to Dr Jospin for him to have a quick shufty at her parts before the shagging began. This was a very good trade for the good doctor who in essence did not give a shit whether the girl had a full house or just a low pair on the venereal scale, because he would make even more money when the shagging machine came back to be cured of his newly acquired ailment. Penicillin was the favoured drug among the detachment personnel.

Between them the girls had every sexually transmittable disease known to man and then some. I encountered a guy in the shower block one morning covering his shaved pubic area with some foul-looking unction. I enquired why he was doing this and he replied, 'Crabs.' I blurted out, 'Yuk, you dirty bastard!' and he retorted, 'That's nothing, it's just as well I didn't have a moustache.' These boys who were so sex starved at home would do anything for and anything with a bit of fanny to get their fill of it in the few short weeks that they were there.

The alcohol that was served in the Chegal establishment was all the different types of spirits, but none of a brand that could be recognised. There was Trois Chevaux beer which was a local brew and quite acceptable, and then there was the Red Biddy wine that was reputedly concocted by the fair Madame Chegal in her back cellar. This wine had certainly never seen a grape. However, as this was the cheapest way to get drunk, it tended to be favoured by the aficionados. Guys who got drunk regularly on this elixir had teeth stained red as if they had been chewing betel nuts all their lives. No amount of scrubbing with normal toothpaste could shift the stains and it had to wear off through the passage of time or until the teeth dropped out. Most of them will have false teeth by this time in any case.

Madagascar is also a place of deep mysticism and the home of Juju that supposedly gave rise to Voodoo in other parts of the world further west. Locally in Majunga this was the origin of all sorts of rumours and tales of ceremonies taking place that involved digging up the bones of the venerated ancestors and polishing them before re-interring them for another year. There were also rumours of dead ancestors being propped up at family get-togethers which celebrated their life and achievements. Whether these rumours were true or not made no difference as they engendered fears and suspicions that there was something sinister about the local religious practices. These suspicions were supported when anything unexpected happened on the island and especially when something happened to the incomers.

Not far from the Camp Britanique was a gnarled old half-dead tree, from the leafless branches of which hung a variety of odd articles, dolls, bottles, a selection of garments, dead animals such as bats, rats and lizards, plus a few other bits and pieces not easily identifiable which were probably best left that way. This was known locally as the Juju tree and was used for the casting of spells to take revenge on enemies, make money, to be cured of something nasty or sometimes just for the hell of it. One of our own warriors, Jimmy Brent, an engine fitter by trade, had visited this tree one afternoon after a liquid lunch.

Most of the guys on detachment were unsure whether they believed in Juju, privately at least. In public of course they declared loudly that it was a load of mince or pish. Jimmy the Valiant was not one of the wimpish persuasion, especially when drink had been taken and on this day it had been well taken. Chest puffed out, chin up and head held high he stepped up to the tree and, showing all his contemptuous disbelief in the black arts, gave it a hefty kick with his size nines. As there were no immediate repercussions, the others who were accompanying him slapped him on the back and praised him for the hero he'd shown himself to be and the happy band made their way back to Camp Britanique to sample the culinary delights created by the camp cooks.

Jimmy got his first course and sat down at a table where his mates were regaling all who would listen with an account of Jim's exploits that afternoon. All went well until, unnoticed by anyone, a piece of ceiling tile worked loose and fell, landing on Jimmy's head, leaving him shocked and face down in his soup. Fortunately the tile was not heavy and the soup was not particularly hot, so James was not physically damaged, However, his mental state was questionable for a while so he took to taking more drink. Once this story had been recounted, nobody ever went near that bloody tree again.

32

The Wing Commander and the Sergeant

Personnel at Majunga could be divided into two groups, the permanent staff who provided continuity in the admin departments and the visiting Shackleton mob who provided the continuity in Madame Chegal's bank account. For the visitors a tour of duty was two months, at the end of which survivors were sent home to recover from the rigours of the constant stress and tension. If you've never seen a man who thinks his credit is about to be cut off at Madame Chegal's you don't know what stress is.

Every rule has an exception and the exception to the two-month detachment rule was one Geoff Spinks, a radio fitter sergeant who had fallen madly in love with one of Madame Chegal's daughters, the beautiful Anne Marie, and therefore he didn't want to go home ever again. He could hardly be blamed as his situation was about as close to paradise as you can get, a beautiful girlfriend, and a mother-in-law who loved him because he was bunked up with her first born and she was raking in the money from the proceeds of alcohol and debauchery. All this combined with a sunny climate.

All this paradise nearly came to a premature end for Geoff when a wing commander came to call. This was the commanding officer of the squadron in residence and he had decided to grab a seat on the crew-change Britannia aircraft to visit his men and pick up some duty-free goods along the way. Crew-change night at Madame Chegal's was a spectacular event. Everyone congregated there, newcomers and homegoers stood shoulder to shoulder and conducted the obligatory handover briefing with their respective reliefs. Some might think this would consist of passing on information about a particularly stubborn technical problem on the aircraft that had been 'red lined' since Pontius Pilot last flew, or the latest news on the political front – not so!

The information that changed hands could be summarised in a short, typical conversation. A newcomer looking around with interest at all the girls displaying acres of brown flesh and white flashing smiles would comment, 'Bloody hell mate, this place is a bit rough!'

Old Hand: 'Nah, the drink is quite cheap and it's OK once you get used to it.'

'How long does that take?'

'About two months.'

'So you're just getting used to it then?'

'Right on mate and am I frigging glad to be leaving.'

'That bird over there looks very exotic, is she going around with anyone at the moment, any chance for me, d'ya think?'

'Yeah, a smooth-talking shit like you should crack it, no bother.'

'Great, what's her name?'

'Gertie la Gon and her mate standing next to her is Sally la Syph.'

'Are those French names?'

'Yeah, sexy ain't they, and they come with a forged certificate of health and a free course of antibiotics.'

At this point the old hand gets bored and changes the subject.

'That's enough about here, what about home, how's my wife?'

'As compared to who?'

This conversation continued in the din of fifty others of equal banality and the row was horrendous. With so many drinks being guzzled it's no surprise that the glasses ran out. This would not normally be a problem but as luck would have it someone chose this exact time to show the visiting wing commander a little Majungan nightlife.

The 'brass entourage' marched into the lounge and grudging bodies separated as the leader made a beeline for the bar where he ordered a beer. The second unlucky coincidence was that he was served by Geoff Spinks who was moonlighting as a barman for his prospective mother-in-law. Geoff passed him a bottle and the wing commander, being a man of culture, requested a glass, to which Spinks replied in a very polite manner, 'I'm sorry sir, we have run out of glasses.' The opening shots having been fired, the verbal exchange continued.

'Sergeant Spinks, surely you can find one somewhere for your CO?'

'Sir, when it's this busy I couldn't find one for Jesus Christ!'

'Sergeant, I'm not Jesus Christ but I'm sure you could find me a glass if you really tried.'

'Sir, even if there was one somewhere I couldn't leave the bar.'

'Sergeant Spinks, I really must insist that you get me a glass.'

Spinks, who had already consumed a few red biddies himself, was now becoming really pissed off with this attitude and blasted back at the wing commander, 'You silly old bastard, there are no glasses to be had – are you deaf as well as stupid?'

At this point the room, which had been growing quieter as people realised what was happening, became totally silent, pins dropping would have been deafening and all eyes were on the wing commander and Geoff. The wing commander, now almost apoplectic, face all red and the veins standing out in his neck, screamed into the deathly silence, 'Flight Sergeant Ward! Flight Sergeant Ward! Where is the blasted man?'

Flight Sergeant Ward was a 'time and motion' man who had been accompanying the wing commander on his tour. He had been dragged along to Majunga to try to make the detachments more cost efficient, as Harold Wilson was now beginning to regret that he had single-handedly declared war on Rhodesia and questions were being asked in the House about the validity and cost of it all.

The flight sergeant had arrived in the bar some time before the wing commander and at this moment in time he was entertaining two of the local lovelies at a table in the corner of the lounge in full view of the assembled masses. Or it would be more correct to say the lovelies were entertaining the flight sergeant. One of them was under the table administering oral sex while her right hand was stuck up the leg of his shorts playing with whatever she found up there. The other girl was draped over him kissing him voluptuously while his hand was down her underwear fingering what ever fingers finger inside ladies' knickers.

Actually, they were not really ladies' knickers but 'Drawers Cellular, Airmen for the use of'. In other words secondhand Aertex underpants that had belonged to an airman who had passed this way at some time in the past. These were high fashion for the ladies in this part of the island as it was apparent that there was nothing scantier or more airy available.

These articles were sold by a very discerning woman who had found a niche in the fashion market, none other than the laundry woman from Camp Britanique. She was a tall and very buxom lass, quite good looking in a Creole sort of way with big facial features and an ever-present beaming smile on her face. She was ensconced in the men's shower block ostensibly to conduct her laundry business from there because of the availability of water and electricity. However, she also had other core business lines as she prowled around the showers to catch her quarry.

'Hello big boy, you want jigajig?' she would say in her French accent.

At this she would expose her melon-shaped breasts. They were melon shaped in the context of watermelons and not the smaller cantaloupe type. They were very firm with charcoal black aureolae that covered a large area and these were topped by nipples that were about three quarters of an inch across and well over an inch long. There must have been many children that had suckled on these breasts but not as many as there were airmen who had. Very few men could resist this extreme temptation.

If her target was up for it, she would accommodate him by bending over her ironing board and allowing him to have his way with her while she laughed her head off. In this way she had put her niche on the market – so to speak!

'You give good jigajig big boy. I plenty satisfied,' she would tell her studs to inflate their egos as their willies deflated but this compliment was usually short lived when they returned to the shower to wash off the sweat of their toils and she would visit the shower next door to ask, 'Hello big boy, you want jigajig?'

And the payment for all this erotic experience? One pair of underpants that she could sell for more than she would get in cash for selling her charms to her customers. This was the benefit of the barter system where services were swapped for goods and the goods sold for money. Everyone was satisfied and there was no tax to pay.

It was because of this enterprising venture that more than half the airmen on the detachment had their genitalia rubbed raw by the constant chafing of their thick khaki shorts, because they had no underpants to wear.

So here was Flight Sergeant Ward with his hand inside a pair of 'Drawers Cellular, Airmen for the use of' when he was summoned by the wing commander. He shooed the girls away and hurriedly tried to stuff his erection back into his shorts but in his heightened state of excitation the erection was fighting back and refused to obey. He did eventually manage to wrap his shorts around the thing but it still hampered his walk. He came crabbing across the floor towards the wing commander almost bent double with a very painful look on his face.

He came up to the wing commander and muttered 'Yes sir' as he craned his neck to look up into the CO's face like some latterday Quasimodo.

'Stand up man, stand to attention, this is a serious matter!'

'I am standing at attention, sir, at least part of me is. I seem to have damaged my back,' he lied.

'Flight Sergeant, you will accompany Sergeant Spinks here to his quarters where he will be under open arrest until he reports to me in the morning. Understood?'

The flight sergeant nodded his head in his bent-over position as if he was genuflecting to some deity.

'Sergeant Spinks, you will report to me at 0900 hours tomorrow morning and I would advise you to pack your belongings as you'll accompany me on the next flight back to the UK. Consider yourself confined to quarters.'

Geoff realised all too late the consequences of his momentary loss of cool and tried to apologise, but to no avail. It seemed that his stay in paradise was over but those observing the expressions on the faces of his fiancée Anne Marie and her formidable mother Madame Chegal, giving the wing commander the evil eye, knew that this battle may have been lost but the war was far from over.

With the celebrations over, Geoff was escorted to wherever bad sergeants go. During the course of the evening, the flight sergeant who was supposed to be guarding Geoff had returned to finish what he had started with the girls. He had to do this so he could regain his sanity and get himself upright once more in the process.

Geoff took his chance and escaped to his 'married quarter', which he shared with Anne Marie, to wait for his fiancée and her mother, but when they hadn't appeared after an hour or so he went to bed. Awakening the next morning he found he was still alone with no trace of mother or daughter.

Geoff duly presented himself at the wing commander's office to find the boss had not had a change of heart and his trip home would be arranged. In recognition of his local 'family' commitments Geoff was given the rest of the day off to pack and to make his farewells.

Arriving back at the house he shared with the Chegal family he found the women had returned and were busy in the kitchen preparing lunch. Naturally he was curious about where they had been all night but when he raised the subject both women just indicated by closing their thumb and index fingers in front of their mouths that it was better he didn't ask any questions and not mention to anyone that they had not got home until after dawn.

That evening the wing commander was invited to have a quiet night at the detachment commander's house rather than causing more ructions by drinking at the lesser mortals' favourite watering hole and ending up sending half the detachment home, thus jeopardising Harold Wilson's pipe dream of diverting the African 'Wind of Change'. If this had happened, Geoff Spinks would not be the only one who was under arrest.

After dinner those present at this auspicious occasion gathered to watch a film in the living room where a projector and screen had been set up. The title of the movie is not known but it must have been extremely exciting because at some point during the show the wing commander decided to quietly shuffle off this mortal coil. Once it was realised that he was not accepting any more drink, it brought the evening's entertainment to an early end.

The wonderful Doctor Jospin was called and pronounced life extinct and the cause as a massive heart attack. The good doctor's experience with airforce personnel until then had consisted of inspecting their pricks and prescribing antibiotics but it was generally accepted that he could recognise a corpse when he saw one.

It wasn't long before the rumour factory got going and very soon the absence from home overnight of the two venerable ladies in Geoff's life and the fact that someone had seen them in the proximity of the Juju tree were taken as evidence that two and two make five. Perhaps the wing commander had overindulged in the sins of the flesh during his visit or he might have just succumbed to a cardiac problem? Nobody wanted to believe that it was just an unrelated coincidence and speculation was rife.

The Britannia aircraft which was to take home the end of tour crew, including the wing commander, had developed an engine fault which required spare parts to be sent from the UK, thereby causing a delay rather longer than would normally be expected. No one was overly worried about the war-worn warriors waiting to go home for a well-earned rest, and in some cases treatment for the odd little thing that was beyond the skills of Dr Jospin, but there was indeed a great deal of concern amongst the brass over the problem of repatriating the late departed leader. This priority was never fully understood by the rest of the personnel and the man himself was not heard to venture an opinion.

The decision was taken that the coffin containing the mortal remains of the recently departed, but still with us in a manner of speaking, should be transported by Shackleton to the island of Gan in the Indian Ocean, once described in a recruiting campaign poster as 'The RAF's own island in the sun'. Gan was an RAF staging post manned by a few stalwarts who welcomed and despatched Transport Command aircraft ferrying servicemen to and from Far East bases in Hong Kong, Singapore and Malaysia. It was hoped a place could be found on one of these UK-bound flights for the wing commander. No one was expected to complain, as he wouldn't require any in-flight rations.

Majunga airfield, as well as being the RAF detachment base, was also the local civil airport and as such was open to the public. This being so, the operation to get the coffin in the Shack was executed in full view of a curious audience comprising airport staff, transiting passengers and local plane spotters.

The coffin was placed on an engine stand, a sort of mobile height-adjustable platform which engine fitters used to access any part of the aircraft engine that needed to be worked on. The stand was towed slowly and reverently by tractor from near the airport terminal across the tarmac to the waiting Shackleton. No hearse, no flag, no guard of honour, just a few men in greasy shorts and shirts following on behind to lift the coffin into the aircraft.

What the spectators thought of the whole spectacle God only knows and He hasn't released the information. The job was done with something less than military efficiency and very little ceremony. A steady drizzle was falling from the sky adding to the solemnity of the situation, making everything slippery and the coffin difficult to grip, it being without handles of any description.

There are only two ways into a Mark 2 Shackleton, the rear entrance via a short ladder which was the usual way, or through the parachute escape hatch in the nose which, as its name implies, is more of a way out. The 'brains' directing the loading operations opted for the escape hatch method which involved heaving the coffin, in an almost vertical attitude, through a hole two feet in diameter, into the bomb aimer's position where there were two willing warriors attempting to pull it in.

The man in charge of the operation, the station warrant officer, or SWO to his friends who were few in number, tried to expedite matters by turning it into a form of drill. This had been his only official job during his tour of duty in Majunga and he was not going to let the opportunity pass without applying his considerable experience in these matters. 'One, two, three, heave, one, two, three, heave' and so on in such a rhythmic chant that the locals took it to be some sort of dance and began to gyrate in time to his voice.

After a while it became obvious that this option was not going to work and that insertion through the rear was the only solution. However, the coffin had now become stuck in the forward hatchway and the sweating, wet and by now disenchanted bearers started to use some very irreverent language and heavy footwork from above in their efforts to extricate the box and contents. The box was finally jerked free and with all the effort being applied in the downward direction, it landed with a thud on the tarmac. There was a stunned silence as all eyes were looking to see whether the box would fall apart to reveal its revered contents.

Fortunately the box held firm and it was once again lifted with solemn reverence, inserted into the aircraft through the rear door and placed atop the radar scanner well, between the beam seats, where it performed sterling service as a card table during the flight. It's a bloody long trip from Madagascar to Gan – in a Shack.

The upshot of all this was that, in all this activity the threats against Geoff Spinks were forgotten about, as the chief witness could no longer give evidence. Geoff did not go home and stayed on for several more months serving beer, servicing Anne Marie and occasionally servicing aircraft, before he bought his discharge from the RAF and married the now pregnant girl.

The wing commander had gone home feet first – was it all down to the power of love and Juju?

33

The Halo of the Reverend Curry

This was Jimmy Curry's third trip to Majunga so he knew the ropes very well and settled back into the routine of visiting Madame's at every opportunity. When, as often occurred, funds were running low but thirsts not declining to match, help was always at hand in the form of the '*bon pour*' meaning drink now, pay later. To prevent the 'tab' rising too quickly to your personal credit limit it was quite common for the warriors to switch from beer to wine, which was less expensive, at least in monetary if not in health terms.

Jimmy, not surprisingly found this to be less than painful, at the point of consumption at least. The liquid served under the name 'wine' had been dubbed by one of the brighter colleagues in a rare flash of original thought as 'Madame's Red Biddy'. It was a dark blood red in colour and very full bodied, just whose body was never established as this stuff left less residue than the acid used by Haigh to dispose of his murder victims. That being said, it's only fair to add that it killed 99 per cent of all known bacteria and not a few viruses. Some believe it would hold its own against most superbugs. This then is what our hero was hoovering down with gusto one night in Madame's, in the sure and certain knowledge that he was free all of the next day with the whole day to recover should he have a little sip too many.

As was his wont, Jimmy was one of the last to leave and grab a taxi home to Camp Britanique. What had slipped his mind was the station commander's inspection scheduled for the very next morning, a time which he intended to spend in bed recuperating from the biddy! Since he was late getting back his room was in darkness and Jimmy didn't want to disturb his mates by putting on the lights. He quietly disrobed, hung his clothes carefully on the floor next to his uniform and with the smugness of one who doesn't have to arise at sparrowfart, slid happily into bed.

Due to his unselfish attitude in not lighting up the room it had escaped his notice that the floor was clean and was not under the usual three feet of shit plus clothes. Thus there was nothing to implant a little nagging doubt in his head that something might be amiss. Nor was he awoken by the hustle and bustle of the others getting ready to leave for work in the morning, and they, being otherwise occupied, took no notice of Jimmy peacefully sleeping, expecting that he would wake up before the inspection began. After all, he was the corporal in charge of the room!

About an hour later the room door was opened letting in a babble of conversation loud enough to penetrate the prostrate man's coma. Phrases such as 'room ready for inspection, sir' were foggily decoded in his brain as he struggled slowly up to a sitting position to find himself staring uncomprehendingly into the face of the station commander.

His face, hair and the whole of his upper naked torso that was visible above the sheet were covered in blood! Thick, red, congealed blood that glistened in the morning sunshine that poured through the window. The pillow was glued to his cheek like some obscene wound dressing.

The station commander, being the first to observe this apparition, let out a shout.

'Good God, is that man all right? He looks like he has been ambushed or run over. Better get the medics around here at the double.' Someone dashed off to get the medic.

Roy Wilstead, who was the duty sergeant of the day as part of the inspection team, noticed something very peculiar. Red streamers of the 'blood' were attached to the cage surrounding the bedside fan and these streamers were wafting in the breeze that emanated from this fan. The clever sergeant put two and two together, some say only because he had done it himself at some time in the past.

'Sir, I think all that has happened is that he has been sick into the fan and has got his own back, so to speak.'

The party observed this possibility and the station commander asked, 'If that's the case why does it look like blood?'

'Madame's Red Biddy,' came the reply.

The station commander, to his credit, considered this stoically, peered a little closer at the apparition and said, 'Corporal Curry, I presume?'

It is to his even greater credit that he was able to control himself until outside the room before bursting into hysterical laughter as did the rest of the inspection team.

As we know to be his wont, Jimmy had consumed too much and

sometime in the night the alcohol won its battle for freedom, causing Jim to sit bolt upright and unleash, under immense pressure, a solid jet of stomach contents bound together by Madame's Red Biddy. The act of sitting up in bed to perform had positioned Jim's mouth directly facing and level with the bedside fan on his locker which had been switched to full blast. The Biddy left Jimmy, hit the fan, performed a perfect U turn and returned whence it had originated. It says much for Jimmy Curry's constitution that he apparently slept right through the entire incident and didn't even wake up when deluged by about a litre and a half of red wine at body temperature.

Jimmy went back to sleep, unaware that he had passed inspection with flying colours.

34

The Darts Match

While Tintown was a good source of entertainment, the beer and wine was still relatively expensive and the ladies of the night did not look all that good in the daylight so a lot of drinking and entertaining was done up at Camp Britanique.

There were dining-in evenings followed by copious drinking and singing but some of the guys tried to spoil this by bringing along their current 'girlfriends'. These girlfriends were jealously guarded and could not be let out of sight, as in the main they had been proven to be free of the diseases that prevailed and therefore were not to be left unattended for other pox-ridden airmen to contaminate. This made good sense but it did not stop the pox-ridden from trying their hand at contamination, even in sight of the boyfriends.

As those of us who had travelled out by Shackair arrived some three weeks after the main body of the detachment, there were those who were already on their second or third dose of the dreaded 'gon' or other things 'nonspecific' and there was no doubt that they didn't give a shit about their own health or that of anyone else. They were singlies and had to get their share when they could no matter the consequences.

I had a friend who was like a terrier in heat all the time in Majunga and he had contracted some filthy STD several times in the few weeks he had been there. This did not seem very healthy to me so we made a pact that on nights when his resolve would be low and he wanted to go down town for a shag he would give me his wallet to stop him being able to afford the price of another dose.

These nights of low resolve normally involved a preliminary infusion of drink somewhere along the line and so it was on this particular occasion when there had been a new consignment of beer brought into the bar and being consumed at a rate of knots by all. These were good nights as everyone enjoyed the banter and the singing. The singing could not have been all that good, however, as at some time during the evening my friend disappeared. I feared for his welfare as he had been well guttered the last time I saw him.

I went back to the room that we shared to search for him but he was nowhere to be seen. I asked several people if they had seen him but in the main they were so pissed that they could not give a shit. Finally one guy said he thought that my friend had gone downtown as he had loaned him some money and had seen him get in a taxi.

Silly bastard! Still, there was nothing I could do, nor wanted to do as he could be anywhere in Tintown by this time. Fuck him, I had not reckoned on him being able to borrow the price of a dose and escape from my custody. I hoped his prick would fall off this time to save him any more bother in future.

The drinking continued until there were only a few of us left. These tended to be the most drink resilient who could continue to sing without the need of a memory. Sometimes the words came out wrong but that did not matter as long as somebody was making a noise.

During a lull in the singing, we could hear this very melodic descant coming from somewhere quite close but in the direction of the jungle where none of us had ever ventured before. We took it that the locals were having a party just like us.

After a few more songs from our company, we listened to the music of the jungle becoming stronger. In our drunken thoughts it was decided that they were trying to outperform us and we had better go down and join their party. We each bought a few bottles of beer to sustain us on our way and to enjoy at our new venue. We set off in search of our new source of entertainment.

The going was difficult as it was dark and nobody had thought to bring a flashlight along. We eventually staggered onto a pathway with the unerring navigational skills of the drunk. However, by this time we were bleeding from the legs, having had to stumble through some pretty ferocious undergrowth to get to where we were at. Where were we at?

We walked along the path with the confidence of the dimwitted until we arrived at the village where the singing was coming from.

The village was just like a set from a Tarzan film. There was a row of huts, some with thatched roofs and some with the ubiquitous corrugated iron. As we walked down through the huts trying to find out where the singing was coming from, we came into the main square in which there was a fire burning and over this fire was suspended a large cooking pot that was steaming and bubbling. I swallowed hard as I thought we had maybe bitten off more than we could chew. Hopefully we would not end up in this pot giving the locals more than they could chew.

However, there is an old adage that says 'When the drink's in – the wits are out' and this was certainly the case on this night. We pressed on with the fervour of a Church of Scotland missionary hell-bent on converting the whole of Africa to Christianity. We had to find out where the singing was coming from so we could let them hear us in full voice.

Eventually we arrived at a hut that was occupied by many people who were singing in a very beautiful way. However, their songs seemed a bit of a dirge and we were resolved to cheer them up a bit.

The door into the hut had the top half open, 'stable door' fashion. We crowded round and peered into the inky darkness and it took several minutes before we could discern first the eyes and then the faces of those inside. Once they had noticed us at the door, they stopped singing and this brought forth cries of derision from our good selves. 'Give us another one,' 'Di yi know "The Wild Rover"?', 'We'll sing one now.'

I tried to hand in some beer into the darkness but no one took it from me. All the more for us then. They probably were pissed on some local concoction – probably from the vast cooking pot in the square. We started to give them a rendition of 'The Wild Rover' and were dancing and passing each other jig style outside the hut and inviting them to come out to join us. They declined our invitation. Unnoticed, a young man had come up to our impromptu party. He had probably been sought out because he could speak English.

'What do you want here?' he enquired. We stopped singing and dancing.

'Well, we were just having a few drinks up at Camp Britanique and we heard this party going on down here. We enjoyed the music so much that we decided to come down and share a few drinks with you guys. Here, have a beer.'

'This is not a party. This is a funeral! One of the children in the village died today and it is a tradition that people stay with the family to console them on the first night of the bereavement. The songs you heard are all funeral songs.'

Christ! I wished the ground would open up and swallow the lot of us stupid bastards. We had better make amends quickly or it may be our funeral that they will be mourning next.

'Aw, look mate, we are really sorry for intruding like this. If we had known this was a wake we would never have come near. We really apologise for this intrusion. We'll go now and leave you in peace.'

'There is no harm done,' said the young man. 'The parents have asked me to thank you for coming to celebrate the life of their child and for singing your songs. You are most welcome to stay and continue if you would like?'

'Thanks very much for the offer, that would be great and I'll sing a couple of songs for them. Have a beer!' This time he took the beer and several other youths started to mill around and were also offered beer.

I sang the only sad song I knew and was very surprised to hear applause coming from both outside and inside the hut. The chorus in the hut started to sing again and all was at peace once more. However, I was still pissed and wanted to make amends for our indiscretions.

'How come you speak such good English?' I enquired of the youth.

'I am training to be a doctor in Nairobi so I need to speak good English. I know a lot of white guys over there so I know how you are when you get drunk. Don't feel sorry about coming here tonight.'

'Have another beer. Here, you guys must be pretty good at throwing darts and things? How about if we arrange a darts match back at Camp Britanique between some of your guys and some of our guys? Have you ever played darts?' I asked while I threw a pretend dart to demonstrate how it is done.

'No, but I am sure we could learn. I would like to do this. How many men should I bring?'

'As many as you like but there are normally four men in each darts team. Come the night after tomorrow and I will have things set up. Sorry once again for this intrusion and give our deepest sympathies to the parents on the death of their child.'

We shook hands and our little band set off along the path leading back to the bar and more drink.

We arrived back in the bar and recanted the tale of our sojourn into the jungle but few if any believed that we could have been that stupid. We could have started a revolution on Madagascar if things had not gone our way. I went off to bed in high dudgeon and fell asleep.

I awoke some time later to see my friend who had absconded to Tintown earlier trying to make his way quietly round my bed to his own. When I say quietly, his 'SSH, SSH, be quiet!' would have woken the dead and certainly woke me.

Something was not quite right. He had someone with him and was trying to guide this someone in the direction of his bed. I switched on the lights to be confronted by the sight of my friend in the company of a young girl and he had his hand down the front of her dress in an effort to guide her to where he wanted her to be.

'Who the fuck's that?' I enquired as it was the unspoken law to forbid the harpies in the bedrooms. 'I hope she's not a prostitute,' I teased.

'She certainly is not!' he stated indignantly ' She's the change from my taxi fare home.' He proclaimed this proudly, as if he had finally beaten the system.

'What ya mean, she's the change from your taxi fare?'

'Well I gave the taxi driver a thousand franc note and he said that he had no change but I could take his wife who was sitting in the taxi with us. So here is my change and I'm goin' to get my money's worth!'

'Not in here you're not! We don't want crabs all over this room because of your financial transactions. Get her out of here and shag her outside if you must.'

'OK, if that's the way you want it I will. I thought that you might want sloppy seconds, there's a lot of change from a thousand francs.'

'Get the fuck out of here and do your stuff!'

He pulled himself up to his full five feet two inches, indignantly turned the girl around, steered her towards the door and disappeared outside.

No sooner were they outside than I heard him shouting and within a couple of seconds he was back inside.

'Christ, that didn't take you long. You must have the shagging stamina of a sparrow.'

'Fuck off, she ran away as soon as we got outside. If I ever see that taxi driver again I'll let his tyres down for cheating me out of my change. Bastard!'

At that he threw himself onto his bed and was asleep before he hit the counterpane. He would not have been able to shag in his condition in any case. The harpy had probably intended to rob him but she was too late to rob him of his virginity.

The night after next, I was in the bar playing darts when somebody came and told me that I had some friends outside and that they were asking for me. Bloody hell, they had taken me up on my offer! Could I run away and hide somewhere? No! I had to face up to what I had done.

I went outside and rounded the building to the rear. Bloody hell there were about thirty locals all carrying homemade spears. What in hell's name had I said to them back at the village? Had I challenged them to a skirmish or what? What was more concerning was, how was I going to buy them all beer?

My 'friend' from the village was leading the group and came forward to shake my hand. He had a big grin on his face and I am sure that he could sense my discomfort.

'How do you like my darts team?' he asked. 'Each one has been hand picked and each has made his own darts.' He shook his spears to indicate that these were the 'darts'.

'Aye, you're well armed I see. Would you like to have a drink?'

'No, we had enough the other night and don't need any more beer.'

Christ, I was saved but I wondered about this confession of 'not needing any more beer'. I had never heard anyone say this before.

The thing was now to entertain them for a while. We set up some car tyres against trees and threw the spears at them. We then hung the tyres from the trees and then threw the spears through the middle. The RAF won, as the guys from the jungle were probably more sophisticated than we were and had not thrown spears for thousands of years.

I then invited the young lad and three of his mates into the bar of the NAAFI and played a game of darts. The rest of his mob stood outside and observed the proceedings through the window. Much to the amusement of the assembled masses, the jungle team had a hell of a job to throw the darts at the board and make them stick. The wall where the board was mounted began to take on the appearance of a severe attack of woodworm, even although it was made of tin. They were giggling and laughing as each other's attempts went flying anywhere but at the board. We played for about half an hour but it was a pretty pointless exercise as none of them could master the skill of throwing the darts with any accuracy – in spite of the expert tuition from us and the constant barracking from the tribal masses outside. However, we had all had a good laugh but it was beginning to wear a bit thin. How to get rid of them courteously?

In the end, I offered them an old dart board that had been lying redundant in the storeroom for ages. I gave them a set of darts and told them to go and practise for a competition to be held at the same time the next year. They took the board and the darts and with many thanks they departed back into the jungle.

I never did get back to that darts match the following year so I have no idea of their proficiency at the board and I have never seen anyone from Majunga competing in any international darts championships so they probably still have not mastered the art. However, I suppose I might have the rather dubious honour of being the one who introduced the game of darts to the people of Madagascar!

Our detachment left Majunga shortly after this and we flew out courtesy of RAF Britannia – the Whispering Giant! At least it was a damned sight quieter and a damned sight shorter than flying Shackair. But never as exciting.

35

The Outcome

The Beira patrols were undertaken by Ballykelly detachments right up to the time when the station closed in 1971. They continued through until 1972 when it was at last realised that they were totally ineffective in stopping the running of oil into Beira for use by Rhodesia. What had all this toil and effort achieved? The answer is absolutely nothing, but it was a stage on which the British Labour government could display the adopted policy of No Independence Before Majority African Rule – NIBMAR. This was probably the first instance of political correctness and was a sop to the growing Soviet accusations of British imperialist colonialism and racialism.

The trade sanctions against Rhodesia lasted right through until final independence was granted in 1980. However, after the declaration of UDI in 1965 a long-term armed resistance campaign led by the marxist-socialist African nationalist liberation movement was waged against the Smith regime. Without support, the Rhodesian government struggled and failed to control this armed campaign which escalated into a full-scale war covering the whole country.

As a result of agreements between the Rhodesian government and some small moderate African national parties, which were not involved in the war, elections were held in 1979. Abel Tendekayi Muzorewa, a United Methodist Church bishop, became the country's prime minister and the name was changed to Zimbabwe Rhodesia.

However, while these elections were declared as non-racial and democratic by the Rhodesian government they were not considered thus by the international community because they had not included the two major marxist-socialist parties. Inclusion of these parties was seen to be crucial as they were critical factors in the armed conflict. It was for this very reason the British government was urged by the international community to intervene and because the armed conflict continued unabated.

The British government was by this time Conservative and led by Margaret Thatcher. They intervened and tried to force a settlement between the 'elected' government and the nationalist fighters. Under the terms of the peace treaty, Britain resumed control for a brief time in 1980 and then granted independence to Zimbabwe Rhodesia that same year. This resulted in the first all-party multi-racial elections being held, which led to much intimidation and violence on both sides of the belligerent parties.

Unsurprisingly the marxist, Robert Mugabe, and his ZANU-PF party won these elections and he became the first prime minister when the country became independent as the Republic of Zimbabwe on 18 April 1980. The rest – as they say – is history.

PART IV

Before the Demise

36

The Troubles

During 1970 the Irish 'Troubles' escalated and this prompted a heightening of security at the Ballykelly base. This didn't seem to amount to much as there were no guards posted at the station gates or anywhere else during the day, but some 'security expert' somewhere decided that maximum inconvenience should be meted out to the already overstretched technical personnel on the base by making them do guard duty during the night. This guard duty was not only on the gate. There were various guard posts positioned around the camp so it took quite a few personnel to cover the fourteen hours or so of continual guard duty. This meant that this bloody onerous duty came round quite often. It was also regarded as a 'sleeping duty' since the rota was two hours on and four off, so it wasn't thought necessary to allow any time off to compensate. A good part of those four hours off were spent eating, showering or just listening to colleagues coming and going as the guards were changed. As a result, the honoured chosen few for the night's festivities would commence guard duties at six pm after a normal day at work on the aircraft, and at the end of a night of little or no sleep would be expected to resume their day job at the usual time.

Perhaps the requirement of the guard duty would have been more readily accepted by the majority of the guys who undertook it if they had confidence that they were to be a deterrent to terrorism. However, in typical RAF fashion the 'powers that be' obviously did not want to offend anyone too much, nor did they want to seem too awfully confrontational. This resulted in the guard outposts being adequately constructed with the usual sandbags and sheets of tarpaulin that would have stopped a speeding bullet if one was ever to be fired. The problem was that the floodlights that had been positioned at great expense around the perimeter fence were facing in towards the airfield and blinded the guards who tried to look in the direction from which any insurgents would be attacking. Not that this mattered overly much because the weapons issued to the guards for the 'Defence of the Realm' were pickaxe handles! Her Majesty must have slept easier in her bed at night as a result of this ring of wood.

When reasonable questions were asked as to why this was, the stock answer was that it was deemed enough of a deterrent that the IRA saw that there were guards in position, and therefore would not attack but would run away and not come back again.

This must have worked because nobody ever attacked the base during RAF occupancy – and this was on an airfield where the public railway ran right across the runway at the western end. The IRA did however wreak havoc elsewhere and one could not help but think that it might have been less socially and politically disruptive if they had attacked the ancient aircraft at Ballykelly.

As the troubles escalated even further, the guards were eventually issued with a rifle without ammunition and then eventually a rifle with five bullets. The bullets were not actually in the rifle magazine but were wrapped up in thick greaseproof paper and sealed inside a thick plastic sack that would have taken a month of Sundays to get into. On top of all this the guards were issued with a walkie-talkie radio that invariably did not work but was supposed to keep each post in touch with the guard command centre. The purpose of this radio was to call to ask permission to retrieve the bullets from their package if the post was under attack. Of course once again the IRA would be good mannered enough to wait until the bullets were calmly, in the face of the enemy fire, retrieved and inserted into the rifle. That is if they could be handled at all because they were so covered in oil to protect them in their greaseproof pack.

The guards were transported and deployed at their various posts and were dumped there quite unceremoniously. First thing was to test the bloody radio but if it didn't work it was hard shit for the rest of that shift. I once had a duff radio and phoned the command centre to tell them, and nearly got my head torn off for 'deserting' my post. The phone was in the Met Office and the guard post was on the roof of this high-security building. Another time I reported a duff radio to the duty sergeant whose job it was to ensure that the guard was in place and was vigilant at all times. The reply that I got was, 'It must have been all right when we gave it to you.' I never saw him again nor did he send anybody else to replace the bloody thing.

The whole thing was a complete farce and pretence at security, and nobody gave a fuck about it. The guys were out there guarding outdated aircraft and their munitions surrounded by a perimeter fence that was full of holes, holding pickaxe handles, with floodlights shining on them making them an ideal and easy target for any terrorist or any passing duck shooter that wanted to take a pot-shot at them. And all this while their families were living in totally unprotected married quarters, near to the base, that would have been an ideal 'soft' target for a terrorist attack. Somebody had a sick sense of humour. If security had been deemed necessary they should have drafted in the professionals of the RAF Regiment to do the job; after all that was their task in life.

When on guard duty, I always tried to opt for the Met Office roof as it was well out of the way, was high up so you could see any approaching vehicles – like the orderly sergeant – and it was easy to get some sleep during the night normally, but not always, with one of the two people manning the post staying awake.

On a particular night, Norman Lindsay and I found ourselves on duty together and we sharp-talked our way into doing the early and then late shift on the Met Office. This would allow us to get into the NAAFI for a few pints on the off-duty time between eight and twelve. The first shift was a pain in the arse as it was boring as hell. I always tried to read a book or do a crossword puzzle but sometimes it just seemed right to stare into the mercury lamps and bemoan our lot. This was one of these nights and by the time eight came around we were both ready for a few pints. Once dropped off at the top of Dukes Lane we headed straight to the NAAFI intending to go for a bite of supper later on.

Almost inevitably we fell into bad company in the bar. It was good company really, but bad if the whole of the RAF in this part of the world depended on quick wittedness and sobriety to fend off the enemy with a pickaxe handle. In any case, we only had eight pints of Guinness each so we were well short of being guttered. We decided to forgo the food as we were already late reporting for the next shift, so we staggered back to the assembly point and bundled ourselves into the truck that would take us back to the Met Office.

On arrival we fell out of the tailgate and were greeted by the lads who had suffered in the cold for the past two hours. At least we would not be cold as we had the price of two bags of coal inside us.

'Where the fuck have youse been? You're bloody late and we're starvin'. We'll be late in relieving you in the morning!'

'Please your fuckin' self, in any case for your information we've not had anything to eat either – so up yours.'

'No, we can smell that you've not been near the mess for your supper. Better watch yourselves as the orderly officer was round earlier and said he would be back.'

'OK, thanks for that – see you later.' They handed over their pickaxe handles and climbed aboard.

The truck roared off and left us in the relative silence. We climbed up to the roof to be out of the wind under the protection of the stockade on top of the building. The stockade was constructed with the ubiquitous sandbags piled to a height of about four feet. Just the right height for leaning on to take aim at the enemy if we had a gun. The sandbags were topped on three sides and over the top with semi-transparent plastic sheeting which was supported at the corners by stout 'four by four' wooden batons. This sheeting gave some protection against the wind unless it was from the unshielded western side that was left open so the enemy could draw a bead on the unsuspecting guards who were lit up by the sodium lamps.

The sandbags were as usual cold and damp but this did not deter Norman from climbing up onto them and prostrating himself along the top in an effort to make himself comfortable. In reality, it must have been as comfortable as taking a cold bath in Lough Foyle but this did not stop him from falling asleep within thirty seconds of pounding the sandbags into submission. This was a fairly precarious position as the top of the sandbags was some twenty-five feet off ground level and there was little to stop him falling off, should he turn over, as the plastic sheeting would have merely given way.

Because I had been toilet trained, I went down from the roof and onto the grass at the side of the Met Office to relieve myself. While carrying out this exercise, I looked up and could see Norman's outline, prone on the sandbags, silhouetted on the plastic sheeting. He looked like a long-forgotten Egyptian mummy laid out ready for burial but the sound of very loud snoring gave the lie to this. I hauled myself back up to the stockade and hunkered down in the corner out of the wind and cold.

The next thing I knew, I was being shaken heavily in an effort to wake me up. It took several minutes to come to my drunken senses and I wondered who was doing this terrible thing to me. I then realised where I was and what purpose I was there for. I looked around to see if Norman was OK but he had disappeared. My first thought was that he had fallen over the side, but then I saw him and he was eating fish and chips. It was he who had been kicking me awake.

'What the fuck's going on, where did you get the food?'

'Our good friend and colleague Roy Wilstead is on orderly sergeant and he has had the good grace to bring us a fish supper each from Ma Hassins.'

'Where's Roy now then?' I asked incredulously.

'He woke me and tried to wake you but there was no response so he left the fish supper and scarpered as he thought that he might have to put you on a charge for being drunk on guard duty.'

'What about you then?'

'I wouldn't have been in any bother as my behaviour was perfectly acceptable – I woke up on demand,' he retaliated indignantly. Little bastard!

We were eternally grateful to Roy Wilstead for seeing the humane side of two drunks being on guard duty at the same time and for not bringing the orderly officer out on his rounds in the dead of night. However, we were even more grateful for the fish suppers.

37

We Are the Champions

Religious bigotry was not an issue among the troops at Ballykelly but neither side was slow at coming forward with statements of their beliefs or to josh with those of the other persuasion. This was done with humour and was seen as serious taking the piss out of each other. This was perhaps unique in the annals of Irish social history because bigotry was real and deep-rooted, as was being demonstrated outside the gates of Ballykelly. Even up to today there has been no real lasting answer to the religious and political divide. This is not surprising, as it is said with reference to Northern Ireland, 'If you think you know the answer, you don't understand the problem!'

The Catholics or 'left footers' were very much in the minority and I suppose in a sense, because of the way that both persuasions lived and had been brought up, they felt somewhat inhibited to give too much retaliation. However, they were given adequate ammunition with the advent of Ian Paisley and his Ulster Unionist Party because it mixed up religion fervour and politics in a similar way that the Republicans did only more surreptitiously.

The big joke of the day was as follows. Supposedly, Ian Paisley was holding a political rally and giving forth with his normal 'fire and brimstone'. He leaned over the rostrum promising that if the audience did not vote for him, they would all burn in hell and there would be much wailing and gnashing of teeth. One wee woman sitting in the front row put her hand up and declared, 'Mr Paisley, ah don't hiv any teeth.' Paisley retorted, 'Teeth will be PROVIDED!'

So 'Teeth will be provided' became a standing joke among the 'left footers' to demonstrate the contempt that they held for this type of political confrontation. However, with all this religious and political interplay going on no one ever lost their temper and life at work went on quite harmoniously.

The same could not be said when it came to sport, especially football and more especially when football meant playing for the station team. Every self-respecting station in the RAF has a football team. However, it is the rule more than the exception that for the majority of the lads who make up this team their skill is vastly outweighed by their enthusiasm. Ballykelly's station team was no different from anywhere else in this respect, indeed this was probably the ONLY thing that Ballykelly had in common with the rest of the service.

Generally the team would be made up of one excellent player, a natural sportsman who was at home on any sports field and won trophies at any sport he turned his hand to; then there would be two or three others who were quite good and also quite keen, and a couple who were middling to average. Since a football team requires eleven members on twenty-two legs this resulted in an exercise called 'making up the numbers'. These numbers were made up by anyone else who enjoyed the sport, preferably had the requisite two legs and wasn't colour blind. It was amongst these stalwarts that talent invariably took a back seat to willingness, the natural law for them being – ability is inversely proportional to enthusiasm.

The physical dimensions of the guys making up the team were, if anything, even more diverse than their skill levels. In height this went between the extremes of Lindsay at the lower end of the spectrum coming in at five feet two inches, to Kerns coming in at six feet six inches, leaving in the middle people like McIlley, whose height fell somewhere between the other two but whose girth was their sum. Personally, I was on the team not because I could play football but because I could remember all the words to the 'Auld Orange Flute' and 'Derry's Walls' so I was good for the entertainment after the match. Kerns and McIlley and a couple others on this illustrious team hailed from the town of Ahoghill in the very heart of 'blue nose' Paisley country in mid Antrim. Another member of the team was Chic McGurk, the man who had introduced me to Ballykelly those long months ago. He was only there to frighten the opposition into submission if they ran into him or he could catch them – he was about as fit as a bean bag.

Kerns, or 'Big Ron' to his friends, was the team captain and tactician and he would spend hours studying the form and style of the opposition before giving the boys a pre-match talk on tactics. He had to discuss the tactics before the match as he always took his top front dentures out when playing and then nobody could understand a word he was saying.

Instructions to his defenders on occasions typified his grasp of the intricacies of top-level football. 'Ye see yon big fella in the number ten shirt? Your job is to stick to him like glue, don't let him out of your sight, if he goes for a shite, you go with him!' Or he would come out with statements like, 'We'll play a three three four formation.'

Everybody nodded but nobody really understood what this meant, nor could keep to any tactics during the game. It wasn't a tactician's game in any case because how can tactics come into play when there are twenty men chasing the same ball all over the park? The only time the team kept any width in the game was when someone had to go to the sideline to evacuate the contents of his stomach.

Notwithstanding, there was one outstanding footballer in H&R who was truly a pleasure to watch, pure poetry in motion. He was an undiscovered George Best clone, a 1960s Beckham even. This boy could attack and score, defend, pass with the accuracy of a smart bomb and he had a body swerve that made defenders seasick. His name was Tommy McIlwrath, by trade an air electrician and an all-round great fella. He never got picked for the team, except when there were not enough to make up the numbers, and that was not often. This could only have happened in Northern Ireland and it might give a clue as to the reason for this strange state of affairs. It was, of course, because Tommy was a 'left footer', not in the footballing sense of the word but the religious. Tommy was a Catholic, and on the few occasions he managed to make it on to the field, his Protestant team mates refused to pass the ball to him under any circumstances.

Of course, life has ways of redressing these little injustices from time to time. It came to pass that, after a long and gruelling footballing season, the Ballykelly team found themselves joint leaders in the local league with a game in hand. The opposition was a local side from just down the road at Limavady and the game was expected to be very tight, or as latter-day commentators love to say, 'It would go right down to the wire.' As the league table stood, the station boys only needed one point to be proclaimed champions so a draw would be just fine. Everybody was quietly confident they could pull it off and a good night of Guinness slurping was anticipated for later on.

To this day it is not clear if papal intervention played any part in events, but an apparently unconnected series of incidents and accidents resulted in the team arriving at the venue a player short and with no substitutes. Naturally Tommy had come along to watch, his loyalty to the team, in spite of his treatment by some of the players, was staunch and true. It was no coincidence that he had his boots and shin pads with him and so, to the great chagrin of some, Tommy was invited to play and proudly pulled on the number ten shirt which, in those days, indicated the position known as 'inside left'. The holder of this position was expected, in conjunction with the number eight, 'inside right', to cover the length of the field, attacking and also helping out in defence when required.

The game was important to both sides for different reasons: the RAF team because they dearly wanted to win the league and the local Limavady team because, although they had nothing to gain for themselves, they preferred to see another civilian team take the title. Memories are long in sport and the locals still remembered the days of National Service when conscripted professional football players turned out for Ballykelly station teams and 'kicked some ass'.

The referee for the game had been specially selected for the two very appropriate qualifications he possessed: he was born and bred in the area but had served in the RAF and at Ballykelly. However, there were some doubts as to which foot he kicked with as he was wearing a green and white hooped shirt. In the event, his impartiality was clearly demonstrated by the abuse heaped upon him by both sides.

The game got off to a slow start, and the only excitement was a couple of the Ballykelly team throwing up their lunches on the sidelines due to the initial physical exertions. Football training was deemed an unnecessary diversion from quality drinking time.

Both teams were testing the water, not wanting to make any silly mistakes from early match nerves, but sooner or later something was bound to happen and it did, big time! During one of the Limavady team's forays into the Ballykelly penalty area the Ballykelly team centre-half, our man McGurk, a known clogger of mean repute whose enthusiasm to skill ratio was 99:1, slid in from behind and took the enemy striker in a way that, off the field, would have got him sent down for about five years without parole. As he came in, feet flying, one set of studs raked the poor lad's left leg from knee to ankle while the other boot nearly caused major testicular and anal restructuring. The most puzzling part of the whole episode was somebody describing it as 'a professional foul'. The incident, which resulted in a penalty, left the station side one goal and one man down, as McGurk got his marching orders. The decision was seen to be perhaps a tad harsh on the part of the referee. The rest of the team, in true sporting spirit, did not complain or perform any histrionics, mainly because of being threatened with further reductions in their numbers. On top of this there were still the doubts about which foot the referee kicked with and they did not want to unbalance the man in case he started to wreak a terrible revenge on this team of blue noses. After all there was still a long way to go.

The contest continued, the station team putting the opposition under constant, intense pressure in spite of their numerical disadvantage until, with a little under five minutes left, Tommy found himself in possession, on the edge of the opponents' box. Had centuries of religious confrontation been forgotten, old bigotries laid aside in the name of sport, had a Protestant colleague passed the ball to Catholic Tommy? The answer, sadly, is no. It was a defensive error, the guardian of the Limavady net mis-hitting a goal kick and sending the ball straight to the talented feet of Tommy who was left with only one defender to get round and beat the goalkeeper. Tommy jinked forward and left the full-back for dead with a classic dummy before placing the ball well out of the keeper's reach to level the score. Surely now his team-mates would at least congratulate him or say 'Well done, boyo!' Tommy was to be disappointed yet again as the others huddled in an ecstatic group shouting and cheering like maniacs but totally ignoring the man who it seemed had won them the championship.

Tommy's sad rebuttal obviously turned quickly to a deep, deep bitterness, watching his team-mates celebrating as he trotted back to his position in the centre circle. As the opposition centre forward tapped the ball to a team-mate to restart the game Tommy shot forward like a sprinter and won the ball. He looked up and paused for a second, then his head went down and he turned and raced for goal, but it was the Ballykelly goal he headed for. Tommy had decided it was payback time for the people who had tormented him for so long on the football pitch and who continued to do so, even though he had probably given them the prize they so desperately sought.

Precious seconds were lost before his colleagues understood the horror that was about to befall, before they could react. They tore across the field intent on intercepting Tommy, but this only gave him the chance to show how good he really was at evading a tackle and keeping the ball like it was glued to his toe. He was lunged at and kicked at from all directions, the shirt he so proudly wore was almost torn from his back but there was no stopping the man as he dribbled round the last line of defence and blasted the ball past his own goalkeeper to snatch defeat from the jaws of victory. He then took off his team shirt to twirl it around his head in an act of triumphalism, revealing to the amazed onlookers a picture of the Pope on the back of his T shirt, and on the front the words 'To hell with King Billy and God bless the Pope.' He could have been forgiven for scoring the own goal but never for this affront to the boys from Ahoghill! There were appeals to the referee to have him sent off for blatant bigotry but this was unnecessary as Tommy waved two fingers in the air and departed the scene of his own volition.

On the day, Ballykelly had accounted for two of the three goals scored but unfortunately not in the same net, so they went home trophy-less. Nevertheless the black stuff flowed that night in the NAAFI bar and soon the rafters roared as the tale was told and retold in ever more embellished versions.

Several Sauls traipsed the road to Damascus that night and were converted, not of course to Catholicism but perhaps to a more ecumenical frame of mind for the next season — some hope!

38

Irish Hospitality

There are many times in life that 'hope springs eternal'. This was very often in the lives of the single airmen at the base and they would take off in forays around the countryside to see if there really were any loose women out there. After all, this was the era of 'free love' but no one was sure if it had reached Ireland yet, or had it become stuck in far-off Sweden?

Such a foray was undertaken one Saturday afternoon when three intrepid stalwarts set off in search of fanny under the disguise of going for a bevy. The usual haunt for this to happen was across the southern Irish border in the little town of Buncrana which was more famous for its Irish broth and Guinness than it was for the abundance of loose women. This being the case, the trio decided to go further afield to the town of Letterkenny some fifteen miles further into the land where all their sexual desires would hopefully be taken care of.

The trio consisted of Steve Bentit, the Reverend Jimmy Curry and Norman Lindsay. Steve Bentit had recently taken possession of a fifteen-year-old Wolseley 1500 that was his pride and joy. Jimmy Curry was there for the drink as he was purported to have a girlfriend back in his native Scotland, however nobody had ever clapped eyes on this girl so we were never sure that she existed. This was despite the fact that Jimmy had fallen down the stairs in Vera's bar while phoning her. There was never any rumour about Jimmy's sexuality but there were rumours that he had become impotent through the imbibing of vast quantities of alcohol. But these were derogatory comments made by those who were jealous of his drinking capacity rather than those who were jealous of his success with the female sex. It was said that, ironically, Jimmy was to be featured in the Guinness Book of Records as the man with the longest period of 'brewer's droop' in history – and there was no evidence to oppose this argument.

Norman Lindsay had been invited along as his lack of altitude at five feet two inches made him fit very snugly under the armpits (Scottish 'oxters') of the other two, so as he could act as a human crutch when either of the other two became legless, which was inevitable. Norman could become just as legless as the others but he soon sobered up once his head had been subjected to the oxters. Single airmen had no access to modern things like washing machines so a civvy shirt had to last at least three wearings, and therefore the sweat and accompanying guff built up in the oxter area. This guff should have been bottled as a sobering influence, as it was more effective than smelling salts were to a dead faint.

Airmen living on the base did have access to a laundry for their airforce clothing and this had to be bundled up in a little roll with a towel wrapped around the outside. A laundry list had to be made out to accompany the parcel and the lot delivered to the laundry store. It could be picked up a couple of days later. Sometimes, the quality of the wash or the ironing was not as it should be and this was met with cries of derision about the use of the service that was supposed to keep the force smart and clean. This despite the fact that clothes became very dirty whilst working on Shackletons and despite the fact that some were too lazy to put their laundry in on a regular basis and would rather wear the clothes until others could not suffer their personal guff any longer. At this point it has been known for guys to rummage in their dirty laundry stash to find the cleanest of the dirty clothes that they possessed.

Complaints about the laundry were not always about the cleanliness of the clothes, others were more particular about how they required their clothes to be prepared. One wag of the 'fairy trades' had written a personal note to the dear ladies of the laundry requesting 'a little more starch on the collars, please'. When he received his laundry back again there was a note inside requesting 'a little less shit on the underpants, please'! He took his complaint to the station warrant officer, who was ultimately in charge of the laundry store, but he only sent him to the sick quarters to get a prescription for his loose bowel and no complaint ever reached the ladies at the laundry. He had to suffer the indignity of limp collars for the rest of his stay at Ballykelly – poor bugger.

It was not unknown for airmen to con married women in the married quarters into doing some of their laundry. This was regarded as a gross misuse of privileges by the husbands as it was seen to be 'gain without the pain' unless there was some other inducement such as a pint of beer or bottle of duty-free spirits.

In the case of the intrepid trio, on this occasion all shirts were clean and the Old Spice aftershave lotion and underarm deodorant were applied, as this was a foray into the female jungle where guffy oxters were not appreciated. However, I could never decide whether Old Spice, liberally applied, was any better than natural occurring guff.

After a late breakfast on this day, the trio set forth in the car in a westerly direction. They had heard the myth that 'Guinness does not travel well' so they wanted to know whether it had reached the far-flung outpost of Letterkenny some twenty-five miles away.

They soon reached their objective, a local hostelry and discovered that, quite beyond comprehension, Guinness was available. As usual they found the local community to be friendly and welcoming. Before long the boys and the residents were engaged in animated conversation covering numerous topics of importance such as sport, the relative merits of Scotch and Irish whiskies and generally just putting the world to rights. As is to be expected, our three lads eventually found themselves with some local boys about their own age and therefore with similar interests, booze, sport and what were the chances of a man getting rid of the dirty water on his spine in a town like this. The local guys said it would be worth staying for a while as there was a dance on later in the local hall which would be graced by the presence of not only the fair maidens of Letterkenny but also the belles from the surrounding villages. A nudge, as they say, is as good as a wink and the unanimous decision was to 'go for it'.

The hosts were inevitably called Patrick and Michael – Paddy and Mick to their friends. Paddy was tall, slim, twenty-something, good looking, intelligent and obviously enjoyed great success with the ladies. Mick was also tall, slim and quite handsome but there the resemblance ended. He was a cheerful and friendly soul but his contribution to the conversation soon made it clear to all that Mick was not the sharpest tool in the shed.

Since it looked like being a marathon session with no possibility of driving at the end of it, Paddy kindly offered to put the visitors up for the night. He had a small farm outside Letterkenny with plenty of spare room for waifs and strays that might not be lucky enough to find a female at the dance friendly enough to share her bed. The drinking continued as late afternoon turned to early and then quite late evening. The group split up, Mick and Paddy to their respective homes to eat and our heroes to find a fish and chip shop, all having agreed to meet up again at the dance.

When Curry, Bentit and Lindsay got to the dance venue there was no sign of Paddy but Mick was well ensconced at the bar and when he saw them enter his face split in a great big welcoming grin. Mick explained that Paddy had probably crashed out, that this was nothing new and it was unlikely he would reappear. When his three guests expressed a little alarm that the sleeping arrangements were out of the window, it was a bit chilly for kipping in an unheated car, Mick assured them there was no problem as they could flop at his place.

Thus reassured the three got down to the serious business of topping up their already overflowing alcohol levels as a prelude to exercising their collective charms on the female population of Letterkenny and district. As most successful Lotharios are aware, a male's attractiveness to the opposite sex is usually inversely proportional to his alcohol intake and the ladies of Letterkenny were no exception to the rule.

The girls of Letterkenny were a fun-loving lot and liked to josh and banter with the lads but their main purpose was to get as pissed as farts, preferably with someone else paying for the drink. The three heroes were naïve enough to oblige and bought a few rounds in the forlorn hope that their generosity would be repaid by the invitation to a bed somewhere not too far distant.

Jimmy Curry fell in with a particularly riotous lot of ladies who sang every song that the band played. They were ladies of mature age but Jimmy hung on to the adage that ladies of this age 'did not smell, would not tell and were as grateful as hell'. One particularly riotous lady was well into her sixties and took to mothering Jimmy in a big way. She finally induced him to get up onto the floor and dance with her. She making a big play of seducing him in a very provocative way. Jimmy did not mind this as it was as close to shagging that he had been in a long time and he was sure that this would be his bed for the night with 'breakfast' thrown in.

They danced quite vigorously for about twenty minutes until the lady had had enough and was glowing with perspiration. She pulled Jimmy off the floor, made him sit down and she sat on his knee.

'Jeez boy, that wis bloody great but it disna half make ye sweat!' she shouted in his ear and at that she whipped off a wig and stuck it on Jimmy's head. She was as bald as a coot and Jimmy nearly jumped out of his skin when he saw this. However, he was quite happy to stay where he was as she was now rubbing his bewigged head in between her cleavage while she joshed with her friends about how this reminded her of having a hairy dick stuck there. Jimmy took it all in good part

271

but his ardour was waning as the effects of the drink were beginning to take over.

She insisted that they dance some more and this she did without replacing the wig. It was firmly stuck on Jimmy's head and quite pretty he looked too. Jiving on the dance floor Jimmy enquired, 'Di yi hiv onythin' else false aboot yi?'

'Aye, mi teeth, an al tak them out fur yi if yi want mi tae gie yi a blow job,' she shouted back as she rubbed his crotch with her hand and noticed the stirrings therein. She winked at one of her pals who was dancing close by.

Although slightly repelled by the thought of being given a blow job by this rather elderly lady who was bald, swathed in whale-bone corsets and smelled slightly of urine overlaid by the sweet smell of cheap perfume, he was not about to miss out because of these few imperfections. The thought of being gummed to ejaculation, no matter who was doing the gumming, brought him back to some degree of soberness and the crotch rubbing gave him an instant hard-on. After all, he wouldn't mind being gummed in the dark outside.

'Ah yer jokin, yi widn'a die that fur me, wid yi?' he slurred hopefully.

'Aye, I wid, c'mon wi me.'

This is not exactly what he had come to Letterkenny for, as in his dreams he had envisaged a somewhat younger encounter but as the Royal Navy fish heads say, any port in a storm – male or female – and the port tonight was to be this toothless mouth.

She led him by the hand towards the stage that had been vacated by the band for the interval and Jimmy followed on, staggering unseeingly like a lamb to the slaughter.

When he recognised where he thought she intended to take him, Jimmy was reluctant to go onto the stage and she assured him that she wanted to take him behind the back-stage curtain.

'It's too cauld tae go ootside!' she declared. 'We'll dae it behind the drapes.'

So round to the back of the stage and she pulled him up the steps leading to the area behind the curtain. It was very dark there.

Jimmy felt her fumbling with his fly zip and then his trouser belt and buttons and then the cold air hitting his nether regions as his trousers and his underpants were pulled down to his ankles. He had a stonking hard-on that had now become free and was looking for a receptacle to keep it warm and make it perform its natural function. Eyes closed he could hardly believe it when he felt his rampant penis being enveloped and exercised by the woman's mouth.

Wig still firmly implanted on his head, he opened his eyes to see that the curtain had been pulled back and he was being ogled by about a dozen women who were by this time giggling and laughing. Even worse, he could hardly believe it when he looked down and saw that instead of being given a blow-job by the woman, she had removed her teeth and had them in her hands. These were what was giving him his penile sensations as she rubbed them backwards and forwards on either side of his erection.

'Fuckin' hell!' shouted the hapless lad as he jumped out of the dental embrace and tried to pull himself together, however he only succeeded in falling over onto his back as he was grabbing for his underpants from around his ankles.

To add to his embarrassment it was at this time that he probably wished that he had put on a clean set of underpants, as the three-day-old skid marks were truly evident, caught in the beam of one of the stage spotlights. This set up a humungous cheer from the ogling audience, with shouts of 'Look, he hisn'a even learn'd tae wipe his arse yet – the poor wee mite.' By this time all the women were in hysterics.

After a while a couple of the women came to his rescue, declaring themselves to be nurses who 'had seen shittier underpants than this'. They helped Jimmy to get his pants up around his waist and then his trousers. They helped him down the stairs and into the toilet where they washed his face in cold water to revive him a little. They took him back to the bar and bought him a pint of Guinness, which more than compensated for all his embarrassment. He was too much out of the game to care in any case.

During this time, Bentit had been sniffing around a slightly younger lady and had been plying her with drinks in an effort to persuade her that she really did need a sleeping companion that night. She seemed keen enough but she was in that maudlin sort of trance that some women get into when they are pissed – incoherently argumentative, eyes half closed, head wobbling and occasionally shaking from side to side as if trying to dislodge a colony of nits from their hair. Lots of finger pointing as the whole of the upper torso seems to defy gravity and rolls around their waist. Fag in one hand, cork tip plastered in lipstick, the lighted end burning into chair or dress, drink in the other, grasped as if it will be the last they are ever bought. And all this while they are sitting down! Bentit finally persuaded her that he was the man of her dreams that night and they departed together into the darkness.

By this time Curry and Lindsay were so pissed that they inevitably ended up empty-handed and muttered 'lucky bastard' as they watched Bentit leave. Consequently they hung onto Mick's shirt-tails and all three staggered their way to his house.

They entered Mick's house, which proved to be very large with a huge kitchen with a great open range, refectory table with chairs and two enormous armchairs. The two musketeers were offered an armchair each, which they sank into and wished Mick a grateful goodnight. Mick left them with the request to 'please be quiet' since he had not been able to warn his ma and his pa that he'd be bringing guests home and he didn't want to alarm them.

This plea was totally unnecessary as the effect of the heat from the open range combined with the alcohol quickly put his audience into a profound coma.

The two slumbered through what remained of the night, Norman in a quiet, genteel manner while the Revd. James gave a passable impression of the Griffon engines which, as an instrument fitter, he sometimes worked on. Now Norman could sleep through a noisy night shift, and often did, frequently only waking up when his fellow shift workers shook him in time to knock off. It wasn't the row created by Curry that woke him up but a noise to which he was not accustomed, the pad, pad of slippered feet quietly descending the stairs, which he was facing. As he opened his eyes a fraction the feet came into view followed by legs clad in thick elasticated stockings all wrinkled at the ankles. Risking a slight upward move of the head he saw an elderly lady stopped halfway down the steps staring at him and Curry as if she'd just found a pair of aliens in her house. Sometime during the night Jimmy had unbuttoned his shirt to the waist so her reaction was not unjustified, because so hairy was this man that he gave a whole new meaning to the expression about not seeing the wood for the trees, the living proof of Darwin's theory, about halfway along the evolutionary scale.

Not wishing to frighten the lady further, Norman stayed quite motionless. There is no knowing what might have happened had he uncoiled to his full height of sixty-two inches. There was no need to worry, however, because at that moment the lady (now identified as Mick's mother) turned to face back up the stairs and called, in a voice that held no trace of concern whatsoever, 'Da, there's two men in the kitchen.' The aforementioned 'Da' then appeared and he was a giant. He was taller and wider at the shoulder than his son and, though advanced in years, gave the distinct impression of being more than confident in his ability to control this situation and one a helluva sight worse if needs be. Jimmy was by now in a semi-comatose state and vaguely aware that something was not quite as it should be – it was beyond his ken why a man twelve feet tall and half as wide should be in his room, standing over him in a slightly menacing way.

Mick was sensibly still abed and no help could be expected from that quarter, so the pair explained as best they could how they came to be there and offered profuse apologies for any worry they had unwittingly caused. The old man acknowledged that 'unwittingly' was certainly an apt choice of word in this case. The two protagonists just nodded, not completely sure what 'Da' meant but with just an inkling that it probably wasn't complimentary. With tensions easing somewhat the lads repeated their apologies and prepared to leave, asking the parents to pass on their thanks to Michael for his hospitality to which the father replied. 'Oi'll certainly be passin sumtin' on to dat boyo!'

Jimmy and Norman headed for the door only to find the route blocked by the broad shoulders of the man of the house. This worried them that perhaps some thick lips or broken noses were coming their way after all but what he said was even more frightening: 'Ye'll not be leaving my house without yer breakfast!'

After a night on the batter till about three am and being woken up at seven, the last thought working its way around the two brain cells currently operating between them was the idea of eating breakfast, but they were too cowardly to refuse. Half an hour later the lady of the house placed before each of them a huge Irish fried breakfast. Instantaneously they both had the same thought: 'Why the fuck didn't he just beat the shit out of us?'

The battle with breakfast having been declared a draw and farewells and thanks completed, the pair were now faced with the problem of finding Bentit and the car.

It didn't matter in which order they were found but it was pretty important they find both. Letterkenny is not a big place so the search was soon successfully completed, with the added bonus that the two items sought were found together, the one inside the other. They spotted the car from some distance away and recognised it as the right vehicle immediately by the colour and registration number. If any doubt remained it was soon dispelled because the shirt flying like a battle ensign from the radio antenna could still be identified as belonging to Steve, in spite of the carrots and tomato skins randomly chucked up over it by his paramour as he tried to grope her on her doorstep some hours previously. He never made it to her bed so any envy on behalf of the other two was unjustified. Hot sick and a cold car were his reward for all his efforts.

Jimmy and Norman defrosted the by now stiffened Bentit slowly, as recommended in the better hypothermia survival manuals. This they achieved by filling the car with organically produced warm air until he showed signs of life by being sick over the dashboard. This set off a chain reaction, and the other two chucked their recently gorged breakfast onto the pavement.

The three then made the return journey to Ballykelly in a quiet, pensive manner – with the windows open.

Recounting their tale of the weekend to their 'comrades' back at the base on the Monday morning resulted in the usual joshing and piss taking. The final outcome was that Jimmy earned himself the title of 'wally wanker', wallies being the Scottish word for false teeth.

39

Engineering Officers

There was probably no greater enigma on the Shackleton operational squadron than the position of engineering officer. Invariably these types were very young and relatively inexperienced in the ways of life that governed such an anarchical institution as Ballykelly's H&R flight. A university degree and an officer's course at Cranwell were no fit training to prepare these young Turks, or perhaps more appropriately turkeys, for the challenges of commanding battle-scarred, experienced and truculent troops. At least they were battle-scarred, experienced and truculent through being ravished by drink and a certain cynicism about their role in life, keeping ancient aircraft airworthy with long hours of unrewarded overtime. All this was for the benefit of a pseudo flying club because very little of importance, apart from search and rescue operations, was ever undertaken.

The boy engineering officer was therefore held in disdain and often outright disrespect, especially when he would try to assert his authority. The most common reason for him to try to assert himself was tardiness of the hung-over troops who had danced the light fandango at the NAAFI dance the night before or had been out all night shagging in Londonderry or Coleraine. Tardiness was very common as the distance between the accommodation and the flight crewroom necessitated a bus to be laid on courtesy of the RAF. This was very unusual in the service and was an indication that the distance to be travelled was indeed very long and would take the best part of an hour to walk should the bus be missed, and missed it was on many, many occasions.

Resultantly, when people were late they were very late and 'necessity being the mother of invention', this led to a bewildering array of excuses being dreamed up by late arrivals. As with every rule, there is an exception and this came in the form of Sean McIlley who rarely made an excuse. Sean could always think fast enough on his feet to come up with a funny, if not quite respectful, answer, delivered with a disarming Irish smile which removed any possible feeling of offended dignity on the part of the engineering officer questioning his lateness. The resulting conversation would be very brief and normally consisted of a one-liner from each participant.

'Late again, McIlley.'

'Me too sir!'

Sean would bluster his way past the officer thereby never giving him a chance to retaliate. The officer would merely scratch his head and walk away looking furtively round in the vain hope that nobody had witnessed this exchange.

On the not infrequent occasions when Sean did not appear at all until after lunch the exchange was modified.

'Where were you this morning, McIlley?'

'Why, what happened?'

This again was greeted by officer scratching his head as he had no immediate satisfactory response. The increasing frequency of Sean's late arrivals was beginning to become an issue and everyone was sure that he would cop it one day and be charged with being late and insubordination. Even engineering officers learn, and he eventually realised that if he worded his side of the conversation with care then Sean would have to play his part and give some sort of excuse or reason for being so late.

The day came when Sean once again ignored his alarm clock and the shouts of his mates to get out of his 'fleapit'. Having missed the transport again, he decided there was no point in risking bodily injury by rushing so he went through his morning toilet routine at his normal pace before leaving for work and a short verbal fencing match with the boss.

As he stepped into the fresh air he bumped into his crony Scouse Dickbury coming in heavily burdened under the weight of a big pile of bed linen and commenting, 'Fucking sheet change duty again, still it's an excuse for an extra hour in bed.'

Scouse dumped the sheets in the barrack room and the two of them set off together down the hill for the long trudge. Like most Liverpudlians, Dickbury possessed a wicked sense of humour that was more brutal than subtle. He started giving Sean a hard time over what was about to befall him when the wrath of their mutual leader came down on his head like the proverbial ton of bricks. As they arrived at H&R, Scouse made a big scene of waving his friend ahead with an 'after you, sir' accompanied by a not very sympathetic grin while staying close behind so as not to miss any of the fun to come.

As the engineering officer spied the pair entering he turned on Sean and said in a very carefully controlled voice that hid some real annoyance, 'OK McIlley, I'm giving you no chances for a smartarse answer this time, just a straightforward question. Why are you late for work this morning?'

'Sheet change duty, sir,' replied Sean in, for him, an unusually serious voice and walked away grinning. The boss, with a face like thunder, repeated the question to Dickbury who, for the first time in living memory, appeared to have lost the power of speech.

There were those who, because of their age, experience and deranged outlook on life, hated authority of any sort and just wanted to get on to do their job without all the rigmarole of service discipline and hierarchy. One of this ilk was a forty-year-old Irish LAC airframe mechanic called Jimmy Kielly. LAC is the second lowest rank in the RAF, so it could be deduced that at forty years old and having been in the service for twenty-two years, twenty of them spent on Coastal Command, ambition was not one of Kielly's strong points. He also regarded himself as being superior purely because of his age and experience and in truth there was nothing that anyone could teach him about Shackletons. Instead of wearing the usual overalls, his normal mode of attire was a khaki dustcoat tied in the middle with baler twine. This mimicked his lord and master Chief Tech Sandlers who was the only man that Kielly respected, perhaps because of the chiefy's similar unconventional approach to service life. So it was very unlikely that Kielly would stand any approach by a boy engineering officer to challenge any point of order like being late for work. In Kielly's eyes there was only one point of order – his own!

However, the engineering officer had the utter temerity to challenge Kielly over his tardiness in his own inimitable way.

'Why are you late for work again, Kielly?'

'It's personal!' replied Jimmy, surly.

'What do you mean "it's personal"? Have you been to the doctor or something?'

'No, I told you it was just personal.'

'Well, if you've not been to the doctor and there is nothing medically wrong you can't just say "it's personal" and expect to get away with it. You had better explain yourself or I will have no alternative but to charge you.'

'Well, as well as being personal it is also very embarrassing.'

'Look, just get on with it or do you want to come into my office to explain – if it is that embarrassing.'

Jimmy leaned towards the officer as if he was taking him into his confidence. 'No, it's all right here. I don't know if anyone has ever told you but I have an enormous penis. Well, I never like to boast about it and I don't like to display it in public as I know to my cost that it causes jealousy and this can lead to adverse reactions among my peers. I mean of course those that are my equal and not those that I meet in the toilet.' The officer looked on, horrified by what he was hearing. He made as if to terminate this line of answer but Jimmy held up his hand and continued.

'Well, this morning I woke up with this enormous hard-on that I couldn't get rid of, no matter how hard I tried to forget it or break its back. As a good Catholic, the very size of the thing and my unclean thoughts were of considerable embarrassment to me. Some of the other guys in the billet were up and about by the time I should have got out of bed but there was no way that I could have possibly exposed my protuberance to them – it would have been unfair and demeaning for them. Demeaning in the sense that they would have cursed God for not giving them a penis like mine. So I just had to lie in bed until the room cleared and I could get out of bed. When I say get out of bed I mean that I slung my penis over the side and it dragged me out after it. It causes me a lot of trouble at times and I sometimes wish that I was just an ordinary bloke with an ordinary-sized penis. I don't know if you have ever experienced any similar sort of embarrassment in your life, sir?'

Chiefy Sandlers had been standing behind the officer all during this interchange and had been urging Jimmy on by making faces and nodding his approval of this piss-taking exercise. The rest of the guys in the crewroom were pissing themselves and trying hard not to laugh by biting their lips but their shoulders heaved uncontrollably and there was also a lot of laughing disguised as coughing.

At this point, the engineering officer wished that he had not started the questioning and that the floor would open up and swallow him. He looked around him with an almost maniacal set smile on his lips and his total confusion was palpable. He had no answer to this revelation and he knew he had been outmanoeuvred by a master. Nothing in his Cranwell training had prepared him for a confrontation like this. He turned on his heel and said over his shoulder, 'Well, don't let it happen again.'

'I'll try sir but it has a mind of its own at times,' was Jimmy's parting shot.

When I related this tale to one of the guys later on he said, 'Fuck off, I've seen Kielly's prick and it's so small he has to sit down to piss.'

The crewroom was the meeting point where sustenance like coffee and tea could be got and the sarcastic interchanges between the various trades and shifts were thrown about. It was also the place that cult figures such as those in the *Magic Roundabout* were revered. There was never any work done at five in the afternoon when that programme was on the telly. There were many that were so in love with Florence that they wanted to see her with her kit off before Zebedee invited her to bed each night. It was during one of these sessions when the crewroom was full.

'What is that fucking awful smell? Has someone shit himself or something?'

'Yeah, I can smell it too! What the fuck is it – has someone dropped a fart? If he has he needs a good pull through because his guts stink!'

'Yuk, fuck a wild man, it's getting worse and it seems to be coming from that direction. Hey Maskell, have you dropped your guts over there?'

Corporal Maskell was an engine fitter and a bluff Yorkshireman to boot who didn't take kindly to any piss taking.

'Fook off, yi bloody great wassak. I've just bin for a shit if tha' must know so there's no way I could be fartin' now, could I?'

Because of this interchange, all eyes were now on Maskell and someone noticed a bit of an anomaly about his person.

'Just been for a shit, have you? You've brought the bloody thing back in here with you – look, you've got a bloody great turd cradled round your neck you dirty bastard.'

'Fook off, you're just takin' the piss!' as he reached behind his neck to be confronted with a soft, squishy, smelly mass that made him pull his hand away very quickly. He looked aghast at the mess on his fingers and realised that it was indeed shit.

'Which one of you dirty bastards did this? You can't go around puttin' shit into blokes' overalls and expect to get away with it. I'll kill the bastard that did this.'

'C'mon Maskell, surely you can recognise it as one of your own, fuck me, it even looks like you.'

By this time Maskell was removing his overalls in some haste and as he pulled himself out of the sleeves, the horrible turd splattered onto the floor with a resounding 'plop' and sat there looking up at its previous owner. Now that he could see the thing and as they gazed longingly at each other there came a faint dawning of realisation of how the turd got into his overalls.

'Fook me, I must have caught me overalls between me arse and the pan and shit into them, stupid bastard that I am. It's a good job it was a solid job, if you know what I mean. It'll be easy to clean off the floor now.'

'Get that horrible thing out of here. Christ, we've missed half of the *Magic Roundabout* because of it. Don't bring your brains in here again, d'ya hear?'

'Fook off!'

40

The Driving Test

Back in this era of austerity there were very few car owners on the base. When Harold Macmillan declared during his time at Number Ten, 'Let us be frank about it; most of our people have never had it so good', one would have thought that he might have thrown in a car for 'most of our people'. This however was not the case and cars were scarce and relatively expensive to buy and to run. Of those that were around on the roads about 90 per cent should have been assigned to a scrap heap many years before but were kept running by injudicious use of glass fibre resin, gun gum and other unsavoury concoctions such as sawdust in the gear box to quieten down worn bearings. Sometimes sawdust was applied to an engine just before the car was sold to hide the minor problem of the knocking of the big end bearings or other some such minor problems. Having applied the sawdust, the engine was unlikely to run for very long but as the car was sold under *caveat emptor* – 'buyer beware' – there was no comeback on the dealer or the private seller.

Whilst on shift at H&R those groundcrew who had a car would spend many hours mending and servicing them, sometimes to the detriment of the work that was supposed to be done on the aircraft. An after-flight service would always take second place to an oil change on the car but at least the chiefy in charge of the shift always knew where to find most of his team when something really needed doing.

Like all young men a car was high on the list of 'wants' but once the bar bill had been paid there was precious little money left to put towards the purchase of one. There were dreamers who saw a car as their passport to paradise by allowing them to get out and chase 'fanny' instead of it having to be bussed in on NAAFI dance nights. However, some others were only at the start of their dreams as they didn't even have a driving licence.

One such as this was Davy Hamilton. Davy, as we have heard, was an engine mechanic but he had undergone metamorphosis and had emerged as a tractor driver and had driven about twelve thousand miles in the year that he had been at Ballykelly. He had achieved this without a civilian driving licence. He didn't know the Highway Code but he could pull a mean train of Houchins or air bottles; however, he had never aspired to towing Shackletons or even the oil bowser.

On one of his frequent visits to my house I persuaded him to apply for his driving test which he did and gave my address as his residence. We spent the next few weeks going through the Highway Code until he was word perfect. He then had the temerity to put his name down for a detachment to America and flew away with the rest of the guys. One would have thought that there would have been plenty of tractor drivers in America.

The notification of the time and place for the driving test duly arrived at my house but Davy was still in the States. However, before cancelling I decided to hold onto the letter until the day of the test just in case he made an appearance and could take the exam.

It was the day of the test and I went to work. Sure enough Davy had made it back and was excitedly telling me about the tractors that they had in the States. It took me a couple of minutes to shut him up and then told him about his test set for three that afternoon.

'Christ, that's great but there's just one wee problem – I don't have a car.'

'Hell, I never thought about that. You can't use your tractor and you can't use my car because it's driver-only insurance. Give me a minute and I'll think of something.'

Colin Hendle came into the crewroom and this spurred me to ask, 'Hey Colin, you've got fully comprehensive insurance for that car of yours haven't you?'

'Aye, so what?' was the very reticent reply.

Colin had a Morris Minor that was the love of his life. He thought more of the car than he did of his wife and what's more he spent more time with the car than he did with her. Every last piece of chrome and paintwork was polished so much that there was more weight of wax than there was of steel. Nor was the engine spared from the constant polishing and the spark plugs fairly gleamed as they went about their business of sparking.

Colin and I had stripped this engine down in his kitchen at home to replace the piston rings and the thing was so clean that we didn't have to put down rags to protect the floor. Each nut and bolt was cleaned to a high degree as they were extracted off the carcass. He physically grimaced as spanners and sockets were applied to the same nuts and bolts as the engine was being rebuilt in case they were damaged or contaminated in some way. This was a man with a serious obsession about cleanliness.

So it was with some trepidation that I said, 'Because we want to borrow it for Davy to take his test in Coleraine this afternoon.'

He blanched to a deathly white and I'm sure I saw a slight stagger as he reeled at the thought of someone else, and a learner to boot, driving his baby. It was therefore no surprise when he said, 'The bloody battery is flat. First thing in the morning it'll start the car as long as it catches first time but the car won't start if the engine is hot.'

'This is just bullshit and he is just trying to wriggle out of lending the car,' I thought, so it was an even bigger surprise when he added, 'You can borrow it if you want as long as I get it back in one piece.'

Christ, he had either gone gaga or he was getting a divorce from the car. Either way it must have been the end of a long and loving relationship. His response immediately put me on the defensive as there was the possibility that there might be a double bluff in there somewhere.

'Are you sure now? We only need it for a couple of hours and will be back before you go off shift. If we're late you can take my car home and I'll pick it up later.'

'Aye, take it but mind what I said about the hot engine. She'll just not start.' He tossed me the keys.

'Right Davy, I've secured your transport to paradise this afternoon so I suppose that we had better try to get the time off. I'll go and see the chief.'

'Hey Chief, Davy's has got his driving test this afternoon in Coleraine, any chance of him and I taking a couple of hours off for him to sit it?' This was directed at Chief Technician Bentley who looked back at me suspiciously with his rheumy eyes and tried to weigh up what particular skive I was up to and furthermore how he could turn it to his advantage. To me at that time he seemed to be ancient, but he had to be under the retirement age of fifty-five, however he had seen the war years and this made him an arch cynic of anything or anybody who had not had this enlightening experience. He had cut his teeth on Spitfires and Hurricanes and he didn't like the modern technology of the Shackleton nor the young whippersnappers who had the audacity to join his air force. We were all good for nothing lazy bastards that would try to take the piss out of him at the drop of a hat. Funnily enough he was right on every count.

'Driving test, is it? Never sat one myself, never needed to, in my day we were all much smarter than you lot. You lot are too bloody soft these days. Too much bloody sex, drugs and stupid music, I was just saying to my daughter the other night, too much sex, drugs and stupid bloody music. What does he want a driving licence for in any case, he can drive a bloody tractor well enough, he should take a job as a bloody farmer that one. He'd be a better farmer than an engine mechanic any day, bloody soft he is. Anyway we've got far too much work on for you two to be skiving off for a bloody driving test.'

I had to agree with most of what he said but I wasn't getting my share of it any more than he was and he could only hope that his daughter was steering clear of it too. Mind, if she was anything like him he had nothing to worry about.

'What job cards are on the go then, Chief? Maybe we can clear a fair amount before you let us go after lunch?'

This was music to his ears. He knew that if we were keen to get away that we would pull the stops out to get the work done for him. He ran his shift as if there was a competition to see which shift could clear the most work and he was always determined that he would win. Like the character played by Jack Hawkins in *Ben Hur*, Bentley was always asking for 'ramming speed' from the poor buggers that had to jump to his commands.

'Well let's see now, there's two double prop changes to be done on Zulu or there's inlet plug changes to be done on two engines on X-ray, or there's a coolant leak to fix on Golf, or there's an engine change on Lima. Christ, those bloody aircrew know how to break aircraft. They wouldn't have got away with it during the war, you know.'

'No I don't know, Chief – before my time.' I had to think quickly about which job I would take on. It had to be one that would satisfy him that he had extracted his pound of flesh but would get us away from the place by lunchtime.

'I'll take the double prop changes if you let us away for the afternoon.'

'That won't do me much good at all because I'll still be short if you both take on that job,' he said, shaking his head.

'No, I didn't mean for both of us to do it, I'll do it on my own and you can get Davy to do the plug changes on X-ray. I'm sure he'll get his arse off his tractor to do that for you.' I looked across at Davy who shrugged his shoulders and nodded in agreement.

I could see that I had struck a fair bargaining position because he thought that there was no way that I could do two double prop changes on my own, never mind complete the task in a morning. This prospect now let him off the hook over refusing to let us go.

'OK, that would seem to be fair. I don't think you will be able to do two double prop changes before close of play today in any case but if you do I will give you the rest of the day off. Mind, I want the engines run after the changes are complete.'

Considering all the countless hours of overtime that I had worked, unpaid and mostly unthanked, this was very big of the old bastard. He wanted a pound and a half of flesh now. Still, I had no choice but to get on with it.

'All right then, let Davy get the prop kit and the new propellers out to the kite before he starts on the plugs and it's a deal. What engines are the props hanging on?'

'Three and four,' he said. At least they were on the same side of the aircraft so it would make the job slightly easier.

'Right Davy, let's get an engine stand and the prop kit out to Zulu and then you can get two sets of props from the engine bay before you start on the plug changes.'

Getting service like this was great, as finding some form of transport to get the equipment out to the aircraft normally took longer than the time to do the job. We booked the kit and the spares out of the stores, lugged them out to the tractor and slung the kit onto the running board. We hitched up a lifting frame and towed it out to the aircraft.

The prop change kit comprised all the large pieces of paraphernalia that was necessary to remove and install the propellers. There were large spanners, long round bars that fitted into the spanners and a very heavy hammer for hitting the long round bars that fitted into the spanners. Because of all the hitting that had gone on over the years the long round bars were no longer round, nor were they straight, in fact they resembled the proverbial dog's hind leg. The fact that they were not straight probably contravened the prop manufacturer's installation criteria, as the correct torque on the propeller retaining nut was achieved by hitting the five-foot-long bar three mighty whacks with the fifteen-pound hammer, so with a bent bar the calibration would be slightly off. This was precision engineering at its finest. However, if the retaining nut locking ring did not fit into place some more hammering had to be done, thereby adding a bit more bend to the bar causing further deviations of the precise tolerances. Another essential piece of kit was a bucket to catch the oil drained from the propeller dome.

We stole an engine stand from one of the other aircraft where somebody was using it but had obviously gone for a cuppa or something. We took it round to Zulu and positioned the stand in front of the number three engine propeller, set down the feet on the stand and secured it in place. We got the kit off the tractor and Davy disappeared at a rate of knots to get the new propellers.

I climbed onto the stand and removed the front propeller spinner after having unlatched the retaining buttons. This then exposed the front propeller dome, the front plate of which was held on by some twenty split-pinned nuts and bolts. In the centre of the front plate there was an oil drain plug that was very ineffective at draining the oil out of the dome. This was because the plug was halfway up the dome and the propeller shafts lay back at a slight angle. This angle caused the thick oil to trickle down the front plate, only to be blown away on the wind without hitting the bucket slung from the dome. The split pins in the nuts on the front plate had to be removed and the nuts undone. Once the nuts were slack the essential bucket was hung around the dome and the front plate loosened by inserting a screwdriver into the joint and giving it a whack with a hammer. On days without wind this allowed the oil in the dome to drain into the bucket, but on windy days the oil splattered wherever it wanted to and it never wanted to go into the bucket. However, the aircraft were normally parked heading into the wind so the oil was normally blown away onto the engine radiators or front cowling.

After the oil had drained the front plate could be taken off and the guts of the dome were removed. The retaining nut locking ring was removed by probing with the bent end of an engineer's scribe. The retaining nut spanner, which was a long cylinder about eight inches in diameter, was then inserted and given several whacks with the hammer to loosen it and then extract it from the dome. The blade racks were then loosened from the translation unit by simply breaking the split pins that were made of a soft metal to facilitate this. They were always a real bastard to extract whole because of their position inside the spinner backplate. The front propeller could now be removed by slinging it to the lifting frame hook and taking up the weight on the winch. The propeller normally had to be rocked backwards and forwards to break the seal between hub and engine shaft splines and once this was achieved the lifting frame was used to pull the prop off the shaft. The prop was laid down on the ground by allowing the winch to free-wheel with the weight of the prop. The lower blade was supported by hand and the assembly would glide to the ground.

The translation unit was then removed from the rear propeller. This exposed the front retaining nut which was removed, and again the rear prop was slung from the lifting frame and removed after the seal between the hub and the rear centralising cone was broken. This prop was laid down in the same way as the first.

Refitting was normally a mirror image of the removal but utilising all the intricate calibrations as described above. The biggest problem on reassembly was the split-pinning of the front propeller rack nuts once they had been located in the translation unit. This exercise had to be done virtually by touch as the nuts were obscured by the spinner backplate. Once the split pins had been inserted by trial and error they then had to be bent over the castellated nuts. This was achieved by using the frame of a small hacksaw specially modified for the job. Sometimes this job was a real bastard as the pins were tight to insert and no amount of tightening or slackening of the nut would accommodate easy insertion, so the pin had to be hammered through, which was no easy job inside the backplate. The other balls-ache was the tightening and torque loading of the nuts and bolts on the dome front plate and again each of these twenty or so nuts had to be split-pinned. The front spinner was then replaced and buttoned up.

I changed the other props and completed this at twelve-thirty. Davy had just arrived and he gave me a hand to get the old props onto the transportation trolley. We lifted the prop kit onto the tractor once again and cleared the pan of all the conglomeration of trolleys, lifting frame and bucket which had caught some oil. The rest of the oil had to be cleaned off the engine cowlings. We nobbled some unsuspecting soul to come and stand by the fire extinguisher while we ran up the engines and put the props through their paces of controlling max RPM, constant speeding at differing engine boost settings and finally through to feathering. Everything was perfect.

We all went round to X-ray and did the engine runs on this kite to prove the efficacy of Davy's plug changes. The magneto drop was acceptable so we had completed our side of the bargain for Chiefy Bentley. We went into the office to sign off the job cards and the aircraft 700. It was a quarter past one.

'What are you two doing with those job cards?' asked a suspicious Bentley.

'We've completed the jobs so we'll just get the paperwork done and then be off for Davy's driving test as we agreed.'

'You can't have done those jobs in that time. Have you run the engines and proved the props and the plug changes?'

'Aye, that we have, so now that we've got signed up we'll be on our way.'

'No, no, I can't let you go at this time, it's far too early, I'll get shot if somebody finds out. You'll have to do something else before I let you go.'

'Aw come on, Chief, we struck a bargain and we've kept our side of it and you've got a lot of work out of us. His driving test is in Coleraine at three and it's now half past one. Who's goin' to know that you've let us go anyway?'

'Look, the engineer on November has just reported the number three engine starter motor has stuck – if you get that going then you can go, OK?'

'OK. Where is the bloody thing?'

'Out on the back pan across the bridge.'

This was good, as it meant we could get there very quickly and we had direct access to Colin's car without coming back into the office.

We went out the back door and across the bridge. There was the aircrew milling about around the aircraft in the sure and certain knowledge that they did not have to earn their flying pay that particular day because of the stuck starter motor. The starter motors were prone to sticking and consequently would not turn the engine whilst engaged with the starter ring. The first thing was to turn the propeller by hand to try to disengage the starter motor gear. This was done but the bloody thing was still stuck.

The next thing was to try to dislodge it by brute force and ignorance. The starter motor was located low down on the starboard side of the engine towards the front. It was a real bastard to get at but over the years innovation had prevailed and the perfect tool had been devised to get at it to give it a real clout. This tool was a 'jury strut' that was inserted in the undercarriage of the Mark 1 and 2 aircraft in case the undercarriage somehow overcame the geometric lock and collapsed. The jury strut was actually two tubes of steel, about three inches in diameter, one inserted inside the other, making an assembly of about three feet long and sprung loaded so it could be compressed for insertion in place when the aircraft was on the ground. There were four jury struts in all, two for each undercarriage. This made a very good and weighty hammer for getting at the starter motor after opening the side engine cowling.

We got a set of stepladders and opened the cover, inserted the strut in the appropriate direction, felt for the starter motor with the end of it and gave it three or four mighty whacks with the strut whilst Davy turned the prop back and forth. This was done with much advice from the aircrew that it would never work. We knew better, as we had a driving test to go to. After about three attempts I thought I heard the motor spring back from the ring. I got down from the ladder and asked the engineer to go and try the engine now. He duly obliged and much to our relief the bloody thing turned over. I replaced the panel, gave the jury strut to one of the disgruntled aircrew and we were free to wend our way to Coleraine. We conveniently forgot to let the chiefy know that we had fixed the engine in case the old bastard gave us another job.

We found Colin's car. Davy was to drive to give him the practice as he hadn't driven since before he went to the States. We packed our overalls in the boot with some trepidation as the overalls were a bit dirty and the boot was immaculate. However, we turned the offending objects inside out so as not to breach the cleanliness code. The car started easily on request and we rapidly departed before the chiefy spotted us.

The drive through to Coleraine was uneventful and Davy was a confident and competent driver. All those hours spent on a tractor had certainly paid off. We arrived in the town centre at about a quarter to three and did a couple of circuits around to get Davy used to the traffic and then we went up to the test centre. The car was parked nose-in near to a wall in the car park.

Mindful of Colin's warning about the car not starting when it was hot I sat in the driver's seat with the engine running while Davy went into the building to carry out whatever formalities had to be carried out. I sat there for about five minutes and Davy came out accompanied by a stern-looking man who was carrying a clipboard. I cleverly deduced that this would be the examiner.

When the two of them came close to the car I jumped out to let Davy take the seat.

'Why is the engine still running?' asked the examiner, in a deep Irish accent.

'Because if we switch it off it's likely that it won't start again due to a defective battery,' I replied.

'You'll need to switch it off so I can see that yon fella can start the car afore we proceed further.'

'But that's the point, with the defective battery the engine probably won't start. Could you not do the exam and then see if he can start the engine at the end of the test?'

'Sur, I'm the bloody examiner and you are not taking the test so I wid be obliged if you'd switch the engine off and let us be about our business.'

I could tell that there was a bit of menace in his voice so I reached into the car and turned off the engine. It seemed very quiet.

'Thank you, sur.' Looking at Davy he said, 'Would you please get in the vehicle and wait for further instructions from me when I have got in.'

I departed and sat myself down on a low wall some twenty feet away on the other side of the car park. I could see the examiner talking to Davy and him nodding in acquiescence. Davy shifted about in his seat and adjusted the mirror, and was obviously getting himself ready for the big event. I heard the click, click, click of the starter motor solenoid that refused to stay in place as there wasn't enough power in the battery to hold it in to turn the starter. This happened a couple of times before the driver's door opened and Davy got out and made for the back of the car.

'Has this car got a starting handle?' he shouted across to me.

'If there is one it'll be in the boot,' I shouted back as I rose and started towards the car.

Davy was rummaging in the boot and I went up to the open door and peered in at the examiner.

'Would it be all right if I gave you a push to get this thing started?'

'Sur, I've told ye afore that you're not the one takin' the test so I would be obliged if you would fuck off and let me run this in my own way.'

'OK, OK, just thought I would ask,' I replied haughtily. I went back to my perch and sat there in a sulk.

Davy found the starting handle and went round to the front of the car. He tried to insert it in the hole in the front bumper but there was barely enough room for him to achieve this because the car was parked so close to the wall. With some struggling he did somehow get the handle into position. However, there was still very little room for him to swing the crank round. When he finally managed to crank the engine the examiner was bobbed around in his seat and the whole thing started to take on the mantle of a circus. The more Davy cranked, the more the examiner bobbed and the procedure was punctuated by curses of

'You bastard!' as Davy's knuckles rattled off the wall or the gravel of the car park surface. The exercise went on for what seemed an eternity but was probably about five or six minutes. This was enough time to reduce Davy to a physical wreck. I am sure he was crying with pain and frustration as he leaned on his folded arm on the bonnet of the car. He had had enough.

The examiner got out of the car and I could see him talking at some length to Davy. I thought that Davy was about to hit him with the starting handle when he reached down and extracted it from the car. However, they both came round to the back of the car and Davy waved for me to come across to the car. As I approached I could see that Davy was nursing some very sore and bleeding knuckles.

'The examiner says that there's not enough time left to take the test now,' said Davy dejectedly.

I was about to get stuck into the man about being so obstinate over switching the engine off when Davy continued, 'but if we can get another battery he has a free slot for another test in an hour. Do you think we can get another battery in that time?'

I shrugged my shoulders. 'We can at least try.'

We pushed the car away from the wall. I still don't know how he had managed to get that handle through the bumper. I think he must have used the handle as a lever to bend the bumper upwards. Even more surprising was how he ever managed to swing the crank in so little space. However, his efforts were not over yet as he had to push the car for a jump start while I sat in the driver's seat. After all, I was the one with the licence. We got the car going with not too much effort and we were off on the quest to find a battery.

'Have you got any money?' Davy asked. 'I've only got some dollars on me and the banks are closed now.'

'Christ, where would I get money from? I've spent my pocket money for this week. Bairns, dogs and singlies cost a lot to feed, you know. Maybe we should give up for now?'

We had just passed a small garage on the main street so I parked and stopped the engine. We went back to the garage where a man was busying himself on the forecourt.

'Hi, we've got a bit of a predicament and wonder if you could help us?' I enquired.

He looked at me with the scepticism of a man who was about to hear some sob story that would tug at his heart strings enough for him to hand over all of his hard-earned money.

'Predicament is it? Aye go on then and let me see if it's a predicament,' he replied cagily.

'Well, my friend here has just been to take his driving test but our car has a flat battery so the examiner has refused to let him be tested until we get a new battery for the car. He's got another test slot in about forty-five minutes but another problem is that we only have US dollars in cash and the banks are closed. Could you see your way to lending us a battery for the duration of the test if we leave the dollars with you as security?'

'Aye, what type of car is it?' was his only and immediate reply.

'It's that Morris Minor sat along there.'

'Oh aye.' He departed into his garage.

We waited for no more than thirty seconds for him to return with a battery clutched between his hands and he laid this down on the ground in front of us.

'Here ye are then. Have ye any spanners tae fit it?' He was offering an adjustable spanner which I took from him as it would prevent dirtying any of Colin's tools.

'It's really good of you to help us like this. Davy will give you the dollars as promised.'

'Don't worry about that, just bring it back when yer finished an' the best o luck tae ye.' He winked at Davy.

Christ, this was some place where there was enough trust to let a battery out the door without any money changing hands. We lifted the bonnet and had the battery changed in a trice. Davy went into the car and it started first time. Eureka, we had done it! We stuck the old battery in the boot on top of our overalls and then went around the town for another mock test. We stopped and started the engine several times just to make sure that it wasn't a fluke the first time. It started every time.

Back up to the test centre and Davy went in to complete the formalities once again. I departed to a café that I had seen around the corner as I thought I should make myself scarce from the examiner in case he took any umbrage out on Davy.

I had ordered a pot of tea and had only just finished the first cup when Davy came into the café. He's crashed the car, I thought, because he had only been away for fifteen or twenty minutes.

'I've passed, I've passed!' he declared jubilantly. 'He only took me round the block, asked for the reverse round the corner, a three-point turn and an emergency stop. I've bloody well passed. I think he felt sorry for me with all that palaver earlier on.'

'Great, congratulations! I don't think he would have passed you just because he felt sorry for you. You did it on your own merit. We'd better get the battery back to the man in case he closes early.'

We went back to the garage with Davy driving minus his L plates. He drove into the forecourt and we were greeted by the owner.

'I see the battery has done the trick then,' he said with a smile. 'Congratulations. There'll be no stopping ye now then.'

'Aye right,' said Davy. 'He was really good givin' me the second chance at the test today. Say, how much do you want for the battery? I could pay for it in dollars if that would be all right. You could exchange them tomorrow.'

'Right, it is secondhand so just give me ten dollars for it an' we'll call it quits. Is that OK by you?'

'Aye certainly,' said Davy, as he handed over the money. 'It was really great of you to loan us the battery in the first place though without any fuss.'

'Oh there was no problem there at all. Yer uniforms sort of give a wee hint of where yer from and I've a brother that works at Ballykelly. Maybe you know him, his name is Bentley – Chief Technician Bentley?'

'That old bastard, he nearly stopped us getting here at all today. We had to escape from him.'

'I see he's not changed then.'

So 'all's well that ends well'. Davy got his licence, Colin got a new battery, and I got shit from old Bentley the next day for buggering off without telling him.

41

The End

I was to complete my nine years of adult service in May of 1971 at the ripe old age of twenty-seven. I had no idea what I wanted to do once I had left the security of the force. I had known nothing else for the past eleven and a half years of my existence and had no appreciation of civilian life at all. Nor did I have any ideas about what I would do in civilian life. I only knew that if I did not leave the force at this juncture I would probably be trapped for the next twelve years at least.

I had been asked if I wanted to sign on for the next term, which would have taken me up to pensionable age at forty. I thought about this but did nothing positive about it. There was a feeling of heading into an abyss that was fast looming and I had no control over it. The magnitude of this situation did not come home until I saw my name on a sheet of paper on a noticeboard and alongside my name was the comment 'natural wastage'. I thought if that was all they thought of me for all my hard work and endeavours over the years, then they could do without me and see where it gets them.

The predetermined leaving date was set for some time in early March of that year as there was annual and demob leave to be taken as well as a resettlement course before the actual day of judgement. Having recognised this predetermined day a whole chain of activities were set to take place to meet the scheduled departure. First among these activities were a series of parties that knocked the hell out of the house.

We had become renowned for our parties, as each one had become better organised and better attended than the last. We had even become so professional at organisation that the carpets in the house, being of the non-fitted sort, were rolled up to the side of the room and served as seats for those who were too pissed to stand. It also meant that all the fag burns were on the back of the carpet. The walls in the house also took a hammering as they were often used for bouncing off.

Fortunately, nobody actually went right through a wall but there were some with severe dents in them.

The favourite food for these parties was soup, chicken curry, spaghetti bolognese or something else that would fill up the 'singlies' who made it all the way up to the married quarters, sober or not. The food was normally consumed in a trice and marauding groups would start to invade cupboards for anything else that was edible.

'Nice bit of liver you cooked up tonight, Pam,' was a comment made to my wife at one party.

'What liver?'

'That liver in the pot on the pantry shelf, we took some out and heated it up under the grill.'

'You daft buggers, that's not liver, they're lights that I cooked up for the dog. It had "Not fit for human consumption" stamped all over it! Still, I don't suppose you lot are totally human anyway.'

There were no after-effects to this gourmet feast which presumably bore out the theory that there was not a human among them.

The parties went on and on and they were becoming a bit wearing after a while. It was very disconcerting when one night I was asked while I was on night shift, 'Are you going to the party tonight?'

'No, where is it?'

'Your house!'

I made sure I was at the party, and that this was the last, as we only had two weeks to go before we were to leave.

Not all the parties were at our house, as some of our friends did reciprocate with get-togethers at their places. These were also attended by marauding gangs of singlies trying to get rid of some of their testosterone along the way. One married woman who was known as 'the squadron bike' was always very keen to have a party as it gave her access to her toyboys. She would get herself slightly drunk and then take on anyone who had the balls and other equipment ready to satisfy her carnal cravings. This flirtation was done in full view of her husband but he was normally pissed by this time and couldn't do much about the proceedings. However, he never condoned her actions and was always willing to stop any impropriety if he could. On one occasion she had coerced, not that much coercing was needed, a willing participant up to her bedroom where there was feverish activity in the kissing, licking and undressing department. Time was short and the act had to be consummated quickly before they could be discovered. But discovered they were, as they heard her husband coming up the stairs, calling her name. In the darkness of the room where seconds ago clothes were being ripped off, now clothes were unsuccessfully being sought for re-donning. This was a doomed exercise as there just wasn't enough time to get fully dressed but the quick-thinking would-be Lothario was highlighted by the shaft of light from the hall once the husband had opened the door to the bedroom. Lothario had no trousers on, and was feeling around the walls of the room asking, 'Where am I? Where am I? I was desperate for a pee and was looking for the toilet.'

The wife had dived under the bed just before the husband switched on the bedroom light. He came into the room, strode across to the bed and lifted up the bedclothes.

'What are you looking for, there's no one else here with me,' said Lothario.

'I'm just making sure that you've not shit in my bed, you dirty wee bastard. I'd rather let you shag my wife than that. You haven't seen her, have you? If I catch her with a bloke I'll knock his fucking block off!'

Lothario swallowed hard and muttered something about 'not having seen her', but he knew that the husband knew he had been with the wife and the wife was probably still in the room. It can only be surmised that he did not want to start an argument during the party, but he was letting her know that he knew about her shagging shenanigans. He left the room and allowed them to get dressed in peace. The next day, however, she was wearing a rather startling shade of eye make-up on one eye.

The next activity required at our place was to paint the house from top to bottom, and in this venture we commandeered the help of those singles who had managed to leave their marks on the walls and doors over the years. We painted the whole house in a day. However, it cost a fortune for all the paint brushes that had to be purchased from the NAAFI as more and more singles presented themselves for duty. The painting spree soon degenerated into another party but at least the walls were clean and the carpet hid most of the spilt paint.

The days moving towards departure were taken up by packing our meagre belongings, although we had moved upmarket and now owned a fridge. At work nothing seemed to change and nobody made any particular reference to the fact that there was anything unusual happening. In truth, there was nothing unusual happening, as people came and went on a regular basis and in this job nobody had an imagination beyond their next pint of Guinness.

I was working as usual right up to the second to last day and on the last day I was trailing round the base getting 'clearance' signatures from all the required sections. I even had to hand in my greatcoat to the stores. There must have been a shortage of greatcoats that year, but whoever got mine got a good one as I had never worn it in my entire service career.

After this exercise I drove down to the H&R offices to say my goodbyes, but there were few people there that I knew, as it was not my shift that was on duty. I shook hands with a few people but I already felt like an outsider as I was no longer part of this fraternity. I left feeling rather saddened and empty.

The next day I 'marched out' of our quarters while my wife and kids were having a cup of tea round at a neighbour's house. The families officer who did the 'marching out' made little comment about how clean the walls of the house were, but he did mention how clean the carpets looked – this was a mystery to me as they had probably had ten years' wear in the two years that we had been in the house.

We piled ourselves into the car, said goodbye to the neighbours and drove away from the place that had given us so much pleasure for the past three and a bit years. I did manage a bit of a smile as we drove away. I had at last managed to get rid of the bloody great pram that had followed us around the world and had been stored in our pantry unused for the past three years. I had sold it to a secondhand shop in Limavady for two pounds. I wonder if it is still in use around that part of the country – either as a pram or some wee fella's cart!

On the seventh of April of that same year the official closing ceremony of RAF Ballykelly took place. I knew they wouldn't be able to carry on without me.

Epilogue

In later years when working in Aberdeen I would occasionally hear the well-remembered growl of the Griffons and would dive to my office window to see if I could spot the familiar shape. More often than not I would manage to see the lumbering beast and my memory would stray back to the good old days.

Conversely, I often played golf at Lossiemouth and the reaction there was completely different, as the Shackletons lined up to take off or land right over the golf course and our heads. Here one was in mortal fear that they might not make it to the runway. There was no memory straying here, as cursing was the order of the day.

During the summer of 1991 we were on holiday around the Moray coast. Whilst at the visitor centre at Culloden battlefield I once again heard the familiar growl in the sky, as one would expect with RAF Lossiemouth being just down the road. It only took a couple of seconds to locate where the noise was coming from. There she was, flying up the firth in all her splendour. There was something different though about this particular sortie for the grand old lady. She had a couple of helicopters buzzing around her, obviously taking pictures as she obligingly swung round a few times over Kessock Island just east of Inverness.

I watched this operation enthralled to see how well the Shackleton looked after all those years. She was nearly as old as I was, but looked in better shape. She had obviously been polished up for this final scene of glory and she revelled in it.

Once the photo call was over she swung out to the west. I watched and listened until I could no longer hear her speaking to me and her profile became an undefined spot in the blue sky. After all we had been through together, twenty-plus years before, I felt very pleased and not a little honoured to have witnessed the very last Shackleton flight from UK soil. However, it was akin to attending the funeral of an old friend

300

and I must admit to having a lump in my throat, as I knew I would probably never see her in the air again. Perhaps one day in the future someone will discover her DNA and be able to clone her for the visual and listening pleasure of future generations.